Clones, Fakes and Posthumans

Thamyris/

Intersecting: Place, Sex, and Race

Series Editor
Ernst van Alphen

Editorial Team
Murat Aydemir, Maaike Bleeker, Yasco Horsman,
Isabel Hoving, Esther Peeren

Clones, Fakes and Posthumans:
Cultures of Replication

Editors

Philomena Essed and Gabriele Schwab

Rodopi

Colophon

Original Design
Mart. Warmerdam, Haarlem, The Netherlands
www.warmerdamdesign.nl

Design
Inge Baeten

Printing
The paper on which this book is printed meets the requirements of "ISO 9706:1994,
Information and documentation – Paper for documents – Requirements for permanence".

ISSN: 1570-7253
E-Book ISSN: 1879-5846

ISBN: 978-90-420-3416-7
E-Book ISBN: 978-94-012-0702-7

© Editions Rodopi B.V., Amsterdam – New York, NY 2012
Printed in The Netherlands

Mission Statement

Intersecting: Place, Sex, and Race

Intersecting is a series of edited volumes with a critical, interdisciplinary focus.

Intersecting's mission is to rigorously bring into encounter the crucial insights of black and ethnic studies, gender studies, and queer studies, and facilitate dialogue and confrontations between them. *Intersecting* shares this focus with *Thamyris*, the socially committed international journal that was established by Jan Best en Nanny de Vries, in 1994, out of which *Intersecting* has evolved. The sharpness and urgency of these issues is our point of departure, and our title reflects our decision to work on the cutting edge.

We envision these confrontations and dialogues through three recurring categories: place, sex, and race. To us they are three of the most decisive categories that order society, locate power, and inflict pain and/or pleasure. Gender and class will necessarily figure prominently in our engagement with the above. *Race*, for we will keep analyzing this ugly, much-debated concept, instead of turning to more civil concepts (ethnicity, culture) that do not address the full disgrace of racism. *Sex*, for sexuality has to be addressed as an always-active social strategy of locating, controlling, and mobilizing people, and as an all-important, not necessarily obvious, cultural practice. And *place*, for we agree with other cultural analysts that this is a most productive framework for the analysis of situated identities and acts that allow us to move beyond narrow identitarian theories.

The title of the book series points at what we, its editors, want to do: *think together*. Our series will not satisfy itself with merely demonstrating the complexity of our times, or with analyzing the shaping factors of that complexity. We know how to theorize the intertwining of, for example, sexuality and race, but pushing these intersections one step further is what we aim for: How can this complexity be understood in practice? That is, in concrete forms of political agency, and the efforts of self-reflexive, contextualized interpretation. How can different socially and theoretically relevant issues be *thought together*? And: how can scholars (of different backgrounds) and activists think together, and realize productive alliances in a radical, transnational community?

We invite proposals for edited volumes that take the issues that *Intersecting* addresses seriously. These contributions should combine an activist-oriented perspective with intellectual rigor and theoretical insights, interdisciplinary and transnational perspectives. The editors seek cultural criticism that is daring, invigorating and self-reflexive; that shares our commitment to thinking together.

Contact us at intersecting@let.leidenuniv.nl.

Contents

Introduction: Cloning and Cultures of Replication

Philomena Essed and
Gabriele Schwab

Cloning technology presents humanity with the very real possibility that it may one day control not only its destiny but also its origin. Human cloning allows man to fashion his own essential nature and turn chance into choice. For cloning's advocates, this is an opportunity to remake mankind in an image of health, prosperity, and nobility; it is the ultimate expression of man's unlimited potential. For their detractors, human cloning and genetic manipulation intrude upon the profound nature of the inherently unknowable; they represent the bottomless depths of human arrogance and irresponsibility.

— Stephens

Cloning technologies have had an almost unparalleled impact on the cultural imaginary and the rethinking of the boundaries of the human. Cloning in agriculture dates back to antiquity, but the assisted manipulation of organisms in order to pre-select their genetic make-up is obviously a more recent phenomenon. Controversies over cloning concern the ethics of creating choice about the genetic characteristics of animals and human beings. Biotechnological cloning is considered controversial for ethical and environmental reasons. Moreover, with the rapid progress of technology, the very nature and boundaries of the human have come into question. Up to now, debates about cloning have almost exclusively focused on its biotechnological dimensions and their ethical implications. *Clones, Fakes and Posthumans* takes a different approach to the question of cloning. Cloning, we argue, is not an isolated biotechnological phenomenon. There are other cloning-like phenomena, such as, for example, copies and fakes of famous art works or designer products. Many cultural forms of cloning have often not really been recognized as such, because they have not been considered part of an encompassing new epistemological configuration inspired by new technologies of replication. We are therefore looking at cloning from a larger cultural and political perspective by asking in what ways technologies of cloning have affected the cultural imaginary more generally. We are posing the question of whether the availability of cloning technologies and the feasibility of the cloning of humans has both been preceded by and then reproduced by a form of "mental cloning" that deeply affects the ways we think about sameness and difference.

Mental cloning, we argue, deeply affects the ways we see. It may shape our vision and indeed create a "common vision" that emerges less from communal negotiations within the public sphere of ways of seeing, but rather from an involuntary absorption of the images (ranging from stereotypical images of others to normative images of self-fashioning) that proliferate in a mass-media culture. The painting by Eritrean artist Josief Habties Indrias we chose for the cover of this volume is titled "Common Vision." We are looking at four overlapping female faces with five pairs of vertically arranged eyes. The faces look like replicas of each other, even though, if we look at them closely, we realize that they are not entirely identical. Since the faces overlap, some of the eyes are shared, if not borrowed.

In the context of the concerns of *Clones, Fakes, and Posthumans,* Indrias's artistic game of doubling raises questions of sameness and difference, questions pertaining to a common versus a unique vision and, more generally, to original versus copy, duplication versus replication, and even tradition versus innovation. Indrias is known to borrow from and rework Byzantine Abyssinian art. We may recognize a contemporary abstraction of traditional African art, including the ornamental eyebrows. The mask-like quality of the faces enhances the effect of the eye's transhuman stare. The theme of copy and replication as well as the creative adaptation of tradition is central to Indrias's work. In today's technologized world, artistic adaptation or, if you wish, the borrowing of eyes, is always haunted by the fate of the work of art at a time of mechanical reproduction. At the same time, however, borrowing eyes may open up the "common vision" to a multiplicity of possible perspectives. Or, in the words of another artist, John Baldessari: "It's like four different sets of eyes perceiving the same world, but differently (John Baldessari about his Goya and Tetrad series at the LACMA exhibition in 2010).

Techniques of replication, however, are one thing in art and quite another in human life worlds. In art, they are predominately related to the adaptation of tradition, the dynamic of original and copy, and the production of seriality. In the life forms that emerge or are imagined in the age of cloning, the control over nature and the negotiation of the boundaries of the human tend to take center stage. In fact, we ask if the debates about the possible and technologically feasible cloning of humans should not be linked to a larger *episteme* in which fantasies of control, if not phantasms of immortality, overdetermine controversies over the boundaries of nature and the human, including the place of humans in nature. Power and control are at the center of these debates and practices. The fact that biotechnological cloning is being developed and advanced by powerful multinational corporations and promoted in late capitalist nations can hardly conceal the underlying colonial heritage with its fantasies of mastery over nature, including life and death.

Ten years ago Jean Baudrillard wrote in *The Vital Illusion*:

> It is culture that clones us, and mental cloning anticipates any biological cloning . . . Through schools systems, media, culture and mass information, singular beings become identical copies of one another. It is this kind of cloning—social cloning, the industrial reproduction of things and people—that makes possible the biological conception of the genome ad of genetic cloning, which only further sanctions the cloning of human conduct and human cognition. (25)

The purpose of this volume is to explore cloning and related phenomena that inform each other, like twins, fakes, replica, or homogeneities, through a cultural prism. What could it mean to think of a cloning mentality? Could it be that a "cloning culture" has made biotechnological cloning desirable in the first place, and vice versa that biotechnological cloning then enforces technologies of social and cultural cloning? What does it mean to say that a culture replicates? If biotechnological cloning has to do with choice and repetitive reproduction of selected characteristics, how are those kinds of desires expressed socially, politically and culturally? Lifting the issue of cloning above the biotechnological domain, we problematize the cultural context, including modernity's readiness to imitate and manipulate nature, and the skewed privileging of desirable socialities as a basis for exclusive replication. We also explore possible relations between a cloning mentality and a consumer society that fosters a brand-name mentality. The construction and (coercive) implementation of copy-prone technological and symbolic items are at the very heart of mass production and the consumer society that have emerged from and seek to articulate, define, and refine modernity and modernization. These phenomena include not only the defining practices of the new reproductive technologies and new consumer cultures; they also affect virtually all other cultural spheres. In this volume, we will look, for example, at new medical technologies and practices, new counterfeit markets based on the production of designer clones and fakes, as well as new missionary practices related to the mass-mediated reproduction of religion.

How does selection take place of the most desirable characteristics of existing beings, objects, practices, behaviors, and cognitions, which then become the norm to be reproduced as the preferred, if not the only kind? Section I of this volume, "Cloning: Technologies, Fantasies and Philosophies of Life," opens with various contributions that address the social, political and cultural ramifications and implications of biotechnological cloning. Section II, "Cultural Cloning," uses the trope and metaphor of cloning to shed a different light on questions of choice and privilege, difference and sameness, normativity and marginalization. It also looks at practices of replication and choice within a consumer culture marked by the fetishization of designer labels. Section III, "Replicating and Marketing Faith," analyzes various religious practices that demonstrate the impact of the new cultures and *episteme* of replication. Finally, Section IV, "The Cloning Imaginary," ends on a more playful note with a story of human cloning that draws out paradigmatic and symptomatic implications of one of the most central cloning fantasies. The story contains three alternative endings, collaboratively produced by different authors, each of whom unfolds a new cultural implication of the fantasy of human cloning.

The volume brings together a range of critical thought that has been formulated in separate areas of scholarship including race and gender studies, whiteness studies, environmental studies, critical theory, communication and media studies, environmental studies, as well as studies of migration and globalization. Given the many possible angles from which to explore technologies and cultures of replication, we selected essays with (inter)disciplinary breadth and thematic variety. Some chapters in this volume give content to what cultural cloning can mean, other contributors theorize about the cultural context in which cloning and cloned desires emerge. Various chapters address the modalities by which replicas become "commonsensical" and, in some cases, hegemonic. This involves viewing, simultaneously, arenas of institutional politics and everyday acts of power. Contributors offer analytical, conceptual and practical tools to re-evaluate critically taken-for-granted norms and criteria of "beauty," "merit," "excellence," "whiteness," "health," "competence," and "fitting in." These notions and others have contributed similarly to shaping a "cloned" profile of the "human," or, more specifically, the "professional," the "family," the "good mother," the "civil," and the "citizen."

There is reason to be concerned about exclusionary profiles, both produced by and serving to summarize and encourage, if not determine, social replications. There is reason to be concerned about "more" of the same material "progress" which goes hand in hand with claims of cultural homogeneity (global culture) and the annihilation of distinct and indigenous cultural values. But we also address opportunities that cloning mentalities create and open new perspectives on what may happen beyond merely normative and hegemonic practices of (cultural) cloning. Some essays assess alternative ways of conceiving and operationalizing biotechnological cloning that may eventually undercut the assumptions and dispositions of cultural cloning and cloning culture. Advocacy of biodiversity and thinking beyond androcentrism and anthropomorphism are cases in point.

For the purpose of analysis, a distinction can be made between *social cloning*— the replication of socialities, with the result of securing spaces of racial, ethnic, gender, and social privilege and, closely related, *cultural cloning* – the replication of norms, values, symbols, legal bodies, practices, political arrangements, procedures, and artifacts with the result of normalizing some, while marginalizing others. Obviously, social and cultural cloning are often intertwined. We suggest that practices rooted in a mental paradigm of cloning, whether they are implemented socio-culturally or biotechnologically, belong to the basic characteristics and systemic phenomena of modern societies.

Within this framework, the volume also makes visible the paradoxical intertwinement of limitless choice and desired resemblance that are constitutive marks of the cultures of modernity. Whether imitation, remake, fake, or replica, the clone, modeled after something or someone else, is not the real thing – at least not the "original" thing. Socio-cultural cloning is the process, if not the condition, of becoming alike while remaining different. Technological sophistication, mass production and consumer demands have made clones and fakes widely acceptable, but a fake is not the same as an exact copy. In the same vein, replicating the success formula of mass pop concerts to proselytize, as Evangelical Christians have discovered, does not make all faith harvesting similar. Replicas come already differentiated, like the many brands of blue jeans, modeled after the original Levi. Cloning as a cultural phenomenon includes more than artifacts. It also involves identities desiring to be or act like others or someone else in particular. Think of the many Elvis Presley or Michael Jackson look alikes and impersonators.

But imitation can also be forced upon populations. Colonization is a case in point. In the development of Western industrialized societies, technology emerged as the driving force of modernization, eventually enabling resources to be generated, replicated and copied indefinitely. The fantasy that resources can be replicated indefinitely is, of course, a highly ideologized construction that has led not only to the subjugation of entire peoples as a cheap labor force, but also to the gradual and increasingly threatening exploitation and depletion of the earth. Seeking to transcend human limitations, the scope of materials manipulated to fulfill the ever-growing needs and greeds of modern and late modern societies has come to include fundamental life processes. Societies marked by modernity have been drawn increasingly if variably into regimes of cloning, marked more and more by the emergence of a culture where competitive creativity goes hand in hand with the commodification of all that is alive. One of the costs is the assault on human and biological diversity. (The recent documentary about assisted human-reproductive technologies, *Frozen Angels,* suggests that, if given the choice of designing babies, 90% of people would choose white and blonde babies.)[1]

The wholesale commodification of goods and life forms relies on the foundations of mass production and mass consumerism. Both laboring bodies and the products enabled by that work are designed to be replicated and sold in a culture of mass consumption in which the "sameness" of what is re-produced becomes the underlying logic of both production and consumption: a *normative* resemblance through which workers, products, commodities, and consumers come to create "cultures of cloning." Mass production in itself is, however, not the same as cultural cloning. But consumer cultures fuel the creation of brand imitation products, the IMB clone being one of the most popularly known examples. Consumerism, and the subjectivities and desires it generates, masks the logic of normative resemblance, if not sameness. The industry around Extreme Makeovers is a case in point. It is the cultural production of "ideal norms" that ties consumerism to the cultures of replication.

The desire to "replicate," even into an imperfect copy, is compelled by ideological constructions around "normative likeness." While Baudrillard was the first to introduce the concept of "social cloning" to mark a cultural desire for sameness, the idea of *cloning cultures* introduces a new turn and new perspectives. The conceptual interventions in this volume, for example, suggest a new focus on the rich literature around "difference." As such, this volume brings together thought-provoking essays that will make visible the myths of homogeneity as well as the paradoxes and multiple dialectical relationships between difference and sameness.

Clones, Fakes and Posthumans consists of 4 sections and 11 chapters that, we hope, will serve as a set of signposts to provide a heuristic basis for a more comprehensive and systematic critical analysis. Section I, titled "Cloning: Technologies, Fantasies and Philosophies of Life," contains four essays by Verena Stolcke, Heleen van den Hombergh, Rosi Braidotti and Gabriele Schwab that focus on the social, cultural and political implications of cloning technologies and genetic engineering, including reproductive and environmental politics.

In "Homo Clonicus," Verena Stolcke makes a threefold argument: she describes the biotechnological facts of cloning with special emphasis on recent developments; she uncovers the set of reasons that may lead to the cloning of humans; and, lastly, she provides the background for gauging the effects that cloning might have both biologically and culturally for consecrated Western notions of sex and conception, parenthood and kin, as well as for gender relations and the dualist notion of the world we inhabit.

For this purpose, Verena Stolcke takes the reader through the biotechnological history of cloning and reproductive technology and points to paradoxes and contradictions in negotiating the power of technology. If cloning desires are (partly) the expression of anthropocentric aspirations to defy the limits of nature, Stolcke notes that, ironically, cloning is "the sensational accomplishment of determinist genetic assumptions translated into material reality in the laboratory by human inventiveness." Cloning technology, Stolcke argues, engenders an unforeseen gender equalizer: human embryo cloning makes sperm dispensable, while female "golden eggs" remain highly priced items in the market economy.

Heleen van den Hombergh links the principles of biotechno-capitalism to the machinery of post-industrial agricultural engineering. In "Gentech Agriculture" she shows how bio-capitalism, a political economy at the heart of cultural cloning, has turned into a "war on diversity." Gentech agriculture goes beyond biotechnological cloning in altering the genetic characteristics of crops in a ways that are irreversible. Van den Hombergh insists on the need to end the divide between human and environmental interests.

The chapter also lays bare the cloning mentality underlying gentech agriculture, namely the principle that human-made *surrogates* can, and therefore should, *replace* natural vegetal reproduction. The victims of this mentality and corporate practice are the poor subsistence farmers. They are "dependent upon agricultural varieties well-adapted to their circumstances which, in practice, is a dynamic process of selection and conservation." According to Van den Hombergh, modernity and the scientific and technological "progress" that is its fuel, have made possible the unimaginable: harnessing extraordinary creativity to the life-giving possibilities of modern medicine as well as deploying that very knowledge to the task of annihilating all human and natural life as we know it.

Rosi Braidotti's essay "Transposing Life" revisits the interconnectedness and complexity of biotechnology and life. Braidotti rejects human-centeredness in favor of embracing "the generative vitality of non-or pre-human or animal life." Cloning technologies and biotechnologies in general might be moving the planet past the stage of anthropocentrism. If the hierarchical ordering of different homogenized categories is a mechanism of cultural cloning, Braidotti's analysis of contemporary political culture points to its contradictions. While acknowledging cloning practices of high tech capitalism, (including replications of US call centers in India or the patenting of genes), Braidotti also sees the diversifying and transformative potential of high tech. Technology seems to serve as interface between pre-human and post-human life. Replication and sameness continue at a time when traditional categories (including race, gender, human, and non-human) fall short in explaining the complexity and multiplicity of connections, of differentiations within categories, and of multiple inter-relations of biotechnological form of life.

A shift is taking place, says Braidotti, from the "sameness" based on reproducing oppositional categories toward the technologically produced complexity of the "inextricable entanglement of material, bio-cultural and symbolic forces in the making of the subject." The current stage of technology, though rooted in paradigms of fragmentation, enables fusion between human, non-human, and other living systems. The ramifications of such fusions for the sustainability of life and the earth have yet to be determined. But there is, according to Braidotti, an opportunity for our societies to rethink and break through entrenched categorical replications that feed into systems of domination.

"Replacement Humans," by Gabriele Schwab, addresses the clone's role in the cultural imaginary, highlighting the fantasies and desires as well as the anxieties generated by technologies designed to facilitate the production and reproduction of sameness. The clone intervenes in the biological as well as cultural politics of reproduction by changing its most fundamental parameters. Schwab argues that the hopes and anxieties that generate the highly ambivalent status of the clone in the cultural imaginary go to the heart of cultural anxieties about the boundaries of the human at the beginning of a new millennium. "Replacement Humans" pushes the boundaries of the modern paradox between determinism and choice when Schwab explores some of the consequences of the popular fantasy in which the loss of a loved one (fate) can be compensated for with a clone of the deceased (choice). Less interested in the feasibility of cloning a "replacement human," the essay rather explores the role of cloning fantasies in the imaginary, if not the political unconscious, of cultures of replication. In this context, she specifically links the fantasy of cloning a replacement human to the "phantasm of immortality that not only does away with death, but also with the pain of loss and the work of mourning." The desire for biotechnological clones and the feasibility of replacement humans promises a profound change in human emotion and in a culturally shared sense of human worth. Like Stolcke, Schwab interprets cloning desires in terms of consumer culture: "Would we slowly get accustomed to considering children as precious, yet replaceable and indeed technologically improvable objects subordinate to the more encompassing logic of a waste consumer culture that needs its war machines and the concomitant militarism of the mind to serve the accumulation of ever more profit?"

The second section, "Cloning Cultures," includes four essays that expand the perspective of cloning toward the social and cultural domain. The leading article, "Cloning Cultures: The Social Injustices of Sameness" by Philomena Essed and David Theo Goldberg has inspired this volume and introduces the concept of cultural and social cloning. While cloning is widely considered as a biotechnological discourse, few have paid attention to the cultural contexts that have made cloning practices and mentalities conceivable. The relation between the biological and cultural considerations of cloning are revealed by the anxieties conjured by the prospect of cloning human beings. Essed's and Goldberg's essay analyzes these anxieties, focusing on concerns about the reproduction of sameness. In this context, they also explore the implications of cloning for issues of social injustice.

In "The Pursuit of Perfection," a collaborative essay by Ross Parke, Scott Coltrane, Robin DiMatte, and Christine Gailey, the authors also highlight social injustices related to the new biotechnologies. In particular, they argue that income, class, race and ethnicity are factors that may severely restrict less affluent or otherwise disadvantaged populations from making use of new available technologies. In this context for example, the authors specifically address the gate-keeping role played by health/medical institutions and service providers. As a unifying theme, they critically examine the concept of the "pursuit of perfection," arguing that the myth of the pre-fect family perpetuates inequalities along racial, ethnic and class demarcations. The normativity of biogenetic parenthood (at least in the West) preceded reproductive technologies, and replications of perfect family images continue to shape the way these technologies are conceived among users. In spite of, or maybe because of, increasing reproductive diversity, the desire to imitate the perfect family model remains pervasive. Moreover, the authors express concern about the "frivolous use" of reproductive technologies "for gender selection and more ominously, selection of infant attributes—both physical and intellectual."

Cloning as gate keeping is the theme of Philomena Essed's essay, but applied to the professions. In "Cloning the Physician" she insists that discrimination *against* non-dominant groups is also indicative of normative preferences *for* imagined perfec-tions such as masculinities, whiteness, European-ness, physical abilities, and high intelligence. Her approach illustrates the combination of cloning socialities—privileged spaces—through the cultural cloning of professional norms, values and behavioral expectations. Thus, everyday racism and genderism operate to secure the replication of physician prototypes. In focusing on the replication of normative prefer-ence as an instrument of socio-cultural cloning, Essed's essay shifts the emphasis away from an exclusive differentialist approach—where difference and how to incor-porate diversity are the focus of attention—toward the deeper, less articulated, prob-lem of hardly contested pursuit of likeness and closeness to an imagined idealized physician. Drawing from concrete examples, she analyzes how masculine (middle-class) whiteness underpins the cultural process relating gender and race to interpre-tations of medical competence. But the notion of socio-cultural cloning also helps to move beyond race and gender critique. "Preference for more of something similar means investing in the continuation of the best and the worst characteristics of cur-rent high status positions including the best and the worst of the social environments in which these positions are embedded." Essed unpacks the social environments that make it possible to continue to replicate dominant practices in the higher profes-sions, including tolerance for humiliating practices and the erosion of humaneness.

Like the other essays in this section, Ackbar Abbas' "Cloning Disappearances, Consuming Fakes" is about the production of sameness in cultures of replication. However, he singles out an instance in which the "pursuit of perfection" in the mar-ketplace overturns conventional notions of corporate capitalist production. In particular, Abbas looks at high end designer brands as the most highly clonable commodities of contemporary consumer cultures. Scrutinizing the emergent markets for cloned prod-ucts, especially in Third World, or less developed countries, the essay explores the relationship between designer models and their fake replicas. As they are traded within the alternative economies of global counterfeit markets, fakes are a way for their creators to relate to the global environment. Many commodities are designed in so-called developed countries and manufactured in developing countries, where the majority cannot afford to consume the very products they make. The transfer of knowledge also creates opportunities. "It is at this juncture that the fake enters to reverse this order of things. It produces objects labeled "Made in Italy" or "Made in France," the design centers of the world, and offers them for sale in China at a fraction of the cost of "the real thing." Thus, the fake obtains economic advantages and effects its own version of "technology transfer"—not in the long term, but right now. Fakes can (relatively) equalize power differences between developed and developing countries not only through financial gains, but also through the development of expertise. Like no other, the faker thoroughly studies and understands the model. But when "faking is no longer confined to the fake, when it is not only the usual suspects who practice it, it is these categories and standards themselves that disappear and everything dissolves into general confusion and easy reversibility. This is the scenario of cloning disappearance." Abbas' perspective on the fake thus challenges conceptions about the global that are often taken for granted, including the nature of value, commodities and the relationship between model and imitator in the age of information.

Section III, "Replication and Marketing Faith," with essays by Rebecca Kugel, Eileen Luhr, and Toby Miller, presents three instances that demonstrate the impact that cultures of replication have on the dissemination of religion. Rebecca "Monte" Kugel's "Civilizing Missions" explores the religious colonization of indigenous peoples in the Americas as an early instance of hegemonizing forced replication. In the early stages of globalization, the differences that constitute the diversities of humans were ranged against an ideal-type. Thus, Western colonizing forces constituted the "primitive" and the "savage" against the measure of an allegedly ideal, civilized human subject. As a result, indigenous peoples were culturally constructed on the basis of an essentialized lack and forever found wanting. Focusing on indigenous American communities, Kugel's case study analyzes how coercion to imitate the norms of Western colonial powers by adopting Christianity served for colonized indigenous communities as an entrance into so-called civilization. Western styles of governance were forced upon indigenous communities, including European patriarchal practices that reinforced male authority while excluding indigenous women. In the same vein, tribal diversity became conceptually homogenized in the Anglo-American 19th century discursive construct and subsequent naturalization of the "Indian." Kugel, however, also shows that, although the conceptual construct and the cultural imaginary of the "Indian" have been "cloned" globally, many diverse tribal communities have not only survived, but are experiencing a powerful cultural revival. This serves as a reminder that "the process of replicating western culture is never a foregone conclusion."

Eileen Luhr's essay "Marketing Religion" focuses on the self-marketing of mega-churches. With the globalization of neo-liberalism, many organizations welcomed clonable elements of marketing models. In a detailed portrait of the replication of successful and popular mass culture formulas into Evangelism, Luhr investigates the Orange County Harvest Crusade. Religious conservatives, she argues, "mastered the cultural formulas of consumerism as they adjusted their witnessing practices to a suburban landscape where civic life increasingly occurred in commercially owned spaces." In this process, Luhr shows, Christian consumerism "sacralizes" popular culture while, at the same time, also imbuing everyday middle class consumption with a quasi-sacred quality. Hidden under the surface of cultural transfers between consumerism and proselytizing is a political message: the protection of suburban whiteness, its middle class family values and economic interests, in the wake of liberal rights at the turn of the century and in an ethnically diversifying California.

Toby Miller's "The 'Yanqui' Make-over" also chooses the mega-church as one of his prime examples. Miller offers a witty analysis of the US national ethos of self-(re)invention, showing how this country of immigration facilitates its demographic differentiation "alongside the need to clone new selves from available models." Miller illustrates his thesis with reference to two techniques of cultural cloning: mega-churches and popular antidepressants. Both, he argues, are designed to create more desirable (white) selves. The mega-church is what Miller calls "a fine instance of cloning, an amalgam of stadium rock and mall dross."

Taking antidepressants as "makeovers" of the self constitutes a new consumer trend, especially popular among the upwardly mobile. Like the evangelical reborn experience, these "new substances, legal and controlled, offer a permanent over-haul" rather than temporary boosts. "These drugs fulfill the meritocrat's dream—to learn the code, to crack the means of making oneself anew." Embedded in US con-sumer culture, antidepressants also serve to pacify (white) anxieties about economic uncertainty and rising numbers of ethnic populations. Less concerned with the actual medical implications of antidepressants, Miller deliberately foregrounds the fan-tasies generated by a culture that increasingly manages emotion and self via phar-maceutical intervention. Like the cultural fantasies that aggregate around cloning and other new biotechnologies, the fantasies about a potential pharmaceutical makeover of the self have a profound impact on the cultural politics of managing emotion as well as, more generally, emergent forms of subjectivity and subjection.

Section IV, "The Cloning Imaginary," ends the volume in a playful way by present-ing a collaborative story in three different versions—"Twin Enemies," "Dead Ringer-Knock Off," and "Destiny-Eternity." This final section of the volume also focuses on prominent cultural fantasies, in this case, specifically fantasies generated by the technological feasibility of the cloning of humans. Based on one of the most promi-nent fantasies in the cloning imaginary, namely the fantasy of self-reproduction through the cloning of a child with the same genetic make-up, this threefold story is subliminally linked to some of the discussions in the essays. Originally, the story emerged in the collaborative research group on "Cloning Cultures" at the University of California Humanities Research Institute that inspired this volume. Gabriele Schwab presented an original story in the context of an exercise with "found objects" of cloning. She translated a recurring fantasy she found in cloning discourses into a narrative to be discussed by the group. Eventually, the group's animated discussions led to two rewritings of the ending that draw out symptomatically different implications of the core fantasy. The story's proliferation along three trajectories that lead to different endings provides a space for looking back at the scholarly interventions in the volume. We hope that our readers will use both the resonance and defamiliarization generated in this imaginary space to think about possible futures and emergent subjectivities in our diverse cultures of replication.

Acknowledgements

Clones, Fakes and Posthumans is the principal product emerging from a three-year collaboration and exchange, initially among scholars at the University of California-Riverside, the University of California Humanities Research Institute and the University of Amsterdam, but gradually incorporating others in the US and Europe. The project, *Cloning Cultures: The Social Injustices of Reproducing Sameness (2002–2005)*, was funded by the Ford Foundation.[2] A Conference, *Cloning Cultures: Normativities, Homogeneities, and The Human in Question*[3] provided the initial forum for a more sustained debate that led to the conception of this volume. While some of the chapters emerged from papers presented at the conference, others were explicitly solicited to broaden and differentiate its scope. We thank the University of California Humanities Research Institute, and in particular director David Theo Goldberg, for serving as the administrative home for the making of this volume. We gratefully acknowledge Piya Chatterjee and Donald Moore as co-organizers of collaborative research groups and events and the participants for stimulating contributions. Thanks go to Adele Clarke, Troy Duster, Ana Paula Ferreira and Gerry Heng who gave invaluable moral and intellectual support to the project. Stephen Becker has been a great style editor. Isabel Hoving encouraged us to consider Thamyris/Rodopi and Murat Aydemar's supportive professionalism proved the case.

Notes

1. For further information, see PBS documentary <http://www.pbs.org/independentlens/frozenangels/>.

2. For further information, see <http://www.ideasandsociety.ucr.edu/> (click Ford grant); University of California Humanities Research Institute <http://www.uchri.main.php?page_id=34> (click grant recipients).

3. See University of California Humanities Research Institute, 13–14 May 2005 <http://uchri.org/main.php?details=50&page_id=88>.

Works Cited

Baudrillard, Jean. "The Vital Illusion." *Wellek Library Lectures at the University of California, Irvine*. New York: Columbia UP, 2000.

Stephens, Patrick. *Navigator* 4.4 (Apr. 2004) <http://www.objectivistcenter.org/articles/pstephens_cloning-new-conception-humanity.asp>.

UCHRI Residency Group. *Cloning Cultures: The Social Injustice of Sameness*. Donald Moore (facilitator), Philomena Essed, Gabriele Schwab, Eileen Luhr, Nancy Postero, Carole-Anne Tyler, Devon Carbado, Saloni Mathur, Michael Salman, and Kim Furumoto (research assistant).

Part One: Technologies, Fantasies and Philosophies of Life

Thamyris/Intersecting No. 25 (2012) 25–44

Homo Clonicus

Verena Stolcke

Adam, we give you no fixed place to live, no form that is peculiar to you, nor any function that is yours alone. According to your desires and judgement, you will have and possess whatever place to live, whatever form, and whatever functions you yourself choose. All other things have a limited and fixed nature prescribed and bounded by Our laws. You, with no limit or no bound, may choose for yourself the limits and bounds of your nature. We have placed you at the world's centre so that you may survey everything else in the world. We have made you neither of heavenly nor of earthly stuff, neither mortal nor immortal, so that with free choice and dignity, you may fashion yourself into whatever form you choose. To you is granted the power of degrading yourself into the lower forms of life, the beasts, and to you is granted the power, contained in your intellect and judgement, to be reborn into the higher forms, the divine.
— Della Mirandola

(Yet) homo sapiens has overcome the limitations of his origin . . . Now he can guide his own evolution. In him, Nature has reached beyond the hard regularities of physical phenomena. Homo sapiens, the creature of Nature, has transcended her. From a product of circumstances, he has risen to responsibility. At last he is Man. May he behave so!
— Handler 928[1]

Natural science does not simply describe and explain nature; it is part of the interplay between nature and ourselves . . . what we observe is not nature itself but nature exposed to our method of questioning.
— Werner Heisenberg

These are two visions of the place of humans in the world five centuries apart. Renaissance humanism exalted human dignity and made Man the measure of all things, a creature endowed with the freedom and capability to forge his own destiny. Thus, the modern subject was born. At first, the exercise of this freedom was thought to be confined by nature and society. Their bodies, sensations and needs as essential features of humans made humankind part of nature. Even so, Man was enthroned as master over nature (Jacob 5–8). With the passage of time, this ideal of freedom became a handmaiden for modern liberal individualism, but by way of a paradox. By the Enlightenment, the modern individual came to be regarded as a substantial entity above and beyond society which he contributed to shape. Yet, individual freedom and self-determination had as their match Man's accountability for his actions (Williams 161–165). Since he was responsible for his merits no less than for his failures, the placement in society of the self-determining individual was, however, credited to his own nature, instead for example, to the socio-political order he precisely helped to forge. In a further conceptual twist, equal rights and justice of all citizens in developing bourgeois class society came to be predicated on cultural and/or natural identity read likeness, inequality and oppression being grounded in moral-cultural differences and/or deficiencies in body or mind. This incongruity between individual freedom to shape one's destiny and collective sameness as a requisite for shared socio-political equality persists in the contemporary contradiction between the arrogant narcissist dream of individual uniqueness and the endeavor to be no different and, therefore, less than everybody else. The growing fear of "the other" represents the extreme opposite of our anxiety to be equal by being like a multitude (Verdú). The tension between individualist singularity and social embeddedness among one's likes in society runs through biotechnology and especially through cloning in more than one sense.

Cloning facts

The biogenetic revolution, which has succeeded in outwitting the very laws of the human condition, is a concrete outcome of the modern Western individual's pursuit of the freedom to redesign himself. The sensational news in February 1997 of the creation of Dolly the sheep, the first mammal cloned from an adult cell,[2] illustrates the vertiginous advances achieved in molecular biology and biotechnology precipitated by modern scientists' fascination with conquering the ultimate secrets of life. Although only a lamb, Dolly the clone is the emblematic image of modern life scientists' incessant quest for transcending nature. Even so, cloning as a metaphor of modernity and its individualist ethic goes only so far. Science and technology are inevitably framed in social relationships and influenced by cultural values without thereby, nonetheless, foregoing its very material implications.

News coverage focused on the powerful emotions, fantasies and fears that Dolly's creation and the potential abuses of human cloning provoked. Disparate concerns ranged from hopes placed in the design in the laboratory of genetically identical human beings, in order either to perpetuate themselves, or to produce a spare self as a reservoir of body parts for regenerative therapy or to replace a loved one (Nussbaum and Sunstein; Kolata *Clone*; Bryan). Whereas opponents objected for ethical reasons, because cloning usurped Divine authority or upset the balance between culture and nature. By contrast, important technical aspects of cloning and associated socio-cultural expectations of biotechnology which could encourage human cloning hardly deserved media attention.

Dolly was a genuine scientific breakthrough in a dual sense. For several decades, scientists had attempted to clone animals (frogs, mice, cattle, sheep, mules) by somatic cell nuclear transfer (Javitt, et al. 11–12; Bloom). However, in 1996, Dr. Ian Wilmut, Dolly's creator, and his team, achieved a qualitative breakthrough in embryology. The team succeeded in overthrowing a consecrated biological principle by turning back the biological clock of an adult somatic cell nucleus to its primitive pluripotent state so that the somatic nucleus began to differentiate anew and gave rise to a complete new organism, a clone.[3]

What is more, Dolly was an ordinary sheep *except for her conception*. Dr. Ian Wilmut's second first was the feat of an *immaculate conception* in mammals. Dolly's conception occurred in the laboratory, not only without coitus but also without spermatozoa, by contrast for example, with *in vitro* fertilization, which is an extra corporeal sexual form of insemination designed to overcome physiological barriers to conception. The description on the internet captured well the drama of the event:

> To clone Dolly, Wilmut and his colleagues took a mammary gland cell from a six-year old ewe. Wilmut then removed the nucleus of a sheep egg cell taken from a different ewe, and inserted the mammary cell into the now nucleus-free egg cell. Wilmut then zapped the two combined cells with a jolt of electricity, and to general amazement the combined cells acted like a fertilized egg cell and began to divide, using the DNA from the mammary cell as its genetic blueprint. He then implanted the new developed embryo into yet another ewe, and in a few months Dolly was born, an exact genetic copy of the ewe from which the mammary cell had been taken. (Mario)[4]

The outcome was a genuine genetic copy of the female somatic cell donor for Dolly also inherited her mitochondria DNA.

It is surprising that cloning as an asexual form of conception has gone largely unrecognized publicly. Of course, spermatozoa are a proverbially as abundant procreative stuff as they are regarded as indispensable. By contrast, Oocytes are scarce. And on account of embryological and biotechnological experimentation, oocytes have become golden eggs of sorts. Hitherto, the notion that mammals, let alone humans, might be conceived asexually sounded like science fiction even to as intrepid a geneticist as James Watson. In 1971, Watson still regretted that the crucial steps in human embryology occurred in the highly inaccessible womb of the human female. "There the growing foetus enlarges unseen, and *effectively out of range of almost any manipulation* except that which is deliberately designed to abort its existence." But he trusted that scientists would soon be able to penetrate the protective abode of the female womb. The rapid progress of *in vitro* fertilization of human eggs, he prophesied, would make embryological development "wide-open to a variety of experimental manipulations," and initiate "a frenetic rush to do experimental manipulation with human eggs once they had become a readily available *commodity*" (50–52).

Nuclear transfer is the critical technique in mammalian cloning through which the intact nucleus of a somatic cell is absorbed into an egg, the nucleus of which has been removed previously. Cloning thus dispenses with male insemination of the oocyte and male participation in conception. Though scarcely perceived by the lay public or acknowledged by the media,[5] in mammalian cloning the male thus becomes superfluous because conception is achieved by substituting somatic cell nucleus transfer for traditional sex. The symbolic dimension of this biotechnological circumvention of traditional *facts of life* in mammals is spectacular. Cloning means reproduction in the most literal sense of creating a practically identical genetic copy of the cloned organism precisely because it is an asexual technology of procreation. François Jacob, the French Nobel prize winner in medicine (1965), regarded this procreative peculiarity of Dolly with an ironic very anthropological twinkle in the eye:

> for a long time we attempted to have pleasure without children. With in-vitro fertilization we have children without pleasure. And now we have come to make children without pleasure and without spermatozoa . . . Evidently this changes family structure somewhat . . . for the moment at least among sheep. (Nodé-Langlois and Vigy)

Dolly, the lamb, let the biotechnological genie out of the bottle of molecular biological research. One evident driving force of biogenetic developments is the confidence laboratories share with multinational pharmaceutical companies and investors in the extraordinary biomedical potentials and the huge economic profits molecular biology and genomics anticipate. Vast sums of public and/or private funding are being placed into genomic research in the United States and, increasingly, also in Europe and Asia ("Biotechnology"; "Schlacht"; Comité; Human Genetics). Intense scientific and intellectual competition for funding and academic prestige fuels a genuine *genomania*.[6] For example, government regulations and funding restrictions in the United States proved ineffective in stopping biogenetic experimentations, while private investments were increasing notably. As a consequence, by the turn of the century, international biotechnological industry was stealing the ground from under the critics of cloning. The ethical and technical reservations vis-à-vis cloning within the scientific and bio-medical community turned around. Biotechnological research moved forward fast and the limelight swung to the extraordinary biomedical potential of regenerative medicine by means of gene and tissue replacement therapy and to cloning as an infertility treatment, thereby pushing earlier fears and ethical objections to human cloning into the background.

Human embryo stem cells: from social order to individual disorders

In November 1998, a new biotechnological breakthrough triggered a burst of fresh research. Two company-funded teams announced that they had isolated and cultured human embryonic and foetal stem cells succeeding in prolonging their undifferentiated state (Vogel; Jasanoff 192). Even Rifkin, a vocal critic of biogenetic research, acknowledged that this was "probably the biggest development since recombinant DNA" (Butler). Embryonic stem cells are unique in that they have the capacity to develop into any type of tissue in the human body. The ability to produce replacement tissue such as muscle, skin, bone and nervous tissue in the laboratory for transplant would revolutionize medicine. New knowledge about cell development enabling the diagnosis of "genetic diseases" such as cancer, Alzheimer and Parkinson disease and even aging seemed to corroborate the dreams of genetic enhancement, individual perpetuation and ultimately immortality.[7]

The achievements of stem cell research also meant a move forward in the individualization of disease. The new notion of "genetic disease" means diagnosing people's ailments in terms of their personal genetic make up, thereby neglecting possible environmental causes. By focusing on individual genetic disorders, the idea of "genetic disease" also encouraged a new individualist eugenics because, by contrast with classical eugenics, biomedical treatment is conceived in strictly individual terms. Regenerative medicine arouses individual's hopes in personalized gene therapy by promising diagnoses and cures which are, however, as Fox Keller warned, highly unrealistic (Keller; Kevles).

Aborted fetuses, "spare" IVF embryos and embryos especially created in the laboratory by inseminating donated gametes had conventionally provided stem cells for research, although not without ethical and technical difficulties. But then, the first cloning of a human embryo as a source of stem cells was made public in November 2001 by scientists working at Advanced Cell Technologies, a biotech company in Massachusetts, U.S.A. This procedure of obtaining stem cells from cloned human embryos raised new ethical concerns. The use of somatic cell nucleus transfer to produce cloned embryos to derive stem cells entails the destruction of all the embryos. For the opponents to any form of cloning, this meant destroying human life.[8] With the success in producing a cloned human embryo, the likelihood that a complete human being could be cloned likewise moved ever closer ("Embryonic"; Human Genome; Jasanoff 193).

Name games

Intense competitive pressures on the biotech industry and on national governments to be first in the biotechnological race collides with ethical concerns and legal regulations. To lessen or circumvent the ethical objections about cloning, advocates of biotechnology have resorted to name games. Words and the combination of words with which we name phenomena in the world shape the way we think and react to them (E. S. Taylor). Defenders and opponents in the debate over cloning employ semantic tricks to justify their respective bioethical positions. Those who favor embryological research coined the category of the *pre-embryo* regarded as a *pre-person* until implantation and the development of the primitive streak around its 16th day, to deny the early human embryo the moral status as a subject of rights.[9] There are even those who propose that cloned embryos are not the real thing, but *pseudo-embryos.* The term *pre implantation embryo* was adopted in a similar vein to facilitate the manipulation of embryos in assisted reproduction (Kischer; E. S. Taylor 117–118).

Advocates also suggested that the publicly less familiar term *blastocyst* be substituted for the *pre-embryo* which still was associated by many with the onset of human life. As human embryo stem cell research advanced, life scientists furthermore decided to dissociate cloning for the purpose of producing embryos for their stem cells from cloning to procreate human beings, by denominating the techniques *therapeutic cloning* by contrast with *reproductive cloning,* respectively, although both protocols differ only in the use to which the cloned embryo is put, to extract stem cells or to engender a mature organism.[10] To decry cloning and stem cell research as assaults on human dignity, their opponents resorted likewise to semantic manipulations. President Bush's Council on Bioethics presumed to shun such "artful redefinitions" such as the above by translating reproductive cloning into *cloning to produce children* and therapeutic cloning into *cloning-for-biomedical-research,* in an endeavor to underline the indefensible risks to human life that either technique involved (Jasanoff 195). In a most recent semantic turn, stem cell researchers dropped the term *therapeutic cloning* altogether in favor of SCNT—*somatic cell nuclear transfer*— a formulation which describes the procedure, but stays away from the ominous ethical connotation of the word "cloning" (Kolata "Name Games").

"I don't think nature is a fixed thing"

Science and technology are then embedded in historical contexts shaped by economic interests, power structures, scientific ambitions as well as socio-cultural assumptions, expectations and desires (Edwards, et al.; Edwards *Born*). The complex intersections between science and society pose major ontological and epistemological dilemmas regarding the manner of analyzing biotechnological innovations in constructivist terms without disregarding the materiality of the momentous transformations biotechnology effects in the *facts of life*.[11] According to Canning, the human body can neither be interpreted as a purely material and biological entity for it is moulded and inscribed by socio-political relationships, nor can its materiality be ignored for it is the arena in which biotechnological innovations occur (Canning).

The British Wellcome Trust carried out the first public opinion study on cloning in 1998. One interviewee declared, "I think nature is not a fixed thing." Modern Western cosmology is actually quite exceptional in that it classifies beings in accordance with whether they are governed by laws of matter or by arbitrary social conventions (Descola). Biotechnology is such a fascinating phenomenon because of the literalness with which it brings together in the ever swifter transfiguration of the *facts of life* the two realms of human experience—that of biology, that which is thought to be inscribed in nature, and that of culture, understood as the domain of human creativity in society—which Western cosmology, in effect, has kept apart, at least conceptually, since Descartes, as though they were obviously distinct and separable dimensions of the human condition. Note in this respect the recent authorization by the UK Human Fertilisation and Embryology Authority of molecular research aimed at producing hybrid human-animal embryos as an alternative source of stem cells ('Press Statement').

But the relationships between nature as opposed to culture and society have been endowed with different symbolic meanings depending on socio-political circumstances and scientific convictions. In the modern Western worldview, nature and culture have been regarded, for the most part, as forces in conflict, with nature being at the service of humans or the laws of nature determining human destiny. The oscillations between human omnipotence and biological determinism forms the scientific and ideological backdrop for biotechnological developments.[12]

A milestone in genetic history was Watson, Crick and Franklin's discovery of the double helix structure of DNA in 1953, which brought new energy to genetic determinism in the form of a theory of life circumscribed to the gene.[13] The confidence in "our genes" not only inspired the human genome project and the biotechnological race to unlock the ultimate secrets of human DNA taken to be the blueprint for *all* life. What is more, the separate organization of fields of knowledge, deepening academic specialization, disciplinary boundary disputes and competition for research funding which turned the severance of nature from culture more relentless, has been extraordinarily productive for the life sciences for it allowed for the intersections, for example, between genetics and technology, between nature and culture, to remain unquestioned and unchallenged (Latour *Nous* 20–21). As a consequence, there are now those, Fox Keller noted sarcastically, who claim that, owing to the progress in molecular biology, the old controversy over nature versus culture has finally been laid to rest—with *nature* emerging victorious! (282, 288).

Cloning is a privileged example of the neglected intersections between nature and culture. Cloning is the sensational accomplishment of determinist genetic assumptions translated into material reality in the laboratory by human inventiveness. As an object of experimentation and knowledge, *nature* has at once a material reality which is irretrievably culturally instructed and constructed.

What will happen with good old sex?

Sex, the source of life, next to death, is among the most glorious and richly symbolized, and emotionally charged materiality in human experience. But sex is not just about humans coming into being as living organisms; it is also about how relationships are thought to be engendered. Even if what is handled in the laboratory is disembodied reproductive stuff, eggs, sperm, embryos, biotechnological manipulations are charged with specific symbolic meanings (Stolcke).

One initial reaction to the prospect of human cloning was to dismiss this probability as science fiction. Caught up in scientific excitement and alarm, few realized that Dolly's inventors had applied for patents in 1997 covering cloning technology not only for animals, but also humans ("Dolly Goes"). In 2005, Dr. Ian Wilmut abandoned research with animals to move to Edinburgh University's Queen's Medical Research Institute having gained permission to clone human embryos! ("Cautious Revolutionary").

The remarkable advances in human embryo stem cell research may have removed reproductive cloning from the public eye. But one serious consideration remained from among the multitude of more or less fantastic scenarios. One observer expressed her suspicion in the journal *Science* in 1997 that though ". . . Like with all breakthroughs it's not possible yet to foretell exactly where cloning will lead;" . . . "there have been whispers that such cloning may one day have a place in giving infertile couples genetic offspring" (Pennisi). The same year, the journal *Nature Biotechnology* drew attention to the "apparently more realistic debates on fertility," that is, the hope that so-called reproductive cloning might serve to cure certain kinds of infertility in humans.[14] Hence, President Clinton's Bioethics Commission proposed that human embryo cloning for implantation be banned precisely because "the history of infertility treatment—especially *in-vitro* fertilization—demonstrated that where there is a sizeable and well-financed demand for a novel service, there will be professionals willing to try to provide it" (Wadman "White House"; "Backing"; Fundación). By the turn of the millennium, British scientists thought that human cloning was inevitable.[15]

To grasp reproductive cloning's genuine potential as a new infertility cure, it must be remembered that cloning is an asexual extra-uterine procedure that makes it possible to create complete organisms which are genetically practically identical to the somatic cell donor.

A passion for genetic descent: pluripotency against infertility

The spectacular advances in embryology and molecular biology encouraged by determinist genetic scientific persuasions implicate first and foremost biological reproduction with its socio-cultural meanings. I have shown elsewhere that the well-established demand for assisted reproduction responds to the powerful and typically modern Western desire for biological parenthood through technological motherhood.[16]

The British Warnock Report of 1984 on the regulation of the new reproductive technologies was quite explicit about this desire:

> Childlessness can be a source of stress even to those who have deliberately chosen it . . . In addition to social pressure to have children there is, for many, *a powerful urge to perpetuate their genes through a new generation*. This desire cannot be assuaged by adoption.

When a child is, however, conceived with donated gametes or embryos and/or is carried to maturity in the womb of a surrogate mother, a socio-legal convention replaces biological parenthood. Conception hitherto requires an egg and a uterus so that motherhood has preserved its *naturalness*, whereas fatherhood by becoming more *artificial* is more fragile. The Spanish law professor Balcells Gorina, a member of the Catholic lay organization *Opus Dei*, was expressing a widespread cultural conviction about legitimate fatherhood when he rejected heterologous insemination—fertilization of a woman with donor sperm—because it constituted adultery.[17] Men, in effect, do appear to be more reluctant than their wives to have a child conceived with donated sperm (Plaza).

Yet, biotechnology found a remedy for paternal dislodgement. Since the birth of Louise Brown in 1978, assisted reproduction has made remarkable strides, especially in the treatment of male infertility. In 1997, a baby girl was conceived by a combination of two pioneering techniques: the freezing of eggs and the injection of spermatozoa, extracted surgically from a man's testicles, into the oocyte's cytoplasm. This technique was called ICSI (intra-cytoplasmatic sperm injection) and had met with immediate enthusiastic acceptance since 1992 when the first successes with sperm injection into a human egg were reported.[18] The use of ICSI before experimental evidence of its safety was available, had to do with men's desire to have biological offspring "of their own blood or genes."

In a letter addressed to the journal *Nature*, French geneticist and member of the French Comité Consultif National d'Ethique Axel Kahn demanded that the report of Dr. Ian Wilmut on Dolly's creation be withheld to gain time for an ethical assessment of the prospects of human cloning because, as he wrote, there prevailed currently a

> strong social and psychological trend towards a fanatical desire for individuals not simply to have children but to ensure that these children also carry their genes,

even when faced with the obstacle of sterility (or death) . . . today's society is characterized by an increasing demand for biological inheritance, as if this were the only form of inheritance worthy of the name. One reason is that, regrettably, a person's personality is increasingly perceived as being largely determined by his or her genes.

This fanatical desire to have biological offspring, sharpened by the renewed confidence in the genetic basis of selfhood and behavior, could become a powerful reason, Kahn thought, to condone cloning of human babies, particularly in the case of severe forms of male sterility such as dysplacia or testicular atrophy:

> Applying the technique used by Wilmut et al. in sheep directly to humans would yield a clone *of the father* and not a shared descendant of both the father and the mother. Nevertheless, for a woman the act of carrying a foetus can be as important as being its biological mother. The extraordinary power of such maternal appropriation of the embryo can be seen in the strong demand for pregnancies in post-menopausal women, and for embryo and oocyte donations to circumvent female sterility. Moreover, if cloning techniques were ever to be used, the mother would be contributing something—her mitochondrial genome. This suggests that we probably cannot exclude the possibility that the current direction of public opinion will tend to legitimize the resort to cloning techniques in cases, where, for example the male partner in a couple is unable to produce any gametes. (2–3)

Therapeutic and reproductive cloning engender embryos whose nuclear genome is entirely derived from a single individual. Clones are genetic copies of the cell nucleus donor. In genetic terms, they are identical twins removed in time rather than genetic offspring. Faced with infertility, the powerful cultural desire to have offspring who carry one's own genes twists genetic reality. Though quite remarkable, it should not be a surprise either that scientific endeavors are underway to satisfy Western bilateral kinship conceptions by means of a biotechnological solution of the *uniparental* origin of cloned progeny. In 2002, a new cloning-derived technique was announced aiming at syngamy (the union of two gametes to form a zygote) between the gamete nucleus from one parent and a somatic cell nucleus from the other to obtain a "biparental embryo"! (Tesarik).

My kingdom for an egg
With ICSI, a single spermatozoa is now enough for a man to have bio-genealogical offspring. Human embryo cloning does not require sperm, but a woman's eggs and womb, donated or rented, are absolutely indispensable. For quite a few people, the fact that no sperm should be involved in reproductive cloning comes as a shock: "I'm getting totally confused here—what about men—how can you have a baby without

men?" one woman interviewed for the Wellcome Trust public opinion study wondered. Another woman asked herself how it would be "growing up and being told that actually you did not have a father at all, genetically." Yet another woman spoke of "male redundancy." Fatherhood is thought to be located in the spermatozoa which, however, cloning makes expendable.[19] Women's eggs, by contrast, are the indispensable, most sought-after and most valuable reproductive stuff of all as biotechnological research gains momentum. When François Jacob quoted Diderot to the effect: "Do you see this egg? With it you can overthrow all the schools of theology, all the churches of the world," he was simply referring to the source of all life, namely the egg (*Logic* v).

The controversy over cloning and stem cell research has focused largely on the moral status of the human embryo ignoring the welfare and rights of women who provide the eggs that are indispensable to produce cloned embryos. Only when the scandal of the South Korean Hwang Woo-suk's false claim to have obtained eleven human embryo stem cell lines in the laboratory broke, did the often fraudulent methods to get hold of oocytes receive some publicity (Galpern and Darnovky).

James Watson was thus wrong when, in 1971, he foresaw that, once they were technically accessible, women's eggs would become a *readily available commodity*. On the contrary, with growing biotechnological demand, oocytes have literally become *the golden eggs*. The need in biotechnological research and infertility treatment for fresh, good quality egg cells is high. Human egg cells are, indeed, fast becoming a *commodity* the price of which is set by supply and demand in more or less illegal egg trafficking on a globalizing market.[20] In the United States, for example, as early as in 1998, a private fertility clinic attempted to outbid the conventional compensation for egg extractions by offering a price twenty times higher in order to attract more donors (Kolata "Price"). Dr. Ian Wilmut proposed recently that women be asked to undergo fertility treatment to donate eggs for research with the British Human Fertility and Embryo Authority's permission ("Cautious Revolutionary"). Other schemes, such as offering cut-rate *in vitro* fertilization at a National Health Service clinic in Great Britain in exchange for donating some of the woman's eggs to science or so-called egg-sharing between couples (Mulligan; Nicholl), are all attempts to improve egg supply by manipulating women without breaking the law.

The biotechnological foregrounding of egg donors is also conditioned by national and international inequalities. An international human egg cell trade is developing which, on one hand, takes the form of fertility tourism to distant or not-so-distant countries where eggs are to be had easily, anonymously, and cheaply and, on the other, poor immigrant women in Europe offer to donate eggs or to rent their wombs over internet to the best bidder.[21]

Economic interests, cultural convictions and ethical objections push the biotechnological cutting edge forever forward. On the biotech experimental front, meanwhile, researchers seek techniques to circumvent their dependence on women's egg cell and embryos for stem cell research. For example, in 2005, a research team at the University of Tennessee announced that it had managed to get human eggs from cultured adult stem cells of egg tissue of five women without destroying the eggs (Sampedro; "World First"). Shortly thereafter, a group of scientists at Harvard University published a technique in *Science* that made possible the production of stem cells from skin cells similar to embryo cells. Dr. Eggan, the head of the team, concluded:

> We must continue research in therapeutic cloning, but the advantage of the new technique is that it does not require eggs. *I don't say this for religious or ideological motives but because eggs are expensive, there are few and they are difficult to manipulate genetically.* (Méndez; Elvira)

Conclusion

I began this essay pointing out an innermost contradiction in modernity. Although humans are thought to be born as free and unique individuals, they find themselves at once entangled in a complex and constraining web of social relationships and symbolic meanings. Cloning culture partakes in this inconsistency in modern liberal ethos and displays it in contradictory manners.

The possibility of genetically producing identical populations in the laboratory has captured many writers' fantasies for some time. Ursula LeGuin was struck by Rattray Taylor's description, in his book *The Biological Time Bomb,* of biology's intrusion in the process by which living beings reproduce themselves and, in 1968 wrote a fable about clones. In the tale, a spaceship from Earth lands on a remote and desolate planet. The astronauts were twelve clones who, for that reason, had a special ability to work as a team. Their assignment was to aid the two technicians in residence to explore and exploit a local mine. But an earthquake destroys the mine, buries and kills all members of the mission save Kaph, "a lost piece of a broken game, a fragment, without experience of solitude, without even knowing how to give love to another individual . . ."[22] Left behind by his cloned twins, Kaph is incapable of acting as an independent individual.

Scholars of the anthropology of kinship such as Sarah Franklin and Marilyn Strathern have suggested, by contrast, that the new reproductive technologies, especially the imaging of embryos in prenatal screening and the extra-uterine manipulation of embryos in stem cell research, reinforce individualism because they erode conventional interactive conceptions of kin relatedness. Beside strengthening a genetic conception of individual identity, the new reproductive technologies appear to underwrite a kind of "post-relational" individualism.[23]

However, both scenarios are one-sided because they are framed in the conventional modern dualism between culture and nature, between personal freedom and genetic determination. Yet modern living is constituted precisely of steering one's way uncomfortably and with frustrations through the tensions rooted in the two contrary modern principles of free will and innate or imposed external constraints. Joshua Lederberg, a leading scientist, warned in the 1960s that biology might be "on the brink of a major evolutionary perturbation" (G. R. Taylor 23). Dolly, the cloned sheep, ushered in the perturbing novelty of the asexual conception of human beings without eradicating the contradictory spirit of modernity. Therapeutic cloning of embryos to obtain stem cells in the laboratory promises individualized made-to-measure attention to and treatment of people's "genetic diseases," thereby cultivating a genetic worldview to the detriment of environmental factors. But this is only one side of the revolution in embryology reserved, moreover, for the wealthy of this world. On account of the typically Western passion for biogenetic parenthood, reproductive cloning of human beings is becoming ever more likely as male infertility increases. This desire for a child "of one's own blood" (now read genes) by means of the most "advanced" biogenetic techniques can scarcely be held back in a society geared to satisfying consumers' every whim. But this wish to "form a family" and have a perfect child "of one's own," which expresses in an especially literal manner the old conventional notion of biological kin relatedness, can hardly be regarded as an individualist quest. Instead, it is one manifestation of the intensely competitive, achievement-oriented but profoundly unequal modern society in which individuals' accomplishments are attributed, paradoxically, to innate capabilities or failings.

Notes

1. Handler was president of the National Academy of Sciences in the 1970s during the recombinant DNA regulation battle. He counted on legislation to be enacted, but thought that the hazards of the technique were largely in the imagination of a small group of scientists.

2. Dolly was born on 5 July 1996 but Ian Wilmut, the head of the Roselin Institute team, postponed its announcement in order to obtain a patent for the procedure. Note also that, in summer 1995, two lambs, Morgan and Megan, had been born at the Roselin Institute, Scotland, carried to term by a "surrogate mother." Their genetic material came from cultured cells originally derived from a nine-day-old embryo instead of having been engendered by the union of a sperm and an egg.

3. Dolly, the sheep, was conceived after 277 trials.

4. But *The Economist* wrote at the time, "One block on large-animal engineering is that the most revolutionary technique in mouse transgenics—called embryonic stem cell technology—does not work in many other mammalian species . . . Nuclear transplantation, Dolly's immaculate conception, may be one way of overcoming this barrier in sheep and other species. Present company not included?" See "Genetic Engineering."

5. See Wellcome Trust, the first public opinion study carried out in Britain.

6. One common reaction to the pressure under which research teams work is manipulation of results. About 15% of researchers are said to modify the design, methods and results of a study to please their funders. See Dean. The human cloning scandal in South Korea is exceptional, but nonetheless symptomatic of the vast sums of money and power at stake. This greatest recent fraud has to do with the frontier of cloning. In May 2004, Professor Hwang Woo-Suk announced publicly that he had obtained 11 different lines of human embryonic stem cells by means of cloning human embryos.

The scientific community was stunned by such an output and immediately started research programs to replicate the results. In October, at the peak of his fame, Hwang Woo-Suk inaugurated an international consortium on human embryonic cells. But then, *Science* which, despite rigorous peer control, had published Hwang's research, reported that there were mistakes in the article. The scandal was doubled. The research results were a fraud and the great number of eggs required had been obtained by coercing young research assistants into donating eggs and by purchase. In the end, Hwang's only demonstrable achievement was the cloning of his dog Snuppy, the result of 1,095 attempts. See "Human Cloning Scandal"; Cyranoski.

7. In 1999, Geron Corporation of California, for example, announced a new technique to obtain *immortal* cells, which could be used to replace stem cells of tissues before they decayed. See Wade.

8. Like voluntary interruption of pregnancy, human embryo research raised again the debate over when human life begins related to setting limits to biotechnological experimentation to protect human dignity without wiping out biomedical research.

9. In 1979, the frog embryologist Clifford Grobstein introduced the word *pre-embryo*. He held that, since identical twins may occur up to fourteen days after fertilization, only a *genetic individual*, not a *developmental individual*, and therefore an embryo, a *person*, is not present. Opponents of human embryo research regard this nomenclature as totally discredited. See Shea.

10. Kolata "Name Games"; Mario; Newman. Scientists consulted by the European Union in 1997 opposed human reproductive cloning, but they did not reject experimentation with human embryos under sixteen days old as long as they were not implanted in a womb. See "Expertos." Drs. Edwards and Steptoe, who had *conceived* Louise Brown, the first test tube baby, were also

approached for their opinions about cloning. Edwards thought that stem cells could be made available through embryo cloning to fabricate organs for transplant. French scientist Jacques Testart was, however, very critical of reproductive cloning. See Postel-Venay and Millet.

11. Haraway's rejection of the nature-culture dichotomy in her endeavor to design a productive politics for the generation of knowledge that bridges the tense opposition in contemporary feminist and general theory between a radically constructivist approach to knowledge as the invariable result of maneuvers of power and feminist capital empiricism, which at more objective demystifications of the *real world* and her emphasis on multiple local knowledges, still strikes me as inspirational. See Latour *Nous n'avons*; Rabinow; Latour *Politics*.

12. Even though dissident voices signalled the beginnings of an epigenetic challenge. See Strohman; Jacob, *Possible* 34. Another distinguished critic of the prevailing genetic determinist paradigm is Richard C. Lewontin.

13. Almost four decades after identifying the double helix, Watson confessed that "We used to think our fate was in the stars; now we know, in large measure, it is in our genes." Watson qtd. Jaroff.

14. See "Thinking about Cloning." For a policy overview regarding the United States, see also Javitt, et al. President Clinton's National Advisory Bioethics Commission heard a wide range of mostly cautious opinions on cloning humans. One bioethicist, however, rejected a ban on reproductive cloning for "cloning should receive the same (constitutional) protection as other non-coital methods of assisted reproduction." See Wadman "U. S. Senators"; "Expertos."

15. More than half of a panel of 32 scientists surveyed by the British newspaper *The Independent* foresaw that reproductive cloning would be attempted within 20 years. See Connor.

16. Stolcke 5–19. Abundant anthropological evidence indicates the enormous cultural variations in notions of kin relatedness and parenthood. Although it is now well established that infertility is distributed about equally between women and men, it is quite remarkable that studies of the culturally differing experiences and attitudes toward infertility should focus almost exclusively on women. See Inhorn and van Balen. Jurists, by contrast, show concern for protecting fatherhood because *in-vitro* fertilization provides women with "a socially adequate instrument to dislodge the husband." See Balz.

17. See Gorina. The term *heterologous* connotes the fact of the subject "belonging to a different species."

18. See "Nace una niña." So spectacular was the reaction to ICSI that Carl Djerassi, inventor of The Pill, turned its development into a play entitled *The Immaculate Misconception,* which was successfully staged in August 1998 at the Edinburgh Fringe Festival <http://www.dejarassi.com/icsi.html:1>. In the meantime, even more sophisticated techniques have been developed to help men to perpetuate themselves. Men who do not produce sperm nonetheless often possess spermatids in their testicles. These can be recovered and their nuclei extracted to inject them into the oocytes' cytoplasm. This method is called ROSNI (Round Spermatid Nucleus Injection). And those men who do not even have round spermatids may also soon have a chance. A method is being developed to recover the most immature cells from the testicles so as to cultivate them in a surrogate testicle, perhaps of a pig or a bull, where they will differentiate and evolve into completely active spermatozoa. See Silver 105–108; Djerassi.

19. See Wellcome Trust 16–18, 41. Men were not asked their opinions about asexual reproduction.

20. Professor Deborah Spar of Harvard Business School has estimated the yearly expenditure for assisted reproduction in the United States alone at $3 million. In 2004, over one million Americans underwent an infertility treatment. In the Ukraine, by contrast, it is possible to rent a uterus for a few thousand dollars. See "Il est né le divin" 51.

21. See "International Human Eggs Trade." Hiltrud Breyer wrote in her role as president of the Bioethic-Intergroup in the European Parliament and a member of the Bündnis 90/Die Grünen. See Cózar. The majority of these women are immigrants who advertise surrogate motherhood on the internet for 15,000 euros; see Belaza. This article refers to internet advertisements, also mostly by immigrant women, for egg donation. Spanish fertility clinics offer, by contrast, compensation of 600 to 1,000 euros per egg extraction. Since the United Kingdom has lifted the anonymity clause on egg donation, fertility tourists to Spain have increased notably. See Tremlett.

22. See LeGuin 186. This first appeared in *Playboy* in 1968, the only time the author used the pseudonym U. K. Le Guin. See also G. R. Taylor.

23. According to Strathern, in this way the embryo is transformed into a unique natural entity detached from its embeddedness in the material womb and within webs of kin bonds. See Franklin. For an excellent French critique of this predominantly British thesis, see Gené.

Works Cited

"Backing for Anti-Cloning Bill Reopens Embryo Debate." *Nature* 388 (1997): 505.

Balz, Manfred. *Heterologe künstliche Samenübertragung beim Menschen.* Tübingen, 1980.

Belaza, Mónica C. "Óvulos a 2.000 euros." *El País* 30 July 2006.

"Biotechnology: Betting on the Genome: The Genomics Gamble." (1997): 767–775.

Bloom, Floyd E. "Breakthroughs 1997." *Science* 278 (1997): 2029.

Breyer, Hiltrud. "Egg Cell Trade Endangers the European Union as a Community of Values." 6 June 2005. 9 Nov. 2006 <www.bionews.org.uk/commentary.lasso?storyid=2602>.

Bryan, Elizabeth M. "A Spare or an Individual? Cloning and the Implications of Manozygotic Twinning." *Human Reproduction Update* 4 (1998): 812–815.

Butler, Declan. "Breakthrough Stirs US Embryo Debate . . . While Europe Contemplates Funding Ban." *Nature* 396 (1998): 104.

Canning, K. *Gender History in Practice: Historical Perspectives on Bodies, Class and Citizenship.* 2006.

"Cautious Revolutionary." *The Guardian* 26 July 2005 <http://education.guardian.co.uk/academicexperts/story/0,,1535747,00,html>.

Comité Consultif National d'Ethique. "Réponse au Président de la République au sujet du clonage reproductive." 22 Apr. 1997 <http://www.ccne.ethique.org>.

Connor, Steve. "Human Cloning is Now 'Inevitable.'" *The Independent* 30 Aug. 2000.

Cózar, Álvaro de. "Decenas de mujeres se ofrecen en España como madres de alquiler." *El País* 30 July 2006.

Cyranoski, David. "Verdict: Hwang's Human Stem Cells Were All Fakes: Landmark Papers Shown to be Fradulent, But Snuppy Turns Out to be a Real Cloned Dog." *Nature* (published online 10 Jan. 2006). 29 Aug. 2006.

Dean, Cornelia. "Investigaciones manipuladas." *El País* 5 July 2005.

Della Mirandola, Pico. *Oration of the Dignity of Man.* 1463–1494.

Descola, Philippe. *Par-delà nature et culture.* Paris: Gallimard, 2005.

Djerassi, Carl. *An Immaculate Misconception.* Edinburgh: Edinburgh Fringe Festival, 1999.

"Dolly Goes to Market: World Patents on Sheep Clones Include Humans." <http://users.westnet.gr/cgian/clonepat.htm>.

Edwards, Jeanette. Born and Bred: Idioms of Kinship and New Reproductive Technologies in England. Oxford: Oxford UP, 2000.

Edwards, Jeanette, Sarah Franklin, Eric Hirsch, Frances Price, and Marylin Strathern. eds. Technologies of Procreation: Kinship in the Age of Assisted Conception. Manchester: Manchester UP, 1993.

Elvira, Malen Ruiz de. "Científicos de EE UU logran células madre sin destruir los embriones." El País 24 Aug. 2006.

"Embryonic stem cell," Wikipedia, the free encyclopedia: 1–3. 1 Sept. 2006 http://en.wikipedia.org/wiki/Embryonic_stem_cell.

"Expertos en infertilidad de EEUU se muestran a favor de la clonación en humanos." El País 8 June 1997: 26.

Franklin, Sarah. "Making Representations: The Parliamentary Debate on the Human Fertilization and Embryology Act." Technologies of Procreation: Kinship in the Age of Assisted Conception. Eds. Jeanette Edwards, Sarah Franklin, Eric Hirsch, Frances Price, and Marylin Strathern. Manchester: Manchester UP, 1993. 96–131.

Fundación de Ciencias de la Salud. Informe sobre Clonación. Madrid, 1999.

Galpern, Emily, and Marcy Darnovky. "Eggs vs. Ethics in Stem Cell Debate." The Nation 29 Nov. 2005. 29 Aug. 2006 <http://www.thenation.com/doc/20051212/galpern>.

Gené, Enric Porqueres I. "Individu et parenté: Individivuation de l'embryon." Corps et Affects. Eds. François Héritier and Margarite Xanthakou. Paris: Odile Jacob, 2004.

"Genetic Engineering: Building to Order." The Economist 1 Mar. 1997: 81.

Gorina, Alfonso Balcells. "La inseminación artificial, zootecnía en el hombre." La Vanguardia 3 May 1980.

Handler, Philip. Biology and the Future of Man. Oxford: Oxford UP, 1970.

Haraway, Donna J. Simian, Cyborgs and Women: The Reinvention of Nature. London: Free Association, 1991.

"The Human Cloning Scandal in South Korea: Toward a Post-cloning Era." Gèneéthique.Bioethic information and analysis newsletter 72 (Dec. 2005). 7 Sept. 2006 <www.genethique.org/en/letters/letters/2005/december.htm>.

Human Genetics Advisory Commission. May 1998: 49–51.

Human Genome Project Information. "Cloning Fact Sheet." 17 Sept. 2006 <www.ornl.gov/sci/technresources/Human Genome/elsi/cloning.shtml,3>.

"Il est né le divin enfant: L'essor du bébé-business." Courrier International 842–843 (21 Dec. 2006 to 3 Jan. 2007): 42–51.

Inhorn, Marcia C., and Frank van Balen, eds. Infertility around the Globe: New Thinking on Childlessness, Gender, and Reproductive Technologies. Berkeley: U of California P, 2002.

"International Human Eggs Trade: Cruel Cost of the Human Egg Trade." The Guardian, digital ed. 30 Apr. 2006. 10 June 2006.

Jacob, François. The Logic of Life: A History of Heredity. New York: Pantheon, 1973. v.

———. The Possible and the Actual. New York: Pantheon, 1994.

Jaroff, Leon. "The Great Hunt." Time 20 Mar. 1989: 62, 67.

Jasanoff, Sheila. Designs on Nature: Science and Democracy in Europe and the United States. Oxford: Princeton UP, 2005.

Javitt, Gail H., et al. *Cloning: A Policy Analysis.* Washington: Genetic and Public Policy Center, 2005.

Kahn, Axel. "Clone Mammals-Clone Man?" *Nature* 385 (1997): 1–4 <www.nature.com/Nature2>.

Keller, Evelyn Fox. "Nature, Nurture, and the Human Genome Project." *Code of Codes: Scientific and Social Issues in the Human Genome Project.* Eds. Daniel J. Kevles and Leroy Hood. Cambridge: Harvard UP, 1992. 291–293.

Kevles, Daniel J. "Out of Eugenics: The Historical Politics of the Human Genome." *Code of Codes: Scientific and Social Issues in the Human Genome Project.* Eds. Daniel J. Kevles and Leroy Hood. Cambridge: Harvard UP, 1992.

Kischer, C. Ward. "The Big Lie in Human Embryology: The Case of the Pre-embryo." 6 Sept. 2006 <http://www.lifeissues.net/writers/kisc/kisc_11biglipreembryo.html>.

Kolata, Gina. *Clone: The Road to Dolly and the Path Ahead.* New York: Quill, 1999.

———. "Name Games and the Science of Life." *New York Times* 29 May 2005.

———. "Price of Donor Eggs Soars, Setting Off a Debate on Ethics." *New York Times* 25 Feb. 1998. 12 Sept. 2006 <nytimes.com>.

Latour, Bruno. *Nous n'avons jamais été modernes: Essai d'Anthropologie Symmétrique.* Paris: La Découverte, 1997.

———. *Politics of Nature: How to Bring the Sciences into Democracy.* Cambridge: Harvard UP, 2004.

LeGuin, Ursula. "Nueve vidas." *Las doce moradas del viento.* Barcelona: Edhasa, 1975. 186.

Mario, Christopher. "A Spark of Science, A Storm of Controversy. *U.S.1 Newspaper* 5 Mar. 1997: 1–6. Princeton U, New Jersey. 16 Sept. 2006 <www.princetoninfo.com/clone.html>.

Méndez, Rafael. "Científicos de EE UU abren una vía para crear células madre sin usar embriones." *El País* 23 Aug. 2005.

Mulligan, Megan. "The High Price of Human Eggs." *Washington Post* 3 Aug. 2006. 29 Aug. 2006 <Washingtonpost.com>.

"Nace una niña concebida de un ovocito congelado e inseminado." *El País* 18 Feb. 1997.

Newman, Stuart A. "Cloning Our Way to 'the Next Level.'" *Nature Biotechnology* 15 (1997): 488.

Nicholl, Heidi. "Payment for Egg Donation Debate Continues." *Progress Educational Trust, Bionews, London* 15 Aug. 2006. 29 Aug. 2006 <www.Bionews.org.uk>.

Nodé-Langlois, Fabrice, and Monique Vigy. "François Jacob: 'Faire des enfants sans plaisir ni spermatozoïde.'" *Le Figaro* 27 Feb. 1997.

Nussbaum, Martha C. and Cass R. Sunstein, eds. *Clones and Clones: Facts and Fantasies about Human Cloning.* New York: Norton, 1998.

Pennisi, Elizabeth. "The Lamb that Roared." *Science* 278 (1997): 2038–2039.

Plaza, Consuelo Álvarez. "La búsqueda de la eterna fertilidad: tensión y construcciones culturales en el sistema de donación de la reproducción humana asistida." Doctoral thesis. Universidad Complutense de Madrid, May 2006.

Postel-Venay, O., and A. Millet. ¿Qué tal, Dolly? *Mundo Científico* 180 (1997): 546.

"Press Statement Regarding Human-Animal Hybrid Research." 8 Nov. 2007 <http:.//www.hfea.gov.uk/en/1478.html>.

Rabinow, Paul. *Making PCR: A Story of Biotechnology.* Chicago: Chicago UP, 1996.

Sampedro, Javier. "Un equipo de EEUU obtiene óvulos de células madre adultas." *El País* 6 May 2005.

"Schlacht um die Gene." *Der Spiegel* 7 Sept. 1998.

Shea, J. B. "The Pre-embryo Question." *Catholic Insight* (reproduced 30 Oct. 2004). 9 Apr. 2007 <http://lifeissues.net/writers/she/she_26pre_embryoquestion.html>.

Silver, Lee M. *Vuelta al Edén: Mas allá de la clonación en un mundo feliz.* Madrid: Taurus, 1997. 105–108.

Stolcke, Verena. "New Reproductive Technologies: The Old Quest for Fatherhood." *Reproductive and Genetic Engineering* 1 (1998): 5–19.

Strathern, Marilyn. *After Nature: English Kinship in the Late Twentieth Century.* Cambridge: Cambridge UP, 1992.

Strohman, Richard C. "The Coming Kuhnian Revolution in Biology." *Nature Biotechnology* 15 (1997): 194–200.

Taylor, E. Stewart. "It's All in What You Call It." Colorado Gynaecological and Obstetrical Society 7. May 2001.

Taylor, Gordon Rattray. *The Biological Time-Bomb.* London: Thames and Hudson, 1968.

Tesarik, J. "Reproductive Semi-cloning Respecting Biparental Embryo Origin: Embryos from Syngamy between a Gamete and a Haploidized Somatic Cell." *Human Reproduction* 17 (2002): 1933–1937.

"Thinking about Cloning." *Nature Biotechnology* 15 (1997): 293.

Tremlett, Giles. "Spain Becomes the Destination of Choice for Fertility Tourists from Britain." *The Guardian* 12 May 2006.

Verdú, Vincent. "El auge del plagio." *El País* 12 Oct. 2001.

Vogel, Gretchen. "Breakthrough of the Year: Capturing the Promise of Youth." *Science* 286 (1999): 2238–2239.

Wade, Nicholas. "Los cientificos ven la inmoralidad en células que se dividen indefinidamente." *El País* 3 Jan. 1999.

Wadman, Meredith. "U. S. Senators Urge Caution on Cloning Ban." *Nature* 386 (1997): 204.

———. "White House Bill Would Ban Human Cloning." *Nature* 387 (1997): 644.

Warnock, Lady Mary. *Question of Life: Warnock Report on Human Fertilization and Embryology.* London, 1984.

Watson, D. James. "Moving Toward the Clonal Man." *The Atlantic Monthly* 22 (1971): 50.

Wellcome Trust, The. *Public Perspectives on Human Cloning: A Social Research Study.* London, 1998.

Williams, Raymond. *A Vocabulary of Culture and Society.* London: Fontana, 1976.

"World First: Scientists Succeed in Cloning Human Embryos from Eggs Matured in the Lab." Copenhagen, European Society of Human Reproduction & Embryology. Press release 29 July 2005.

Thamyris/Intersecting No. 25 (2012) 45–60

Gentech Agriculture

Heleen van den Hombergh[1]

While beginning to work on this article, the title of a book I ran across long ago came to mind: *Rape of the Wild*. The authors (Collard and Contrucci) explored the common cultural foundations and expressions of man's violence against nature and animals. Much like other philosophical scholars of the time (Merchant; Warren; Haraway; Achterhuis), they addressed the logic of domination of man over the natural world and what is considered "male" over what is considered "female," a logic based on the normative dualism rooted in Western philosophy since the 16th and 17th centuries. It is found in expressions such as: "force nature to serve you and make her your slave."[2] The scholars argued that this logic of domination is reflected in science and technology and the intent of its owners to control and exploit the natural world with them—a natural world which, in both Western and non-Western philosophies, is associated with "the female." Based on a vast set of quantitative data, policy reports and academic articles, others have shown that, especially because of gender division of responsibilities, labor and control over natural resources, environmental degradation and pollution in practice are felt most severely by poor women (Dankelman and Davidson).

The decline of biological diversity is a case in point. In many parts of the world, women have more diverse tasks and responsibilities than men in the provision and production of food, fodder, fiber and medicine, This is often reflected in a wider knowledge of plant species and their use, and a stronger interaction of women with plant as well as ecosystem diversity (Abramowitz; Shiva). Decline of this biological diversity is often first felt by women as it affects their work and income but, finally, by all who are dependent upon natural resources for their livelihoods. In times of drought and famine in Eastern Africa, women's knowledge of edible parts of bushes and weeds has often come to the rescue. In times of accelerating climate change, the variety of choices for land users in vulnerable areas becomes even more vital to their survival.

This article is about Gentech Agriculture. What does this type of agriculture have to do with the philosophical concepts and effects of environmental decline on poor women? Genetic engineering (GE) goes beyond cloning, the technique through which more individuals are made from the same embryo, which are "copies of the original." GE is a technique that makes it possible to change the genetic characteristics of an organism by inserting alien DNA into its cells—DNA which may be from a species that could never cross with the manipulated species through nature. For example, GE has produced a tomato with the gene of a fish and cotton with built-in insecticide. Unlike cloning, with genetically engineered organisms the next generations take with them the altered composition, although little is known of how the genetic composition develops over time. Genetic engineering is already widely applied to agricultural production such as soy, corn, cotton and canola (rapeseed), the first commercial planting having taken place in 1996. Many other crops are following.

This technology has led to fierce debate and protests. The most worrisome feature of genetically modified crops is their ability to contaminate and reshape conventional, traditional or wild varieties of agricultural crops and associated life forms, taking with them the "alien" elements and their unknown behavior in the genome. Knowing that there are strong economic powers behind the rapid spread of GE crops around the world, this fact provoked my memory of the book mentioned above; would it lead to "rape of the wild"? As I will argue, active influence over policies by the GE lobby, coercion by contamination, and threats of punishment for those who want to take safety measures are all part of what one might call a downright war on diversity.

This article is neither meant to deny the benefits of agricultural technologies nor to deny that there may be beneficial agricultural technologies based on GE beyond us even for the poor. Neither is it meant to settle the scientific controversies and uncertainties over the risk aspects of GE—not in the least because of the lack of independent scientific data available to date. Instead, this article focuses on the coercive principles and practices involved in corporately controlled GE agriculture, the violation of the precautionary principle by the release of GE crops and seed into the environment and food chains, and the risks this may pose to global diversity in its many aspects.

Claims and counter-claims

The possibilities of gene technology in agriculture give rise to expectations. Claims have been made by its proponents that GE will end vitamin A deficiency among the poorest of people, make formerly barren dry and salt lands cultivable, make pesticides superfluous and even solve world hunger. However, these arguments have been opposed fiercely, and resistance to the application of GE in agriculture is growing as its areas and crop experiments are extending. Arguments challenging the notion that GE technology will solve hunger have included the following (Rosset). First, there is enough food for everyone worldwide, but poverty, inequality and lack of access to food, or land upon which to cultivate it, cause hunger. What's more, over-production and dumping of food, caused by unfair trade rules, also cause hunger instead of solving it, because local producers are pushed out of the market. This does not eliminate the need to increase productivity, especially in some sub-Saharan countries. The question is if expensive GE technology is the answer or if low-cost technologies plus a set of infrastructural measures and redistributive policies can deliver more gain for the poor (Rosset; DeGrassi; Lappé, et al.).

Secondly, GE poses a series of risks to farmers, biological diversity and possibly consumers. Some of these concerns will be further reviewed below; here they are presented with a birds-eye view. Many farmers have opted for GE agricultural seeds, either because of their herbicide tolerance (no weeding needed in soy or canola cultivation) or their pest-resistant characteristics (less chemicals in cotton and corn). The real industrial objective of genetic engineering in agriculture, however, seems to increase farmers' dependence on seeds and chemicals. Resistance of pests to the built-in insecticides of GE crops, such as cotton and maize, occurs rapidly, and costs per hectare increase when pest outbreaks occur because more pesticides are required instead of less. GE yields often have been disappointing or have simply failed to date (Rosset; CSA), posing extra risks to the resource-poor, but that is not the main problem. Because of the contamination risks involved—the transfer of genes from GE crops to others with unknown effects—the cultivation of GE crops poses a potential threat to agro-biodiversity, which is crucial for risk reduction and future experimentation in agricultural systems of the poor specifically. As I will discuss below, this is especially important in risk-prone, dry, areas and in the face of climate variability and change. Also, wider ecological risks present themselves related to the unforeseeable interactions of the crops with other organisms, such as insects and other animals. Furthermore, by investing in costly GE research, public institutions expend scarce funds, while existing technologies offer ample opportunities for improvement if sufficient public funds are made available (Pretty and Hyne; Hickey and Mittal; Rosset).

Because of the perceived disadvantages and risks, coalitions of scientists, consumers, farmers, environmental organizations and indigenous communities have opposed the release of GE crops and seeds into the environment. Many of them have promoted "biosafety" legislation: the precautionary approach applied to GE technology. One of the targets of policy advocacy surrounding genetic engineering in agriculture has been the Cartagena Protocol on Biosafety, a supplementary agreement to the UN Convention on Biological Diversity. It is meant to address the potential risks posed by the transboundary movement of "genetically modified organisms" (GMOs, or LMOs—Living Modified Organisms; the term GEOs is not used). Created in 2000 and ratified by 134 countries, the Protocol establishes an Advanced Informed Agreement procedure and sets minimum standards for national biosafety legislation. Considerable political influence on the Protocol was exerted by environmental NGOs, especially during the phase of agenda-setting (Arts and Meck). Further elaboration of the precautionary aspects of the Protocol, and the national biosafety legislation efforts based on its standards, are contentious fields of transnational advocacy these days. In terms of international agreements, consumer awareness especially in Europe (Oosterveer) and farmer awareness in some countries, the anti-GE and pro-biosafety movements have come a long way. However, the counter-reaction of the seed industry and GE proponents is very strong in both policy and practice. As I will argue, coercion is one of the major strategies to push the technology into the world, and reap the related profits.

Homogeneity: What's New?

In the estimated 100 million hectares of GE crops cultivated in the world in 2006 (ISAAA), herbicide resistance and insect resistance were the two most important traits. The major GE crops grown were herbicide tolerant—more specifically "Roundup Ready"—soy and canola, and insect resistant—called "Bt"—corn and cotton. Roundup is the brand name of an herbicide (or weed-killer) produced by agritech giant Monsanto. "Bt" stands for *bacillus thuringiensis*, a plant-inserted bacteria resistant to a particular pest. Other major agricultural crops to which GE is applied are rice, squash, and papaya, but the latter are not yet cultivated on a large scale (AFAA). Moreover, many experiments take place with other cereals, pulses, roots and tubers, vegetables and fruits, as well as with pharmacrops manipulated to serve medicinal purposes (Meijer and Stewart).

As with High Yielding Varieties (HYV) of crops promoted during the Green Revolution and beyond, agricultural species are manipulated to emphasize particular traits. With conventional breeding techniques used to produce HYV, these effects lasted for several crop generations until the existing positive traits of a crop were strengthened. With GE technique, inserting new traits is possible with a flip of the switch in the laboratory, a switch that nature could never turn.

One gene, one trait?

The principle of GE technology is: one gene inserted, one trait added. However, as critical biotechnology scholars have argued, by changing one gene, the whole genome is changed with unforeseen consequences (GRAIN). Also, the traits achieved, such as pest resistance, are not necessarily sustained, because pests become resistant. Neither is the targeted pest necessarily the local problem. For example, Bt-cotton in

India has suffered from low production rates—with cotton bolls falling off unexpectedly and, in some areas, pest attacks have intensified despite the built-in bacteria, as Bt targeted the wrong disease or the pests became resistant (Das). In Indonesia, negative results have also been found. In other places, such as South Africa, the crop seems to have benefited farmers (Meijer and Stewart), although others (DeGrassi) have critically reviewed this claim.

Central to the whole argument is that the "one gene, one trait" principle also denies the ecological effects of GE crops because of their interaction with pollinating animals, livestock, soil and their potential out-crossing with conventional and wild relatives. Greenpeace and Genewatch UK reported more than 100 cases of contamination and 27 illegal releases of GE crops into the field in more than 40 countries since the beginning of commercial cultivation. One third of the cases involve maize, followed by soybean and canola (Greenpeace International). According to the authors, this is often due to poor quality control measures.

Out-crossing with wild relatives is a serious risk in centers of origin of crops, such as maize, which originates in Mexico, soy in China, cotton in some parts of the U.S.A., and for newer GE crops: potato in the Andes, sorghum and cassava in Sub-Sahara Africa, and rice in various parts of Asia (Greenpeace). Contamination or wiping out of these (semi-) wild and diverse stocks would place the potential for future plant breeding in serious trouble. Failing harvests and sudden pest attacks may become economic, ecological and social problems, but wiping out genetic stocks for future use would be a long-term food security disaster. This is the major risk, especially for the poor in vulnerable ecological areas. They are dependent on agricultural varieties that are well adapted to their circumstances. In practice, this is a dynamic process of selection and conservation. Living and working in close relationship with these crops is a vital matter of both cultural identity and survival.

Bt rice from China and the U.S. is a major concern of GE opponents now, as it concerns the most important staple crop in the world and a basis of many cultures. Rice diversity is not only feeding, but also providing income and cultural identities to people throughout Asia and beyond. It is because of these strong cultural and economic connections to crops that genetic contamination of maize which happened in Mexico has caused outrage among farmers and ecologists. The contamination was found to be widespread (Quist and Chapela), despite the prohibition of GE products in the country. As with canola, avoiding contamination by GE varieties of conventional or traditional maize is impossible or, at least, very difficult as it out-crosses very easily and its seed travels very far. It is also not easy to maintain the GE traits of maize because of this, but this does not mean that de-contamination of stocks is a settled matter. Some NGOs have begun to concentrate on experiments with decontamination of GE infected crops, next to supporting farmers to save their varieties of seeds in banks.

Seed saving, seed banks and participatory breeding

Seed and gene banks are important safeguard measures for agricultural biodiversity. Saving and exchanging agricultural seeds are still common cultural practices, especially in poor areas. In Central Mali, community seed banks set up with the help of civil society organizations,[3] sometimes contain up to 40 varieties of sorghum, 28 varieties of millet, 30 varieties of rice, 7 varieties of okra, and various varieties of sesame, maize, peanuts and other crops. As rainfall over the past years has declined below 350 mm annually in some areas, I found during a field visit in 2006, that old sorghum varieties which earlier suffered from too much rainfall, had now been revitalized for use, as currently used varieties did not withstand the drought. In 2006, a citizen's jury in Mali ruled against GE technology for that country among others, because of such values of agro-biodiversity (HED). In Mali, as well as Zimbabwe, during agricultural seed fairs where hundreds of farmers were present, it was mostly women who won the prizes for the best and most varied seed stocks, related to their roles in diverse food production. It is these stocks and this knowledge about cultivated and wild varieties that are very important in times of crisis when adaptability is a matter of survival. It is then that one can be skeptical about "pro-poor" GE technology, advertised by some development specialists, as long as and as far as contamination of poor people's seed stocks is a risk, and de-contamination as a technique is not yet established.

Participatory plant breeding, where researchers support farmers to improve their own genetic materials in agriculture, delivers promising results to improve productivity, among others in the Philippines.[4] However, farmer participation in research is not a panacea for avoiding problems when GE seed enters the scene and contaminates current stocks. If risk can really be controlled, GE might have potential for the future, for example with pest resistant bananas, which are sterile and do not risk outcrossing. In crops such as sorghum and millet, however, the precautionary approach is vital, as they are basic to food security but highly prone to cross-pollination with GE relatives. In order to serve the poor, any technology must satisfy a number of criteria such as being demand-driven and sustainable (DeGrassi) and being applied under a number of political and infrastructural conditions (Scoones). (Other longer-standing technologies (Pretty and Hyne), or new and less risky ones may turn out to be cheaper and serve the purpose of crop improvement better than GE.[5]

Monopoly: two traits, vast areas, few owners

Commercial planting of GE crops began in the mid-1990s, and the pace of extension rose rapidly afterward. So far, the two traits of widely commercialized crops are: herbicide tolerance (about $\frac{3}{4}$ of the area) and pest resistance, sometimes in combination. The major crops have been Roundup Ready soybean (57% in 2006), Bt-maize (25%), Bt-cotton (13%) and Roundup Ready canola (5%) As previously mentioned,

Roundup Ready refers to the tolerance of the crop to the herbicide Roundup, Bt refers to a built-in pesticide called bacillus thuringiensis. In 2006, the U.S.A. (55% of the world area), Argentina (20%), Brazil (10%), Canada (6%), India and China (4%) were the leading growers of the crops mentioned—with Paraguay and South Africa adding to the list (ISAAA).

However, irrespective of whether countries are opting to grow GE crops, most are faced with increasing global trade in agricultural commodities and food—also food aid—containing GE material. The growth of a globalized biotechnology industry and the growth of trade in GE crops and seeds requires countries to develop regulatory systems, forcing them to consider the effect that imports of GE products might have on the sustainability of their agricultural systems, on food security and biosafety, and on their current and future position in global agricultural trade. An additional question for developing countries is whether they should devote scarce financial, institutional and R&D resources to developing GE crops domestically. The potential for pro-poor GE crops has been widely alleged by supporters of the technology, but the evidence remains mixed and is heavily contested. DeGrassi shows for several GE crops that they do not meet six criteria, which could reflect "pro-poor" potential in Sub-Sahara Africa: demand driven, site-specific, poverty focused, cost effective, institutionally sustainable, and environmentally sustainable.

Monsanto's monopoly and the revolving door

Beside the production and environmental risks GE cultivation presents, dependence on multinational firms poses a potential problem to farmers. A small number of multi-national corporations play a pivotal role in research and development, and dominate commercialization and global trade in GE crops and food. Since 2003, the world's top-10 seed companies have increased their control from one-third to one-half of the global seed trade; and the top-10 biotech enterprises have raised their share from just over half to nearly three-quarters of world biotech sales (Etc Group "Oligopoly" 82; Etc Group "Oligopoly" 91). While corporate and technological concentration take place in various industrial sectors, in the GE seed and agrochemical sector this con-centration is extreme, with Monsanto controlling almost the total GE soy and canola market and selling the herbicide to which the crops are tolerant—Roundup. In 2002, Monsanto was second in the world in terms of seed sales with a value of U.S.$1600 million, and third in agrochemicals with U.S.$3088 million (Etc Group "Oligopoly" 82). Once it merged with Seminis in 2005, Monsanto topped the list of seed compa-nies with estimated seed sales of U.S.$2803 million. It dropped to fifth place in agrochemicals that year, despite its growth to U.S.$3180 million in sales. It was bypassed by Bayer, Syngenta, BASF and Dow (Etc Group "Oligopoly" 91).

Friends of the Earth International noticed (!!!!) the powerful political influence of the company, and identified so many of Monsanto's coercive practices, that it has published a special brochure about this company (FOEI). Greenpeace and others have followed the company's activities with scrutiny. Resistance to the release of GE crops into the environment has had effects in terms of consumer awareness, farmer resistance (for example in Indonesia), and has halted GE wheat research in Europe but, so far, has not broken down Monsanto's strong position and influence at all. One of the secret accomplishments is that Monsanto has managed to install a revolving door between its corporate headquarters and most U.S. government agencies that regulate its products (Koons Garcia). For example, during the first Bush Jr. administration, after Food and Drug Administration (FDA) scientists protested the lack of regulation of GE foods, the agency hired a former Monsanto official to write a new, industry-friendly FDA policy for GE food crops. A former executive vice president at Monsanto has been back and forth between Monsanto and the U.S. Environmental Protection Agency (EPA) three times (Koons Garcia). The head of the U.S. Department of Agriculture (anno 2005) was a former Monsanto executive; so was one former Secretary of Commerce. Whatever the reason, the U.S. EPA and Food and Drug Administration determined that GE crops and the foods produced from them should be classified under the rubric "generally recognized as safe". These products require no labeling, no traceability (of where they come from), no corporate liability in case of negative effects and no ongoing collection of data on health effects (ibid). In June 2006, the Center for Food Safety in the U.S. filed a lawsuit against the Food and Drug Administration for its laxness.

Other GE seed and chemical giants include Syngenta, DuPont and Bayer. A study by the PANOS Institute in developing countries revealed that biotech companies and scientists have much better access to the powerful ministries of agriculture, commerce and science than do NGOs, which tend to find more echo in the much less powerful ministries of environment and public health.

Coercion: policy, law and . . . disorder
Hardon and others have outlined how the Intellectual Property Rights attached to GE crops have moved out of control and affect farmers' choice and freedom in seed selection, storage and exchange. The section below will show how plant patents are a driver behind the expansion of the sector.

Cloning and genetic engineering in agriculture are acts of choice for the optimum characteristics of seeds according to a certain preference. It has been widely argued that developing countries should be able to choose whether they want to start working with the technology or not. Often, the question is whose choice this represents. In the case of GE agriculture, the core of the problem is the breakdown of individual choice, which the release of various GE crops can imply. Because of the contamination and invasion risks involved with many GE crops and seeds, the release of them into the environment may pose strong constraints to choice of the individual farmer, collectively organized farming, and indigenous communities, as well as consumers. The defense of their crops against intrusion of genetically engineered ones by so-called "co-existence measures" is very complicated in practice or, in the case of crops such as rapeseed, even impossible. Biosafety legislation and regulation as well as co-existence measures are policy inventions that may create only the illusion of control, as the GE seeds travel and mix with others through wind, animals, transport, and even deliberate acts of contamination, which are very difficult to contain. Its control is complex and costly, and this, even in the EU, proves hardly possible to implement. Furthermore, in some countries, biosafety legislation is rather a framework for facilitation to GE technology—its drafting may or may not be actively supported by U.S. AID and the World Bank—rather than a regulatory framework to defend the enactment of choice in a country or region. This way, preference for uniformity of one set of actors may wipe out the preference for diversity of many others. Coercion is an important trait of the GE power complex to break the resistance that has been built up by the movements and coalitions against GE expansion.

Eight coercive characteristics

In June 2006, the international programs department at Oxfam Novib[6] organized an international meeting, attended by more than 20 internationally operating networks and organizations, about the global state of affairs concerning biosafety regulation and implementation (Van den Hombergh). We also looked at the problem of force and coercion. Drawing from our own state-of-the-art inventory prepared for this meeting and published data,[7] at least eight characteristics of coercion can be identified, embedded in the principles, policies and practices of GE agriculture and trade.

1. *Contamination in the field.* The inherent, hard-to-avoid contamination by cross-pollination or invasion from GE crops into fields with conventional, traditional or wild stocks. Examples include rapeseed/canola contamination in Canada, maize contamination in Mexico and Spain, and soy contamination in Brazil.

2. *Post-harvest mixing.* The contamination of seed stocks during transport, storage or otherwise. Contamination of stocks of maize seed has been found in 11, mostly northern, countries. Rice sold for consumption has been found contaminated with a GE variety from the U.S. that was not approved for human consumption in at least 19 European countries. This also happened elsewhere in the world—for example, in food aid to Ghana and Sierra Leone. The same kind of event occurred with a Chinese GE rice variety (Greenpeace international). The main cause is the lack of capacity, resources or willingness to control the movement of GE seed and crops, even when parties have signed the Biosafety Protocol.

3. *Indiscriminate herbicide spraying.* Not yet widely reported, but noteworthy, is that herbicides are used more indiscriminately in GE herbicide tolerant crops. One of the

effects is the potential destruction by herbicides of adjacent stocks that are not tolerant to the chemical. This has led to health problems and forced migration of families living next to Roundup Ready soy fields in Paraguay, after which soy producers would have claimed their lands.

These three events may be accidents, but consider the following:

4. *Aggressive litigation*. Claiming of patent rights by industry over even haphazardly (!) GE-contaminated stocks. This has led to lawsuits and fines for farmers who did not want the GE crop, but cultivated it against their will because of cross-pollination or invasion into their fields. Many—at least tens, some say hundreds—of such lawsuits have been filed against farmers in Canada and the U.S.A. from 1998 to date.
5. *Political lobbying across borders*. Active involvement of GE proponents in biosafety and trade legislation, especially in developing countries, designing legislation for facilitation instead of regulation of the technology in the country (in Western African countries). The example of revolving door practices between the GE industry and controlling bodies in the U.S.A. was mentioned above.
6. *Coercive international extension*. The introduction of GE seed against the will of countries through food aid (various African countries) and contamination of stocks in resistant countries (such as occurred with soy in Brazil).
7. *Using the inability to control*. The administrative limitations on biosafety regulation and arranging for co-existence of GE and non-GE crops are huge, especially in developing countries. This regulation is an additional burden they cannot afford and which will most likely lead to hardly any control in practice (throughout the developing world, but also in Europe).
8. *Violating international environmental policy*. The active fight of GE proponents against precautionary policies of the EU and elsewhere, such as Sri Lanka, through (threats with the rulings of) the World Trade Organization, or through regional or bilateral trade agreements and other measures in which the acceptance of GE products is explicitly or implicitly arranged.

More examples of all of these characteristics of coercion can be cited; more monitoring and study is required, however, to duly inventorize their scope. Below, I mention four cases in which various of these coercive elements are staged.

Lawsuits of Monsanto against farmers in the U.S.A and Canada
Engineered seeds are patented and these patents must be paid for, which is part of the business rationale and the basic principle of the GE industry's profit. If farmers choose to cultivate the GE crop, they can make the choice of whether or not the fee is worth paying. But, if stocks are contaminated by invasion of GE plants and/or horizontal gene transfer from the GE variety into the traditional/conventional ones,

paying the patent becomes a source of conflict. GE giant Monsanto has found an interesting source of income in taking farmers who cultivate their patented crop to court. No matter if they cultivate it willingly or unwillingly.

One case known worldwide is the case of Percy Schmeiser, on whose Canadian farm Monsanto found "their" GE variety of Roundup Ready canola. Schmeiser argued the seed entered against his will. The company took him to court for illegal use and refusal to pay the fee and fine. The Supreme Court judge ruled that it did not matter if the GE seed entered Schmeiser's fields against his will or not, he cultivated it illegally and, therefore, had to pay. The Monsanto Canada Inc. v. Schmeiser decision made headlines around the world because, for the first time, a company won control over the higher life form—in this case, the plant—that contained its patented gene, and not solely the gene itself. And it also made headlines because the farmer was fined even though he did not want to cultivate the plant at all. Encouraged by success, Monsanto is now said to have filed more than 100 lawsuits against farmers in the U.S.A. and Canada, attempting to claim its patent rights over GE corn using the same argument.

Soybean expansion in Latin America

GE soy cultivation, representing 60% of worldwide GE cultivation, comes with a package deal. GE soy is engineered to be tolerant to Roundup. No matter how much is sprayed, the soy survives while weeds and other plants die. This makes it possible to cultivate the plant without weeding and much plowing, enabling the cultivation of vast areas of land. This happens especially in Latin America: in Argentina, but increasingly also in Paraguay and Brazil, soy occupies vast areas of land. Opposition has focused mostly on the deforestation caused by the extension of soy cultivation in the Amazon, but also to the social problems caused by expansion into new areas. To a lesser extent, attention has been drawn to the pollution by Roundup in adjacent areas, causing crop failure and health problems among the neighbors.

Both Roundup Ready seed and the herbicide are sold by Monsanto, the largest industrial giant in GE technology. The Intellectual Property Rights over the seed—laid down in patents—belong to Monsanto, as in the Roundup Ready canola case discussed. GE soy has spread willingly and unwillingly over the countryside in Argentina. Monsanto did not succeed in claiming its "rights" in that country as the Argentine government refused to pay a bulk fee for patents on GE soy among others, because the process takes place beyond its control. In reaction, Monsanto withheld soy shipments from Argentina in 2006, before the ships could harbor in Europe, in order to force IPR-related payments in 2006. In Brazil, the cultivation of GE soy was prohibited by the state, until the level of contamination of soy stocks with its GE variety—probably originating from neighboring Argentina—had reached such a level in 2004, that the government felt it better allow it. First it was allowed for one crop cycle, then for another one, then for an indefinite period. Finally, the Brazilian government gave up its resistance.

In defense of Intellectual Property Rights: Terminator Technology

Next to actual seed and chemical sales, plant patents are a major driving force behind the GE seed industry. They affect the right to selection, storage and free flow of seeds among farmers (Hardon). Terminator technology, officially Genetic Use Restriction technologies (GURTS), is a type of technology by which genetically engineered seeds or crops become sterile and unusable after one cycle. It is developed by agrochemical and seed industry leader Monsanto among others. GURTS are meant as a measure to protect IPRs of the seeds industry—in its first phase, around 1999, it was therefore called Technology Protection System. In practice, this technology means that farmers cannot select and save the seeds for a next cycle. Some have promoted this technology as a "biosafety measure," because the seeds, which are genetically engineered, die and thus will not contaminate other stocks. However, it is uncertain if and to what extent this sterilization will actually occur. An estimated 30% would live on, according to the inventor of the term *Terminator Technology*, the NGO Etc Group. What happens when the seeds cross out with other varieties and what happens to animals and humans eating from these stocks? The risk to food security may be very high, because of the plants "killing themselves," because of the related unknown agronomic, health and ecological risks, and also because farmers become dependent on agribusiness to buy their seeds anew every year. Including—and this is crucial to the argument—the farmers whose stocks may be contaminated with the seeds and did not even choose the technology. The risks are so high that a worldwide moratorium on this technology was put in place, which was almost lifted after a strong industrial lobby in 2005 and early 2006. A broad coalition campaign, involving clearly visible grassroots actions in Brazil, where the decisive meeting took place in March 2006, resulted in a continuation of the ban on Terminator Technology for the time being.

Resisting the resistance in Europe: the WTO dispute

Resistance may be most widespread in Europe since the early days of commercial cultivation (Oosterveer). Strong regulation resulted in a *de facto* moratorium until 2004. After the lifting of this moratorium in 2005, cultivation of small areas of Bt maize began in Portugal, France, and the Czech Republic (AFAA). Field trials in France included maize, grape, poplar, sugar beet and tobacco among others. However, consumers throughout Europe have been successfully influenced by the anti-GE movement, and are still negative about the technology so far as their own food is concerned. That EU livestock is fed by Argentine and Brazilian GE soy seems to be less of a concern. In any case, it is more difficult to detect as labeling of GE fed meat is not required.

With the lifting of the de facto moratorium, many farmers and consumer groups in Europe have reacted by promoting and achieving the creation of "GE-free zones". The precautionary policies in the EU and by some of its national members were challenged again by the U.S., supported by Argentina and other GE producing countries, through a complaint to the World Trade Organization in 2003. The final ruling passed down in autumn 2006 contains more than 1000 pages of text and does not give the U.S. its way in all aspects; however, among other things, it questions the use of the precautionary approach by the EU. The precautionary principle is important from an environmental point of view. It is laid down in the widely agreed 1992 Rio Declaration on sustainable development, underlined again by the UN Convention on Biodiversity and worked out in more detail for GE technology in the Cartagena Protocol for Biosafety. It states that, in case of scientific uncertainty combined with high potential risk, one can—and should—decide for safety. Outraged by the challenge, a campaign was launched against the complaint with the slogan "Bite Back—WTO hands off our food," which was underwritten by 750 organizations allegedly representing 60 million people.[8] The final verdict of the WTO panel was rendered in September 2006. In more than 2000 pages, it assessed three issues for their compliance with WTO rules: (1) the EU's alleged general moratorium on biotech approvals, (2) its failure to approve a number of specific biotech products (referred to as "product-specific measures"), and (3) national-level bans in several EU member states on the marketing and import of specific biotech products which had already been approved at the EU-wide level. The panel concluded that general and product-specific moratoria had led to an "undue delay" in the completion of the EU's approval procedures for biotech products. The panel rejected the EU's defense of the national-level bans as precautionary measures, arguing that sufficient scientific evidence was, in fact, available to carry out an adequate risk assessment. Greenpeace, Friends of the Earth Europe and the Institute for Agricultural Trade Policy criticized the panel's ruling for undermining the Cartagena Protocol on Biosafety and the precautionary approach. In particular, they attacked the panel's conclusion that it was not obliged to take into account the Protocol or the Convention on Biological Diversity since not all of the parties to the dispute were also parties to these agreements(!) (ICTSD). Some have called the U.S.-EU battle a GE Cold War (Meijer and Stewart), and it cannot be denied that precaution can be used as a protective trade measure by the EU and others. However, in the context of other elements of coercion, the last mentioned argument in the verdict of the WTO panel rather echoes the image of rape, where the offenders may have charges dropped because they never signed an agreement against this practice, even though they committed their crimes in a territory where rape is against the law. Instead, the victims are punished for trying to protect themselves? One hundred thirty-four countries have ratified the Biosafety Protocol, but the U.S. and some other GE giants have not, and this—according to the panel's logic—would give them the right to expand their preferred technologies into other countries even against their will. The complaint and part of its outcome can be regarded as another case of U.S. unilateralism versus UN consensus, maybe more complex even than military warfare, but likewise resulting from the "revolving door" between policy and the industry.[9]

Final note: a War on Diversity?

I began this article by mentioning the book *Rape of the Wild*. The over 100 GE contamination events that could be reported to date mostly concern cross-pollination of cultivated crops and post-harvest mixing of seeds, with some occurrences of contaminated wild relatives of plants. It is the inherent and inherited logic of domination of man over nature—and of industry over agriculturalists and their livelihoods—that finds a unique and potentially dangerous expression in GE cultivation and trade. Backed by the risk of contamination, gentech agriculture is the expression of Cloning Culture in *ultima forma*—reaching farther than cloning deep into the nature of production and reproduction of organisms and increasingly monopolizing power over this production behind the doors of laboratories of only a few companies.

If the coercive practices described, violating the widely endorsed precautionary approach, are pushed forward, GE poses a serious threat to global diversity: culturally and ecologically and, in the end, to food security. Even if the technology were to have positive potential in the future, under current power dynamics—and with Intellectual Property Rights attached—GE is a tool of economic warfare most of all— not just a Cold War, but also a War on Diversity with potentially far-reaching implications in the conflict zones. Those most probably affected include: organic and poor farmers, and—because of the gender division of labor, responsibility and control over resources—women, who may experience the severest effects, especially on agrobiodiversity which a victory of GE—a monoculture in every sense of the word—risks to imply. Pro-Poor GE technology—in which some development specialists tend to believe—under current conditions is a *contradicio in terminis*. Rather, special effort is required to defend the agriculture of the poor against further genetic erosion, and to promote low-risk technological experiments for crop improvement, especially in the face of climate change and its expected effects in Africa and Asia.

Notes

1. The author works for the Netherlands Committee for IUCN (the World Conservation Union) as coordinator of the Nature and Poverty knowledge and learning network, and carries out additional academic work. Most of the information and ideas are derived from her work with international partner organizations in Oxfam Novib from 2002 to 2007. The author wishes to emphasize that the views expressed in this article are not necessarily all shared by the leadership of either IUCN or the Oxfam federation.

2. Francis Bacon qtd. in Achterhuis.

3. Run by the Community Biodiversity Development and Conservation programme of Mali, part of an international CBDC network; project visit by author in June 2006.

4. With CBDC Philippines managed by the NGO Searice, for example.

5. Such as marker-assisted breeding.

6. Together with the Dutch HIVOS-Oxfam Novib Biodiversity Fund.

7. Since then, Greenpeace International, "GM Contamination Report 2006."

8. See <www.bite-back.org>.

9. This revolving door between the GE industry and U. S. policy was strongly argued with names and figures by Koons Garcia. See also the website Mindfully <www. mindfully.org>; and FOEI.

Works Cited

Abramowitz, J. "Biodiversity and Gender Issues: Recognizing Common Ground." *Feminist Perspectives on Sustainable Development.* Ed. W. Harcourt. London: Zed and Society for International Development, 1994.

Achterhuis, H. "Van moeder aarde tot ruimteschip: humanisme en milieucrisis [From Mother Earth to Spaceship: Humanism and Environmental Crisis]." Inaugural address. Wageningen Agricultural University. 29 Mar. 1990.

AFAA. "Uptake of GM Crops in 2005." *Biotech Bulletin* 17. Kingston: Agrifood Awareness, 2006.

Arts, B., and S. Meck. "Environmental NGOs and the Biosafety Protocol: A Case Study on Political Influence." *European Environment* 13 (2003): 19–33.

Center for Sustainable Agriculture (CSA). "The Story of Bt Cotton in Andhra Pradesh: Erratic Processes and Results" (Feb. 2005).

Collard, A., and J. Contrucci. *Rape of the Wild: Man's Violence Against Animals and the Earth.* Bloomington: Indiana UP, 1988.

Dankelman, I., and J. Davidson. *Women and Environment in the Third World.* London: Earth Scan and IUCN, 1988.

Das, K. "Bt-Cotton Cultivation: Fact and Fiction." *InfoChamge News & Features.* Delhi: Nehru U, Sept. 2005.

DeGrassi, A. *Genetically Modified Crops and Sustainable Poverty Alleviation in Sub-Saharan Africa: An Assessment of Current Evidence.* Africa: Third World Network, 2002.

Etc Group. "Oligopoly." *Concentration in Corporate Power.* Communiqué issue 82. Mexico: Etc Group, Nov.–Dec. 2003.

———. "Oligopoly." *Concentration in Corporate Power.* Communiqué issue 91. Mexico: Etc Group, Nov.–Dec. 2005.

FOEI. "Who Benefits from GM Crops? Monsanto and the Corporate-driven Genetically Modified Crop Revolution." Nigeria: FOEI, 2006.

GRAIN, "Blinded by the Gene," Editorial. *Seedling* July 2003.

Greenpeace. "Centres of Diversity: Global Heritage of Crop Varieties Threatened by Genetic Pollution." Berlin: Greenpeace, 1999.

Greenpeace International. "GM Contamination Report 2006: A Review of Cases of Contamination, Illegal Planting and Negative Side Effects of Genetically Modified Organisms." UK: Greenpeace, 2007.

Haraway, D. *Primate Visions: Gender, Race and Nature in the World of Modern Science.* New York: Routledge, 1989.

Hardon, J. "Plant Patents Beyond Control: Biotechnology, Farmer Seed Systems and Intellectual Property Rights." No. 2. Wageningen, The Netherlands: Agromisa Foundation, 2004.

HED. "African Farmers Say GM Crops are not the Way Forward." Press release. International Institute for Environment and Development. 29 Jan. 2006.

Hickey, E., and A. Mittal. "Voices from the South: The Third World Debunks Corporate Myths on Genetically Engineered Crops." *Food First, et al.* May 2003.

ICTSD. "Biotech Panel Calls on EU to Conform with WTO Rules." *Trade BioRes.* 6 Oct. 2006 <www.icsd.org>.

ISAAA. "Global Status of Commercialized Biotech/GM Crops." ISAAA brief 35-2006 (2007).

Koons Garcia, D. *The Future of Food.* DVD, Lily, 2005.

Lappé, F. M., J. Collins, P. Rosset, and L. Esparza. *World Hunger: Twelve Myths.* 2nd ed. New York: Grove & Earth Scan, 1998.

Meijer, E., and R. Stewart. "The GM Cold War: How Developing Countries Can Go from Being Dominos to Being Players." *Review of European Community & International Environmental Law* 13 (2004): 247.

Merchant, C. *The Death of Nature: Women, Ecology and the Scientific Revolution.* New York: Harper, 1980.

Oosterveer, P. "Global Food Governance." PhD thesis. Wageningen U, 2005.

Panos Institute. "The GM Debate: Who Decides? An Analysis of Decision-making about Genetically Modified Crops in Developing Countries." *Panos Report* 49. London: Panos Institute, 2005.

Pretty, J., and R. Hyne. *Reducing Food Poverty with Sustainable Agriculture: A Summary of New Evidence.* Essex: Centre for Environment and Sustainability, U of Essex, 2001.

Quist, D., and I. Chapela. "Transgenic DNA Introgressed into Traditional Maize Landraces in Oaxaca, Mexico." *Nature* 414 (2001): 541–543.

Rocheleau, D. "Gender Complementarity and Conflict in Sustainable Forestry Development: A Multiple User Approach." Paper. IUFRO World Congress. Montreal. 5–11 Aug. 1990.

Rosset, P. "Transgenic Crops to Address Third World Hunger? A Critical Analysis." *Bulletin of Science, Technology and Society* 25 (2005): 306–313.

Scoones, I. *Can Agriculture Technology be Pro-Poor?* Brighton, UK: Institute for Development Studies, 2003.

Shiva, V., ed. *Biological Diversity: Whose Resource, Whose Knowledge?* New Delhi: Vedams, 1994.

Van den Hombergh, H., ed. "Report of the Workshop Biodiversity, Biosafety and Sustainable Trade held in Mbour, Senegal." Oxfam Novib and Hivos. Internal document. May–June 2006.

Warren, K. "Feminism and Ecology: Making Connections." *Environmental Ethics* 9 (1987): 3–20.

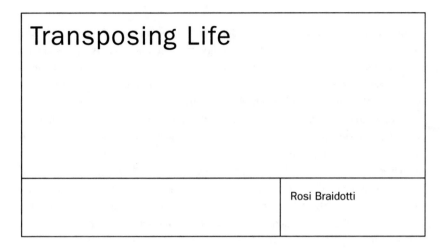

Transposing Life

Rosi Braidotti

Genetic bio-capitalism is less of a concept than a web of multi-layered and contested discourses and social practices focusing on the management of Life and living matter. Contemporary genetics, bio-technologies and their convergence with information technologies are central to the shift toward the post-human politics of "Life" as "Bios" or "Zoe," which I aim to discuss in this essay. The mutual interdependence of living beings and technologies creates a new symbiotic relationship, which displaces both the humanistic assumption about "Man" as the measure of all things and also the anthropocentric hubris that automatically positions the "Human" at the center of all discursive and social practices. A radical critique of anthropocentrism leads to the recognition of the entanglement of material, bio-cultural and symbolic forces in the making of subjectivity and contemporary social practices. This is what I refer to as "zoe" or non-human life (Braidotti, *Transpositions*).

The notion of the post-human as both post-humanism and as non-anthropocentrism lies at the core of a number of scientific discourses about Life, in social and political theory as well as cultural critique. This emphasis on Life forces was both announced in and renewed by post-structuralist philosophies of bio-power, which emphasize the play of differences, the work of resistance and the production of alternative subject positions. A reference to Foucault may well be de rigueur here, but his unfinished project on bio-power is one of a number of significant explorations in critical and anti-essentialist vitalist politics which grew on the far left of the European political spectrum and in Europe-based Continental philosophy through the 1970s and 1980s. Gilles Deleuze's notion of radical immanence ("L'immanence" 3–7) and Irigaray's experiments with the sensible transcendental are other significant models (Braidotti, *Metamorphoses*).

Michel Foucault reads bio-power in the frame of his analysis of both the cultural logic and the political economy of modern governamentality. This encompasses the management of all the living resources that compose a people, not only those covered by the sociological categories of class, gender, race and ethnicity, but also some more visceral or elemental ones. These have to do with the sheer bodily materiality, or corporeality, of the subject. They are the generative, living forces of individuals as members of a species, which are bio-political *par excellence* and thus both propel the production of and escape the control by discursive practices. Bio-power tends to turn all subjects into disposable bodies, yet it does so with striking degrees of internal differentiation and, more importantly, it encounters resistance at all levels. The focus of a Foucauldian analysis falls upon the technologies of subject-formation and their complex webs of social relations. In a theoretical move that runs alongside feminist and postcolonial analyses, without ever acknowledging them, however (Braidotti, *Patterns*; McNay) Foucault foregrounds the importance of micro-instances of power and locates resistance at a suitably molecular level. The workings of bio-power are best exemplified by relatively recent discursive phenomena such as population statistics, public public health (mental as well as physical), sexology and the gradual elimination of anomalies, defects and malfunctions among the population in a proliferation of techniques for disciplining embodied subjects, which amounts to a "soft" eugenics.

The Foucauldian take on bio-power not only refines our understanding of the all-pervasive techniques of control and surveillance, including those that are self-implemented, but it also has another merit. It highlights the paradoxical proximity of social practices that are related to death in the sense of elimination, exclusion and even extermination. The politics of bio-power affect the subjects who are allowed to survive, as well as those who are doomed to perish. It is a rather brutal regime of gradual, all-pervasive selection, which takes the form of distributing and controlling the entitlement to "life" understood as survival and perpetuation. Giorgio Agamben develops this aspect of Foucault's work and I will return to it later. It is the case that one cannot deal adequately with the social and political implications of bio-politics without raising the question of death and ways of dying: necro-politics and bio-power are two faces of the same coin. I do not think, however, that we need to diversify our thinking and terminology about death, so as not to reduce it to either radical exteriority or to the metaphysics of finitude, but rather take it in as a vital component of our biogenetic system. I shall not, however, pursue this line further here.

The theoretical legacy of Foucault's project on contemporary bio-governamentality is problematic. The unfinished nature of Foucault's project has been complicated by two elements: the first is the split that has occurred between the so-called "second" Foucault—who through the history of sexuality defined as technologies of self-styling, posits a new model of ethical inter-relation—and the earlier Foucault, who concentrated on the analysis of power formations and patterns of exclusion. This split reception institutionalizes a new division of labor between power analyses on one hand and ethical discourses on the other. This meta-ethical turn is useful in stressing the need to elaborate new systems of values that reflect the changing structures of subjectivity. It also creates, however, an unresolved tension in relation to the first phase of Foucault's work, more centred on power. It is, therefore, urgent to assess the state of the theoretical debates on bio-power after Foucault, especially in terms of its legal, political and ethical implications.

The second problematic element in the reception of Foucault's bio-power is the rapid rate of progress and change undergone by contemporary biotechnologies and the challenges they throw to the human and social sciences. Here Foucault's work has been criticized, notably by Donna Haraway, for relying on an outdated vision of how technology functions. It is argued that Foucault's bio-power provides a cartography of a historical moment that is now past. Haraway's work itself offers a stark contrast in that it also starts from the assumption that "life as a system to be managed, a field of operations constituted by scientists, artists, cartoonists, community activists, mothers, anthropologists, fathers, publishers, engineers, legislators, ethicists, industrialists, bankers, doctors, genetic counsellors, judges, insurers, priests, and all their relatives—has a very recent pedigree" (174). In other words, contemporary science has moved beyond Foucault's bio-power and has already entered the age of "the informatics of domination", which is a different regime of discourse, visualization and control. Deleuze and Guattari (Anti-Oedipus; A Thousand Plateaus) also analyze this new formation of power over life in their work on capitalism as schizophrenia and move beyond the Foucauldian framework. They provide the single most coherent analysis of materialist vitalism, or "Life" in a post-anthropocentric vein. More on this later.

A central element of discrepancy between Foucault's bio-power and the contemporary structure of scientific thought is the issue of anthropocentrism. Contemporary technologies are not man-centered, but have emphasized the mutual interdependence of material, bio-cultural and symbolic forces in the making of social and political practices. The focus on life itself as zoe or post-human force encourages a sort of bio-centered egalitarianism (Pearson, Viroid Life), forcing a reconsideration of the concept of subjectivity in terms of "life-forces."

It dislocates but also redefines the relationship between self and other by shifting the traditional axes of difference—genderization, racialization and naturalization—away from a binary opposition into a more complex and less oppositional mode of interaction. Bio-politics thus re-locates the Same-Other interaction and inaugurates alternative modes of relation in multiple, non-dialectical and complex ways. These "hybrid" social identities and the modes of multiple belonging they enact are not based on the reproduction of sameness, but rather on the recognition of incommensurable difference as constitutive of the Self-Other relationship. They may constitute the starting point for mutual and respective accountability, and pave the way for an ethical re-grounding of social participation and community building. More on this in the conclusion.

Life as Zoe

In light of these critical considerations, I want to propose a shift of emphasis away from the residual Kantianism of the late Foucault and argue for a neo-vitalist perspective that combines Deleuze with feminist, post-colonial and race theory. This shift implies a change of emphasis from the classical and highly formalized distinction between "*bios*" and "*zoe*." I value *zoe*, as vitalistic, pre-human and generative life, rather than *bios*, the political discourse about life. I want to defend the argument that the emergence of *zoe* results in the need for a shift of paradigm about bio-politics in general and for the politics of difference more specifically. Let me expand on this.

The emergence of vital politics, or "life itself" (Rose), scrambles the relationship between Same and others which had already become unsettled in postmodernity. The relationship to woman/native/nature, which mark respectively the processes of sexualization, racialization and naturalization—albeit in the non-dialectical, deconstructive, affirmative or rhizomatic manner made current by poststructuralist analyses—not only confirms the power of the One and hence the replication of Sameness. The whole frame of the interaction is rather reorganized in relation to the emergence of *zoe*, so that what returns as a major concern is the "other" of the human defined as the anthropo-centric vision of the embodied subject. This is the other face of *bios*, that is to say *zoe*, the generative vitality of non- or pre-human or animal life. This pre-human force combines in surprising ways with the non-human potency of contemporary technologies. They converge upon the production of discourses that take "Life" as a subject and not as the object of social and discursive practices and contribute to the making of the post-human predicament.

The political economy of this shift of perspective in bio-genetic capitalism is complex. The bio-technological interventions neither suspend nor automatically improve the social relations of exclusion and inclusion that historically had been predicated along the sexualized, racialized and naturalized lines of demarcation of "otherness." In some ways, the ongoing technological revolution merely intensifies the patterns of traditional discrimination and exploitation (Eisenstein; Shiva; Gilroy).

As a consequence, critical social and cultural theory need to develop new tools for the analysis of power over living matter in the complex frame of the new global world order, at the same point in time when the very notion of *bios/zoe* or life is called into question in a variety of ways. For instance, this emphasis on life as *bios-zoe* opens up the eco-philosophical dimension of the problem, which inaugurates alternative ecologies of belonging. It shifts toward the recognition of the inextricable entanglement of material, bio-cultural and symbolic forces in the making of the subject. It is a sort of bio-centered egalitarianism which, as Keith Ansell Pearson (*Germinal Life*) suggests, forces a reconsideration of the concept of subjectivity in relation to the "others" of the human, the vegetable and the environment: all of them being "life-forces" that displace anthropocentrism. It also marks a post-secular turn that acknowledges the emergence of the Earth as a planetary political agent and hence of new modes of panhuman inter-connection. Let me explore this point further with a series of selected examples.

Embodied capital

The work of Franklin, Lury and Stacey shows that the global economy entails the cannibalization of nature by a market ruled by short-term profit based on bio-genetic matter. This process is matched by an increased degree of control, reterritorialisation and, consequently, re-invention of nature. However, refigured and saturated with technological culture, "nature" also resists. It is more than the sum of its marketable appropriations and remains an agent that acts beyond the reach of commodification. The point in case here would be environmental catastrophes and the extent to which they exemplify the co-presence of nature and culture in contemporary global risk societies (Beck, *Risk Society*; *World Risk Society*). I refer to this surplus vitality of living matter in terms of *zoe*, post-human life, as opposed to the discursive production of meanings of life as *bios*. I will return to this.

Franklin argues that contemporary technology-driven societies develop and are supported by a genetic social imaginary that rests on the equation between the genetic code or DNA and marketable brand names. Genes are capital. Thus, contemporary car engineering, for instance, is visually marketed in a genetic format, which stresses the industrial transmission of inherited traits through careful selection and manufacturing of strengths and weaknesses. This commercialized version of social Darwinism adds a touch of irony to the widespread idea of the "next generation" of electronic gadgets, computers, cars or whatever.

Accordingly, the political economy of the bodies-technologies interaction has undergone a paradoxical evolution. In the historical phase of modernity, the machine provided a sort of body-double which, as the site of imaginary projection, was both genderized and eroticized. Examples of this are the female robot in Fritz Lang's film *Metropolis* (Huyssen) or the virile locomotives in Eisenstein's cinema (Braidotti, *Metamorphoses*). In post-modernity, however, this relationship changes: electronic and digital machinery and their post-human bodies are figures of complexity, mixture, hybridity and interconnectivity (Halberstam and Livingston). As such, they do not provide a smooth surface for projection, are not positioned comfortably within the gender polarity, nor are they particularly sexualized. Contemporary technology marks instead a systematic scrambling of codes (Hayles), hence a space of sexual indeterminacy, undecidability or trans-sexuality.

This is echoed by the notion of stepping beyond gender, which is highly dominant in contemporary advanced cultures. This fantasy is conveyed both in the dominant molar mode by the social imaginary about cyborgs and in the more radical minoritarian mode by feminist, queer and other counter-cultures. This blurring of the boundaries of gender and sexual difference, in the sense of a generalized androgynous drive, is characteristic of post-industrial societies (Lyotard) and hence cannot be assumed to be intrinsically transgressive. In fact, queering identities can be seen as a dominant ideology under advanced capitalism (Braidotti, *Metamorphoses*). This sexually indeterminate or transsexual social imaginary may appear at first to blur or interfere with the replication of sameness, or cultural cloning, which is so central to the political economy of advanced capitalism—as it was to the old phallo-logocentric world order. On closer analysis, however, it does nothing of the sort. The discourse of indeterminacy and of degrees of in-between-ness goes hand-in-hand with the brutal return of sexual polarizations and rigid gender roles, both in the West and in the rest.

This can be demonstrated with reference to contemporary global politics. The so-called "clash of civilizations" is postulated and fought out on women's bodies as bearers of authentic ethnic and religious identities. The painful paradoxes implied here can be shown by the claim made by the anti-feminist and arch-conservative President George W. Bush, that he invaded Afghanistan also to liberate the Burka-clad Afghan women. This is a racist and sexist manipulation that aims to justify one of the many commercially-driven wars of conquest. Another would be the charge—made during the Iraq war—that the European Union has become feminized or effeminate and hence has lost the edge in military leadership to the far more virile U.S.A. The global political arena posits both gender dichotomies and sexual difference defined as the specificity of separate gender roles as the terrain on which power politics is postulated. In a context of racism, xenophobia and global degradation of the status of women and children, this type of gender politics results in mutual and respective claims about authentic and unitary female identity on the part of the "liberated" West and of its allegedly traditionalist opponents. They are mirror images of each other and engender specular forms of fundamentalism.

This schizoid double-pull of simultaneous displacement and re-fixing of differences, including the binary gender opposition, is one of the most problematic aspects of contemporary political culture. It is also the key to its vehement anti-feminism, in that it erodes the grounds for the affirmation and the empowerment of embodied and embedded feminist political subjects. In this context, the maternal function and hence the reproduction of the human in its bio-cultural mode has become simultaneously disengaged from the female body—in bio-technologically assisted reproduction—or in technophilic social practices that actualize "the desire to be wired." Motherhood has also, however, been re-naturalized in a number of paradoxical variations ranging from fundamentalist religious convictions to secular affirmations of

being "proud to be flesh." These paradoxical patterns reflect the schizophrenic double-pull that marks the global era. The simultaneous occurrence of opposite effects
defeats the logic of excluded middle and fits in with the manic-depressive alternation
of euphoria and melancholia, which is the political economy of affectivity in advanced
capitalism. To translate this into the language of nomadic subjects: the pull toward
traditional or reactive values (Molar, sedentary, linear, static, replication of Sameness)
is balanced by a more progressive and active drive toward more innovative solutions
(Molecular, nomadic, dynamic, positivity of incommensurable differences). The molar
line of reterritorialization and the multiple lines of becoming are contiguous, but they
trace altogether divergent patterns. Keeping these two lines well distinct qualitatively,
while respecting the simultaneity of their occurrence is an analytic necessity, albeit a
challenging one (Braidotti, *Transpositions*).

The immaterial labor of the digital proletariat
A second example of this political economy of bio-genetic capitalism is the analysis
of the labor and economic politics of the globalized world, as exemplified by those
who are marginalized. A significant case is provided by the workers in call centers
who cater to the information society by processing phone inquiries from selected
locations miles away from the callers' homes. Denounced strongly by Arundhati Roy,
these "call centers" or data outsourcing agencies are a multi-billion dollar industry
that has attracted a great deal of critical attention in both mainstream and alternative media (Biemann). This kind of service industry labor presents a number of
features that are reminiscent of the exploitative work conditions of former industrial
culture, but also innovates on them.

In their work replying to phone enquiries, indigenous workers simulate the
Western consumers whose queries they are handling. This strategy is not mere
impersonation, for there is no visual or physical contact between the parties involved.
Nor can it be seen as a form of identification, as the workers need not feel or experience themselves as being from a different culture/nation in order to fulfil their con-
tractual obligations. It is rather like a logistical issue: working in a call center is about
carefully orchestrated simulation that plays on the accent, the affected knowledge of
local weather, lifestyles, cultural traditions and enforced cheerfulness. As such, it
requires a radical "Othering" of oneself, or a mild form of schizophrenia, which is not
a masquerade in the ironical sense of self-exploration, but reification of the worker's
own life-world. Not unlike characters in a chat room, call centre workers perform their
labor market persona in such a way as to emerge from the process neither wiser nor
enriched (especially considering that workers in these call centers are paid one-tenth
of their Western counterparts), but rather firmly located as "the emerging digital proletariat that underpins the new world economy" (Biemann 85). Another significant
example of the same phenomenon is the extensive reliance of the computer games

industry on test-players drawn from mostly male youth in former Eastern Europe. Playing computer games up to 15 hours a day at a time—in an industry that operates continuously, 24 hours a day, seven days a week—for wages of about U.S.$130 a month, these digital workers have invented the virtual sweatshop (Harding).

This is today's immaterial variation on the theme of bodily exploitation, which fits into the global marketing of both material commodities and of Western lifestyles, cultures and appropriate accents. Hardt and Negri stress the immaterial and affective nature of this labor force which trades phonetic skills, linguistic ability and proper accents services, as well as requiring attention, concentration, high spirits and great care. This *tour de force* by the digital workers of the new global economy rests on an acute and explicit awareness of one's location in space and time, and yet it functions through border crossings, nomadic shifts and paths of deterritorialization. The allegedly ethereal nature of cyberspace and the flow of mobility it sustains are fashioned by the material labor of women and men from areas of the world that are thought to be peripheral. The collapse of the binary opposition of center-periphery introduces a new fluctuating continuum between discrete spaces in the global economy. This space of fluctuation is racialized and sexualized to a high degree and it is exploited accordingly, thus reproducing traditional relations of power that defy the complexity of the very material conditions that engender them.

Bio-piracy
The third example I want to quote is what Vandana Shiva has called bio-piracy, namely the plea for bio-diversity in global culture by resisting the practice of patenting bio-technological products. Shiva connects this practice to European empire building over the last 500 years and sees a continuum between them and the policies of the WTO and the World Bank. In a Foucauldian shift, Shiva links bio-piracy to the individualist philosophies of Locke, Hume and other "fathers" of liberalism, arguing that their theoretical works both reflect and legitimate capitalist appropriation of the world's resources and the eviction of others. These individualist theories are still operational in contemporary legal practices and institutions such as intellectual property rights and the policies of the World Trade Organization and the GATT apparatus. What marks specifically the present historical era, argues Shiva, is the fact that the target of capitalist looting has shifted from the former colonies to the "new frontiers," to the "natural resources" represented by human genetics in general, and women's reproductive powers in particular. Capital, as I argued earlier, is the generative power of living matter and the resilient vitality of "Life." The self-generative power of living matter is both denied and enhanced by patenting and branding for the sake of corporate profit. Life, as both *bios* and *zoe,* actualized in seeds and cells, is cash.

In Shiva's assessment, "bio-piracy," as the ultimate colonization of the interior of living organisms, not only destroys bio-diversity, endangering the many species that used to live on this planet. It also threatens cultural diversity by depleting the capital of human knowledge through the devalorization of local knowledge systems and world-views. Eurocentric models of scientific rationality and technological development damage human diversity. The patent system legalizes bio-piracy, spreads mono-cultures and homogenization in both nature and social systems. The strategy of resistance proposed by Shiva is globalized eco-feminism.

In a significant divergence of opinion with Shiva; Franklin, Lury and Stacey point to a structural ambivalence in the political economy of advanced capitalism. They argue that, as a privatized icon for commercialized biodiversity, the seed connects the old Universalist idea of "nature" to the financial reality of global culture. Just as the Humans have their Genome project, plants have their Heritage Seed catalog, which patents a number of seeds. They are advertised as organic, home-grown, but also ancient and, as such, the repository of old lore and cultural authenticity. This holistic ethos guarantees both the perpetuation of the species and the preservation of techno-culture. The reproductive female body as a whole is the seed which corporate capitalism wants to patent and eventually clone, according to the paradox of a new global compound of nature/culture that is naturalized and commercialized simultaneously. In both cases, however, the seed as the gene conveys the notion of purity of the lineage and of direct genetic inheritance.

In other words, in the era of globalization, the very notions of cultural diversity and local knowledge systems can be seen as one of the products of advanced capitalism, not as its excluded others. Diversity, including indigenous or authentic local culture, has become a highly valuable and marketable commodity. In its commercialized form, it has increased the uniformity of consumers' habits, while sponsoring the proliferation of "local" differences or micro-diversities. The global market is fuelled by "differences," so that the "local" is a political space constructed by the global flows of capital (Hardt and Negri). Because the proliferation of local differences for the sake of marketability is one of the features of the global economy, one must beware of taking any claim to local cultural identity and difference at face value. All identities are in process and, consequently, are inherently contradictory. They are best approached in an open-ended and contested manner, in keeping with the cognitive and figural "style" of philosophical nomadism and its transposing method (Braidotti, *Metamorphoses; Transitions*).

The plight of animals
The paradoxes and contradictions of our post-human historical condition are brought into stark evidence by the status of animals, which provides my last illustration. If people in war-torn lands such as Afghanistan are reduced to eat grass in order to survive (*Guardian Weekly* 3–5 Jan. 2002), the former herbivore bovine animals of the United Kingdom and parts of the European Union have turned carnivore. Our agricultural

bio-technological sector has taken an unexpected cannibalistic turn by fattening cows, sheep and chickens on animal feed. This is not the least of the paradoxes confronting the critical thinker and the aware citizen these days. Animals (mice, sheep, goats, cattle, pigs, rabbits, birds, poultry, and cats) are bred in industrial farms, locked up in battery-cage production units reminiscent of torture chambers. Paradoxically, however, because they are an integral part of the bio-technological industrial complex, more animals enjoy peculiar privileges. Thus, livestock in the European Union receive subsidy to the tune of U.S.$803 per cow. This is not so remarkable when compared to the U.S.$1,057 that is granted to each American cow and U.S.$2,555 given to each cow in Japan. These figures look quite different when compared to the Gross National Income *per capita* in countries such as Ethiopia (U.S.$120), Bangladesh (U.S.$360), Angola (U.S.$660) or Honduras (U.S.$920) (Guardian Weekly 11–17 Sep. 2003).

Animals provide living material for scientific experiments. They are manipulated, mistreated, tortured and genetically recombined in ways that are productive for our bio-technological agriculture, the cosmetics industry, drugs and pharmaceutical industries and other sectors of the economy. The monitoring group "Gene Watch Outs" places their numbers at a half million per year; other animals, such as pigs, are genetically modified to produce organs for humans in xeno-transplantation experiments (*Guardian Weekly* 23–29 May 2002). Animals are the mass of tradable disposable bodies of many species, which are inscribed in a global circulation. They are also sold as exotic commodities and constitute the third largest illegal trade in the world today, after drugs and arms, but ahead of women. Cloning animals is now an established practice: Oncomouse and Dolly the sheep are already part of history; the first cloned horse was born in Italy on May 28, 2003. It took more than 800 embryos and nine would-be surrogate mother mares to produce just one foal (*Guardian Weekly* 14–20 Aug. 2003). These developments are in keeping with the complex and dynamic logic of contemporary genetics, which confront us with non-linear ways of conducting science that are better rendered as transpositions (more on this term below). Bio-genetic capitalism entails the commercialization of life forms in all their complexity, through a series of systematic but scattered modes of appropriation.

The emergence of *zoe*

The series of examples I have provided illustrate the perversity of contemporary bio-capitalism. Its political economy consists in multiplying and distributing differences within categories and species only for the sake of profit. It produces ever-shifting waves of genderization and sexualization, racialization and naturalization of multiple "others," while de-materializing them. It has thus effectively disrupted the categorical distinctions that used to exist among the empirical referents of Otherness— women, natives and animal or earth others—and the processes of discursive formation of genderization/racialization/naturalization. Once the empirical referents and the discursive processes are de-linked, advanced capitalism looks like a system that promotes feminism without women, racism without races, natural laws without nature, reproduction without sex, sexuality without genders, multiculturalism without ending racism, economic growth without development, and cash flow without money. Late capitalism also produces fat-free ice cream and alcohol-free beer next to genetically modified health food, companion species alongside computer viruses, new animal and human immunity breakdowns and deficiencies, and the increased longevity of those who inhabit the advanced world. Welcome to capitalism as schizophrenia!

This colossal hybridization effort also means that the political representation of embodied subjects can no longer be understood within the visual economy of bio-politics in Foucault's sense of the term. Nor is it just *specular* anymore in the psycho-analytic dialectical scheme of oppositional recognition of self-and/as other. It has rather become schizoid, or internally disjointed (Deleuze and Guattari, *Anti-Oedipus; A Thousand Plateaus*). It is also *spectral* (Derrida) living beings are represented as a self-replicating system that is immersed in a visual economy of endless circulation. Contemporary embodied subjects have to be accounted for in terms of their surplus value as genetic containers on one hand, and as visual commodities circulating in a global circuit of cash on the other. Much of this information is not knowledge-driven, but rather media-inflated and thus indistinguishable from sheer entertainment. Today's capital is spectral and our social imaginary is forensic (Braidotti, *Transpositions*) in its quest for traces of a life that it no longer controls.

The Life that inhabits us is not ours: we are just time-sharing it. Life is half animal, *zoe* (zoology, zoophilic, zoo); and half discursive, *bios* (bio-logy). Whereas philosophy has always upheld this classical distinction in a strict hierarchical order that privileges the latter, contemporary critical theory is calling for a serious restructuring of this relationship. *Zoe* is no longer the poor half of a couple that foregrounds *bios* defined as intelligent discursive life. The spurious humanism of centuries of Christian indoctrination about the centrality of "Man" has worn rather thin. The mind-body dualism, which had historically functioned as a shortcut through the complexities has lost credibility. *Zoe* as post-human force is now the central concern: it covers the entire animal and Earth's others. This used to be called "Nature" and be constructed as the constitutive outside of the human polity. Now, *zoe* no longer marks the outside of the subject. We can therefore speak of a generalized "becoming infrahuman" of Life—so much so that this category has cracked under the strain and has splintered into a web of interconnected effects.

Life, encore
Different theoretical positions have emerged in recent scholarship about bio-politics in biogenetic capitalism. For instance, some thinkers stress the importance of moral

accountability as a form of bio-political citizenship, thus re-asserting the notion of "Life" as "bios," that is to say an instance of governmentality that is as empowering as it is confining (Rose; Rabinow; Esposito). This neo-Kantian school of thought locates the political moment in the relational and self-regulating accountability of bio-ethical subjects that take full responsibility for their genetic existence. The advantage of this position is that it calls for a higher degree of lucidity about one's bioorganic existence—which means that the naturalist paradigm is definitely abandoned. The disadvantage of this position, however, in a political context of dismantling the welfare state and increasing privatization, is that it allows a neo-liberal perversion of this notion. Bio-ethical citizenship indexes access to and the cost of basic social services such as health care to an individual's manifest ability to act responsibly by reducing the risks and exertions linked to the wrong lifestyle. In other words, here bio-ethical agency means taking adequate care of one's own genetic capital. The recent campaigns against smoking, excessive drinking and overweight constitute evidence of this neo-liberal normative trend that supports hyper-individualism.

A second important group is formed by feminist, environmentalist and race theorists who have addressed the shifting status of "difference" in advanced capitalism in a manner that respects the complexity of social relations and critiques liberalism, while highlighting the specificity of a gender and race approach. In feminist theory— a relevant area of scholarship that I find missing from far too much of the scholarship on bio-politics, globalization and technology studies—this point has been taken quite seriously (Haraway; Gilroy; Benhabib; Butler; Braidotti, *Metamorphoses*; Grosz; Barad). Feminist, environmentalist and race theorists have addressed the shifting status of "difference" in advanced capitalism in a manner that respects the complexity of social relations and critiques liberalism, while highlighting the specificity of a gender and race approach (Gilroy; Essed and Goldberg; Braidotti, *Metamorphoses*; Butler; Grosz).

A third grouping takes its lead from Heidegger and is best exemplified by Giorgio Agamben. It defines "bios" as the result of the intervention of sovereign power as that which is capable of reducing the embodied subject to "bare life," that is to say "zoe." The vitality of the subject is identified with its vulnerability and thus reduced to its propensity to death and extinction. Bio-power leads primarily to necro- or Thanatos-politics. The horizon of mortality overrules any positive potential in *zoe*. This reduction, combined with a cross-reference to the political theology of Carl Schmidt results, among other things, in the indictment of the project of modernity. As I indicated earlier, I find this over-emphasis on mortality both unwarranted and inadequate in relation to the positive potential of *zoe* as non-human life, read with Nietzsche, Spinoza and Deleuze.

A fourth significant community of scholars works within a Spinozist framework, and includes Deleuze (*Difference; Logic*; "L'immanence"; Deleuze and Guattari,

A Thousand Plateaus), Guattari, Glissant, Gatens and Lloyd, Hardt and Negri, Balibar, Colebrook, Grosz, and myself. The emphasis here falls on the politics of life itself as a relentlessly generative force and on the interrogation of the shifting inter-relations between human and non-human forces. Let me expand on this position.

As I stated before, the key to the biogenetic shift is the overturning of anthropocentrism. Post-structuralism initiated this critique by declaring, with Foucault, the "death" of the humanistic subject of knowledge. We are experiencing a further stage in this process and, as the rhizomic philosophies of Deleuze and Guattari point out, we are forced to confront the inbuilt anthropocentrism, which prevents us from relinquishing the categorical divide between *bios* and *zoe*, and thus makes us cling to the superiority of discursive power, rational consciousness, and human agency. The monist political ontology of Spinoza, revisited with contemporary concerns and frames of reference, can rescue us from this contradiction, by providing a continuum through the theory of radical immanence. Accordingly, Deleuze dissolves and re-grounds the subject into an eco-philosophy of intensive becoming. This takes the form of a strong emphasis on the pre-human or even non-human elements that compose the web of forces, intensities and encounters that contribute to the making of nomadic subjectivity (Braidotti, *Metamorphoses; Transpositions*). *Zoe* refers to the endless vitality of life as continuous becoming. Guattari refers to this process as a transversal form of subjectivity or "trans-individuality." This mode of diffuse yet grounded subject position achieves a double aim: firstly, it critiques individualism and, secondly, it supports a notion of subjectivity in the sense of qualitative, transversal, and group-oriented agency.

Let me emphasize a number of features of this neo-vitalist, anti-essentialist cartography that takes life as the subject of critical theory. The first point is that the technological subject is, in fact, an ecological unit. This *zoe*-techno-body is marked by the interdependence with its environment through a structure of mutual flows and data transfer that is best configured by the notion of viral contamination (Pearson, *Viroid*), or intensive symbiotic inter-connectedness. This nomadic eco-philosophy of belonging is complex and multi-layered.

Secondly, this environmentally-bound, bio-genetically constituted subject is a collective entity, moving beyond the parameters of classical humanism and anthropocentrism. The human organism is an in-between that is plugged into and connected to a variety of possible sources and forces. As such, it is useful to define it as a machine, which does not mean anything with a specifically utilitarian aim, but rather something that is simultaneously more abstract and more materially embedded. The minimalist definition of a body-machine is an embodied affective and intelligent entity that captures, processes, and transforms energies and forces. Being environmentally bound and territorially based, an embodied entity feeds upon, incorporates, and transforms its (natural, social, human, or technological) environment constantly. Being embodied in this high-tech ecological manner means being immersed in fields of constant flows and transformations. Not all of them are positive, of course, although in such a dynamic system this cannot be known or judged *a priori*, but has to be experimented with and assessed *a posteriori*.

Thirdly, the specific temporality of the subject needs to be re-thought. The subjects are evolutionary engines, endowed with their own embodied temporality, both in the sense of the specific timing of the genetic code and the more genealogical time of individualized memories. If the embodied subject of bio-power is a complex molecular organism, a bio-chemical factory of steady and jumping genes, an evolutionary entity endowed with its own navigational tools and an in-built temporality, then we need a form of ethical values and political agency that reflects this high degree of complexity.

Lastly, this ethical approach cannot be dissociated from considerations of power. The *bios-zoe*-centered vision of the technologically mediated subject of post-modernity or advanced capitalism is fraught with internal contradictions. Accounting for them is the cartographic task of critical theory.

This relocation of the subject also entails a number of methodological consequences about the status of social and political theory itself. The key idea of transposition as a method is that it allows us to leap from one discursive code to another, re-telling, re-configuring, and re-visiting the concept, phenomenon or event one is analyzing, as if from different locations. It is related to Spinozist perspectivism (Gatens and Lloyd), but infuses it with a nomadic spin, which establishes multiple connections and lines of argument. Resolutely non-linear, it works by the eternal return of multiple differences, not of Sameness: it is a creative mimesis, not static repetition. Re-visiting the same idea, project or location from different angles is therefore not merely a quantitative multiplication of options, but rather a qualitative leap of perspective. This leap takes the form of a hybrid mixture of codes, genres, or modes of intellectual apprehension. A higher degree of interdisciplinary effort is needed in social and political thought: more akin to transversality and boundary-crossings among a range of discourses.

Because transposition is a way of reworking the interrelation among different differences (sexualization, racialization, naturalization), it is grounded in critical theory and, more specifically, in transnational feminist theory, environmental thought and critical race theory. All these share a passionate commitment, not only to dislodge "difference" from its hegemonic position as an instrument of world-historical systems of domination, exclusion and disqualification. They are also determined to prevent the discursive replication of sameness under this play of differential discourses. They do so by inscribing complexity, multiplicity, and internal contradictions at the heart of the subject of knowledge, thereby showing it for the messy and makeshift assemblage it is.

A third requirement follows from the process-oriented structure of this approach, namely the emphasis on processes and interconnections. This requires an effort of our conceptual creativity in order to learn to think differently about us. Such a transformative epistemological project mobilizes more than the cognitive or epistemic qualities of a subject. It also calls for its affective or intensive resources, for the courage to negotiate the often dramatic shifts of perspective and location which are required for the implementation of a process-oriented (as opposed to concept-based and system-driven) thought. As a term that relies on both genetics and music, "transpositions" (Braidotti, *Transpositions*) is a useful tool.

Conclusion

Far from precipitating us into an abyss of amorality, nihilism, and methodological anarchy, a bio-genetic, vitalist view of the subject fosters the possibility for more situated forms of interaction and situated micro-universals to emerge. A post-anthropocentric approach to the analysis of "life itself" is a way of broadening the sense of community by acknowledging its non-human components. For instance, contemporary science and biotechnologies affect the very fibre and structure of the living, creating a negative unity among humans. The Human Genome project, for instance, unifies all the human species in the urgency to organize an opposition against commercially-owned and profit-minded technologies. Franklin, Lury and Stacey refer to this situation as "pan humanity," by which they mean a global sense of interconnection between the human and the non-human environment, as well as among the different sub-species within each category, creating a web of intricate interdependences. Most of this mutual dependence is of the negative kind: "as a global population at shared risk of global environmental destruction and united by collective global images" (Franklin, Lury, and Stacey) There are also positive elements, however, to this form of post-modern human interconnection. Franklin, *et al.* argue that this universalization is one of the effects of the global market economy.

The paradox of this new pan-humanity is not only the sense of shared and associated risks, but also affirmative elements, such as the pride in technological achievements and in the wealth that comes with them. Equally strong is the drive to elaborate systems of value that reflect these transformations. The state of the debates on these issues in fields as diverse as environmental, political, social, and ethical theories, to name just a few, shows a range of potentially creative positions. From the "world governance idea" to the ideal of a "world ethos," through a large variety of ecological brands of feminism, the field is wide open. Powerful claims to non-Western forms of radical neo-humanism and planetary cosmopolitanism have been made by feminist and race theorists, such as Gilroy and Shiva, as a way of recomposing human ties in the global era.

In other words, we are witnessing a proliferation of locally-situated Universalist or pan-humanist ethical claims. Far from being a symptom of relativism, these claims assert the productive force at work in contemporary subjectivity. They constitute the starting point for a web of intersecting forms of situated accountability, that is to say an ethics.

Zoe power keeps the "human" hanging between a future that cannot provide a safe guarantee and a fast rate of present change that demands one. This tantalizing situation expresses the perverse logic of bio-capitalism as a regime that points toward possible futures, while blocking and controlling access to them in such a way as to make sure that "life" never reaches the higher levels of intensity of which it is potentially capable. Working toward social relations and cultural practices that empower us to act affirmatively is the essence of a neo-Spinozist ethics of becoming.

The whole point is to elaborate sets of criteria for a new ethical system to be brought into being that steers a course between humanistic nostalgia and neo-liberal euphoria. In my view, that can only be an ethics that takes life (as *bios* and as *zoe*) as its point of reference, not for the sake of restoration of unitary norms or the celebration of the master narrative of global profit, but for the sake of elaborating sustainable modes of transformation and becoming.

Works Cited

Agamben, Giorgio. *Homo Sacer: Sovereign Power and Bare Life*. Stanford: Stanford UP, 1998.

Balibar, Etienne. *Politics and the Other Scene*. London: Verso, 2002.

Barad, Karen. "Posthumanist Performativity: Toward and Understanding of How Matter Comes to Matter." *Signs* 28 (2003): 801–831.

Beck, Ulrich. *Risk Society*. London: Sage, 1992.

———. *World Risk Society*. Cambridge: Polity, 1999.

Benhabib, Seyla. *The Claims of Culture: Equality and Diversity in the Global Era*. Princeton: Princeton UP, 2002.

Biemann, Ursula, ed. "Raqs media collective: 'A/S/L.'" *Geography and the Politics of Mobility*. Vienna: General Foundation, 2003.

Braidotti, Rosi. *Metamorphoses: Towards a Materialist Theory of Becoming*. Cambridge, UK: Polity, 2002.

———. *Patterns of Dissonance*. Cambridge, MA. Polity, 1991.

———. *Transpositions: On Nomadic Ethics*. Cambridge, UK: Polity, 2006.

Butler, Judith. *Undoing Gender*. London: Routledge, 2004.

Colebrook, Claire. *Understanding Deleuze*. Crows Nest, NSW: Allen and Unwin, 2002.

Deleuze, Gilles. *Difference and Repetition*. Trans. Paul Patton. London: Athlone, 1968. Trans. of *Différence et repetition*. Paris: Presses Universitaires de France, 1968.

———. "L'immanence: une vie . . ." *Philosophie* 47 (1995): 3–7.

———. *The Logic of Sense*. Trans. M. Lester and C. Stivale. New York: Columbia UP, 1990. Trans. of *Logique du sens*. Paris: Minuit, 1969.

Deleuze, Gilles, and Felix Guattari. *Anti-Oedipus: Capitalism and Schizophrenia*. Trans. R. Hurley, M. Seem, and H. R. Lane. New York: Viking; Richard Seaver, 1977. Trans. of *L'anti-Oedipe: Capitalisme et schizophrénie I*. Paris: Minuit, 1972.

———. *A Thousand Plateaus: Capitalism and Schizophrenia*. Trans. Brian Massumi. Minneapolis: U of Minnesota P, 1987. Trans. of *Mille plateaux: Capitalisme et schizophrénie II*. Paris: Minuit, 1980.

Derrida, Jacques. *Specters of Marx*. New York: Routledge, 1994.

Eisenstein, Zillah. *Global Obscenities: Patriarchy, Capitalism and the Lure of Cyberfantasy*. New York: New York UP, 1998.

Esposito, Roberto. *Bios. Biopolitica e filosofia*. Torino: Einaudi, 2004.

Essed, Philomena, and David Goldberg, eds. *Race Critical Theories*. Oxford: Blackwell, 2002.

Foucault, Michel. *The History of Sexuality Vol. I*. Trans. Robert Hurley. New York: Pantheon, 1978. Trans. of *Histoire de la sexualité I: La volontée de savoir*. Paris: Gallimard, 1976.

Franklin, Sarah, Celia Lury, and Jackie Stacey. *Global Nature, Global Culture*. London: Sage, 2000.

Gatens, Moira, and Genevieve Lloyd. *Collective Imaginings: Spinoza, Past and Present*. London: Routledge, 1999.

Gilroy, Paul. *Against Race: Imaging Political Culture Beyond the Color Line*. Cambridge, MA: Harvard UP, 2000.

Glissant, Edouard. *Poetics of Relation*. Trans. Betsy Wing. Ann Arbor: U of Michigan P, 1997.

Trans. of *Poetique de la relation*. Paris: Gallimard, 1990.

Grosz, Elizabeth. *The Nick of Time*. Durham: Duke UP, 2004.

Guardian Weekly. 3–5 Jan. 2002: 2.

———. 23–29 May 2002: 10.

———. 14–20 Aug. 2003: 2.

———. 11–17 Sep. 2003: 5.

Guattari, Felix. *Chaosmosis: An Ethico-aesthetic Paradigm*. Sydney: Power, 1995.

Halberstam, Judith, and Ira Livingston, eds. *Posthuman Bodies*. Bloomington: Indiana UP, 1995.

Haraway, Donna. *Feminism and Technoscience: Modest_Witness@Second_Millennium.Female Man_Meets©_OncoMouse™*. London: Routledge, 1997.

Harding, Consult Luke. "Delhi Calling." *Guardian Weekly* 25–31 Mar. 2005: 17.

Hardt, Michael, and Antonio Negri. *Empire*. Cambridge: Harvard UP, 2000.

Hayles, Katherine. *How We Became Posthuman: Virtual Bodies in Cybernetics, Literature and Informatics*. Chicago: U of Chicago P, 1999.

Huyssen, Andreas. "The Vamp and the Machine: Fritz Lang's Metropolis." *After the Great Divide: Modernism, Mass Culture and Postmodernism*. Bloomington: Indiana UP, 1986. 65–81.

Irigaray, Luce. *An Ethics of Sexual Difference*. Trans. Carolyn Burke and Gillian Gill. Ithaca, NY: Cornell UP, 1993. Trans. of *L'éthique de la difference sexuelle*. Paris: Minuit, 1984.

Lyotard, Jean Francois. *L'inhumain: causeries sur le temps*. Paris: Galilée, 1998. Trans. Geoffrey Bennington and Rachel Bowlby.

McNay, Lois. *Foucault and Feminism*. Cambridge, MA: Polity, 1992.

Pearson, Keith Ansell. *Germinal Life: The Difference and Repetition of Deleuze*. London: Routledge, 1999.

———. *Viroid Life: Perspectives on Nietzsche and the Transhuman Condition*. London: Routledge, 1997.

Rabinow, Paul. *Anthropos Today*. Princeton: Princeton UP, 2003.

Rose, Nicholas. "The Politics of Life Itself." *Theory, Culture & Society* 18.6 (2001): 1–30.

Roy, Arundhati. *Power Politics*. Cambridge, MA: South End, 2001.

Shiva, Vandana. *Biopiracy: The Plunder of Nature and Knowledge*. Boston: South End, 1997.

Springer, Claudia. *Electronic Eros: Bodies and Desire in the Postindustrial Age*. Austin: U of Texas P, 1996.

Replacement Humans

Gabriele Schwab

". . . Is cloning the death or the apotheosis of individualism?"
— Adam Phillips (88)

"Same, same but different!"
— A waiter in Thailand when asked to describe two of the dishes on the menu

In the wide range of debates about cloning, one spectacular cultural fantasy often takes center stage on the utopian scene of imagined reproductive politics: the fantasy that one day it may become possible to clone one's own child. Rather than envisioning these clones as "duplications," that is, gene-technologically fabricated identical twins, they are imagined as potential replacement children designed purposefully to compensate for the death of another child. In case of the original child's death, so the fantasy goes, the cloned child is supposed to help the parents cope with an otherwise unbearable loss. Welcome to the arrival of the child in the age of biotechnological reproduction!

Debates about human cloning have profound ethical consequences that cannot yet be fully explored. Interestingly enough, some religious leaders cautiously embrace the possibility of human cloning. For example, Rabbi Elliot Dorff holds that cloning a human child would be "legitimate from a moral and a Jewish point of view" (National Bioethics 175) under certain circumstances. As an another example of ethically justifiable cloning, the National Bioethics Advisory Commission lists the cloning of a dying child so long as the procedure is safe for the child created by cloning. The Commission then adds: "Other conditions include the protection of the created child's rights and the lack of acceptable alternatives to cloning persons in such cases" (National Bioethics 176). One may indeed wonder how broadly "the created child's

rights" would be defined and what would constitute a "lack of acceptable alternatives." In sharp contrast to this perspective and cavalier rhetoric about the human
rights of a clone, Jean Bethke Elshtain in "To Clone or Not to Clone," develops a reading of Stanislaw Lem's *The Star Diaries* in order to discuss the cultural fantasy of
cloning as a defense against human loss and grief. On Lem's imaginary planet Panta,
the worst of crimes is "the crime of personal differentiation."[1] By eliminating individuality, the inhabitants of Panta aim at achieving the highest degree of social interchangeability in a culture in which functions and roles can be exchanged at any time.
While the traditional roles of family members are maintained—there are still fathers,
mothers and children—those who perform these roles change every day. The social
interchangeability of people profoundly changes the structures of feeling and affect
that govern relationships.

> Affection, respect, love were at one time gnawed by constant anxiety, by the fear
> of losing the person held dear. This dread we have conquered. For in point of fact
> whatever upheavals, diseases or calamities may be visited upon us, we shall
> always have a father, a mother, a spouse, and children." As well, there is no "I."
> And there can be no death "where there are no individuals. We do not die. (183)

Elshtain astutely grasps here what I consider the most fundamental cultural fantasy
attached to cloning: a phantasm of immortality that not only does away with death,
but also with the pain of loss and the work of mourning. "All feelings are entirely
abstract. One never needs to grieve or to mourn as everyone is infinitely replaceable"
(183). This scenario, Elshtain points out, is no longer confined to science fiction, but
enters the actual debates about cloning:

> It was anything but amusing to overhear the speculation that cloning might be
> made available to parents about to lose a child to leukemia or, having lost a child
> to an accident, in order that they might reproduce and replace that lost child. (184)

Questioning the ethics of such a politics of substitutive reproduction, Elshtain writes:
"This image borders on obscenity. Perhaps we need a new word to describe what it
represents, to capture fully what order of things the cloning of children in order to
forestall human loss and grief violates" (184).

This question of what order of things is violated in the fantasy of the cloning of
children as replacement children lies at the center of the following reflections. I need
to emphasize from the outset that I am not concerned with the reality of cloning
humans, with its technological feasibility or its biogenetic effects. I am well aware of
the fact that, even though it has become technologically feasible, cloning humans is
something that belongs to a very distant future. I am also well aware of the fact that
no cloned child would be a true replacement of a lost child since no clone would be
the same as the original. I am also aware that scientists have abundantly demonstrated

that the personality and talent, let alone destiny, of a clone will be entirely different from the original. I agree with Dan W. Brock who, in *Cloning Human Beings: An Assessment of the Ethical Issues Pro and Con*, claims that the desire for a cloned replacement child is based on a deep confusion:

> Cloning such a child would not replace the child the parents have loved and lost, but would only create a different child with the same genes. The child they loved and lost was a unique individual who had been shaped by his or her environment and choices, not just his or her genes, and more importantly who had experienced a particular relationship with them. (148)

However, the very irrationality of the fantasy of cloned replacement children betrays its deeper anchoring in the cultural unconscious. Rather than exploring the reality of cloning, I am therefore interested in the ongoing cultural fascination with cloning as a technique for the production of replacement humans. I attribute the tenacity of this fantasy against all better knowledge to the fact that cloning is unconsciously held as a magic cure that defies death and forestalls grief. Perhaps we need to explore the idea of replacement humans in the context of a larger cultural fascination with seriality. Artists such as Andy Warhol are fascinated with the seriality of the face in the age of its technological reproduction. Cultural icons such as Elvis Presley and Michael Jackson elicit an unending series of impersonators. Films such as *The Matrix* that feature cloned serial characters become cult films. If the 19th century was haunted by the notion of the double, perhaps we are in the process of becoming haunted by the specter of a potentially endless series of clones. I am interested in exploring both what the fantasy of cloning replacement children responds to cultur-ally and what it generates in terms of new structures of feeling and/or new cultural phantasms. If, as Michelle Rosaldo argues, feelings are "social practices organized by stories we both enact and tell" (143—quoted in Woodward p. 28), then the stories we tell about cloning not only *respond* to feelings such as grief over a lost child; but also they generate new feelings such as, for example, that the child is replaceable. The feelings organized and generated by stories about cloning are not just individual. They are social and transgenerational, affecting not only the generation of those who contemplate the increasingly feasible practice of cloning humans, but also the gen-erations to come that may well include—if the stories are right—the first generation of human clones. The very wish to clone a replacement child to offset the grief for the loss of a child would, in fact, transmit the legacy of grief and transgenerational trauma to the cloned child. Elshtain puts this in the most drastic terms:

> These poor children of our fantasies and our drive to perfect and our arrogant search for dominion: What are we to say to them? Forgive us for we knew not what we were doing? That tastes bitter on the tongue. We knew what we were doing and we did it anyway. (185)

Not surprisingly, the question of psychological harm plays a prominent role in debates about cloning. In *A Rush to Caution: Cloning Human Beings*, Richard A. Epstein asks the rather blatant but not necessarily obvious question: "What we have is the creation of one new person whose genetic component is identical to that of another human being, alive or dead. What, we may ask, is the harm in all that?" (268). The National Bioethics Advisory Commission lists a whole series of possible harms caused by cloning, including psychological harms deriving from the clone's supposedly "subordinate and derivative place" (Epstein 269). The report quotes values such as "the right to ignorance" propagated by philosopher Hans Jonas or philosopher Joel Feinberg's claim to a "right to an open future." Finally, they quote philosopher Martha Nussbaum's defense of the "separateness of persons" (Epstein 270). In a similar vein, Brock discusses the predictable psychological distress and harm to the potential replacement child:

> The later twin might feel, even if mistakenly, that her fate has already been substantially laid out, and so have difficulty freely and spontaneously taking responsibility for and making her own fate and life. The later twin's experience or sense of autonomy and freedom might be substantially diminished, even if in actual fact they are much less diminished than it seems to her. She might have a diminished sense of her own and her own uniqueness and individuality, even if once again these are in fact diminished little or not at all by having an earlier twin with the same genome. (155)

We may notice that, here and in debates about cloning more generally, old Enlightenment categories and values such as identity, autonomy, uniqueness, individuality and freedom return with a vengeance. At the same time, as Adam Phillips remarks, "With the advent of cloning [. . .] a whole range of political and psychological vocabularies are stopped in their tracks" (89). Debates about cloning, in fact, sit squarely with current debates about identity and identity politics, individuality and individualism as well as difference and otherness. It is as though debates about the "ethics of cloning" bring to the fore a return of forgotten, willfully abandoned or perhaps repressed discourses and values attached to the singularity of individuals. Even postmodern subjects who may easily abandon their sense of a bounded identical self in favor of a freely flowing continual self-fashioning or becoming, might become squeamish at the idea of encountering identical copies of themselves on the street corner. Doubles, let alone serial replicas, are uncanny and belong to the stuff of gothic novels and horror films. Yet, they are also infinitely fascinating and tie into primordial recesses of narcissism. Culturally moreover, doubles and copies are widely used to protect against loss. Almost like in a fairy tale, the fantasy to replace a lost child or to reawaken the dead belongs to the order of magical thinking. The question is: What happens if the realization of such a fantasy seems to be technologically feasible? The relevance of this question pertains despite the fact that the fantasy itself is based on a psychological confusion. It pertains because it can be read as a symptom that tells us about the emergence of new structures of feeling and new emotions related to loss, death and, indeed, human mortality as such.

In order to understand these new structures of feeling, it might be worthwhile looking at a more conventional scenario that addresses a related psychological dynamic. The phenomenon of replacement children is not new and not directly related to cloning. Rather, cloning gives it a new turn or, if one likes, a new edge. The wish to replace a lost child is, of course, as old as history, and diverse cultures have developed manifold practices designed to fulfill this wish. Even the widespread custom of naming a newborn child after a dead relative, while cast as a commemorative practice, bears traces of a more subliminal replacement fantasy. Yet, the specific forms the wish for replacement children assumes are highly culture-specific, emerging in the cultural imaginary predominately among peoples who have lost children during colonization, war, genocide and periods of starvation or epidemics. It is also a common wish in environments with high infant mortality. The cloning debates, by contrast, emerge in late 20th century in highly industrialized capitalist societies with their standard one- or two-child families, and the ensuing intense cathexis of each individual child. Moreover, it is psychologically highly significant that the fantasy of cloned replacement children predates the actual death of a child. In other words, the child is considered to be "replaceable" from birth and this fantasy inevitably colors the relationship to the actual living child. We may only begin to imagine what it would mean in psychological terms if the parents and the child or children lived with the actual knowledge that the genetic material for their cloned copies hovered somewhere in limbo, always available to be used on demand. Most likely, this scenario would, in a curious inversion of the temporal logic of generational succession, create a kind of haunting, not by the dead but by the not yet born. In other words, we would have to face the reality of a hauntology from the future.

In what follows, I will look at the psychic life of "natural" replacement children as a historical background to explore the cultural imaginary of cloned replacement children. In recent decades, we have seen the advent of a rich body of literature and autobiographies featuring replacement children. One of the most prominent examples is Art Spiegelman's famous cartoon *Maus* in which he reveals that, through his whole life, he has been haunted by the specter of his dead brother Richieu who died in Auschwitz before Art was born. In his parents' fantasies, Richieu appears as the ideal child with whom Art could never compete. Interestingly, Spiegelman chooses to cast his Jewish characters as mice and their Nazi persecutors as cats or pigs, a de-individualizing technique that uses seriality to produce the effects of characters that all look visually like clones of each other. The only character not portrayed as a mouse, but represented by a copy of an actual photograph is Richieu, Art's phantom brother. Similarly, a recent memoir by French psychoanalyst Philippe Grimbert also tells the story of the author's relationship to a phantom brother who died in Auschwitz. In Grimbert's case, his parents tried to keep this brother's existence and death a family secret, despite the fact that they saw young Philippe obsessively engaged in a ghostly competition with an imaginary brother. The crucial turn in Philippe's life follows a friend's revelation of this secret when Philippe is fifteen years old. His memoir describes the path from shock and alienation from his parents to mourning and integration.

In addition to fiction and autobiography, a growing arsenal of psychoanalytic literature has emerged describing the particular identity trouble of so-called replacement children. The role they are assigned in parental fantasies is intimately tied to the traumatic loss of a previous child. It is with these literary and theoretical reflections on replacement children in mind that I would like to pose the question of how the fantasy of cloning one's child may affect our sense of individuality and bounded life as well as, ultimately, our sense of the boundaries of the human. It is important to understand that, with the fantasy of cloning one's own child, we are no longer merely dealing with a psychological problem. At stake is, I think, a much larger cultural and, for that matter, eminently political and ethical issue, namely our culture's changing relationship to loss, death, mortality and mourning more generally. As soon as cloning became technologically feasible, the figure of the clone almost instantly advanced to the status of a cultural icon, promising—or threatening—to change some of the most fundamental parameters of biological and, as many argue, cultural reproduction. My concern here is not with actual cloning, but with the cultural fantasy of cloning and the special case of cloning a replacement child. The prospect of a gene-technological reproduction of virtual replacement children heralds an emotional economy in which one's child is fantasized as infinitely replicable and therefore replaceable. Films such as the block-buster *The Matrix* that figure the horrors of an army of identical cloned replacement children, serially produced like conveyer belt merchandise, already bring us, I think, to the threshold of imagining serial clones of children hovering in virtual existence, ghosts of a technologically feasible human autopoiesis.

Let there be no misunderstanding: I am fully aware of the fantasy's irrationality. We know that no cloned child would ever be the same. Difference would not only assert itself in the particular expressions of genetically identical material, but also in environmental, historical and cultural circumstances. But this is not my point. Fantasies have always not only defied reality testing, but also at the same time produced reality effects. The impossibility of an identical replication of a human being has never prevented parents from developing fantasies of a replacement child. What I want to address is a psychic, often unconscious economy of seriality and substitution. Since, in the unconscious, the boundaries between discrete entities are permeable and affective energies flow freely between them, people in fantasies, especially unconscious ones, may become exchangeable also. Most of us have dreams that condense very different people into one and the same figure. Similarly, our unconscious affective economy can condense different children into one and the same child, regardless of their concrete material differences. Psychoanalytic theories of "replacement children" are based on extensive clinical work with children who experience psychological problems related to the fact that they were meant to replace a child who had died before they were born. In an essay entitled "The Replacement Child: Variations on a Theme in Individual and Collective History and Psychoanalysis," Leon Anisfeld and Arnold Richards provide a provisional definition:

> In the narrowest sense, a replacement child is a child born to parents who have had a child die and then conceive the second child in order to fill the void left by the loss of the first. [. . .] The psychological dynamics of the parents, who have themselves, survived the trauma of the real or symbolic death of a child, mediate between the sick or deceased child and the sibling who is his or her surrogate. (2)

The replacement child is then conceived and born in response to a traumatic death that cuts off the path to mourning and grief. Unconsciously taking in their parents' fantasies, these children often grow up in confusion about their identity and sometimes gender. Supposed to live someone else's life, they never quite come into their own. The death of a child is always a wound and an outrage, an improper death, a death that haunts parents, siblings or entire communities. Parents are not supposed to survive their children and therefore may give in to the temptation to try to undo for themselves and their affective life what should not be. However, the attempt to undo a child's death by replacing it, even if only in fantasy, entails a refusal to mourn this child properly and integrate the fact of his or her death. Replacement children thus bear the burden of an inability or refusal to mourn. In extreme cases, they are the products of a manic defense against death. Fantasies of replacement children commonly abound after histories of human violence and war. They materialize in survivors as psychic attempts to deny, undo or merely bear the effects of the violence of humans against other humans. On the surface, it might look then as though fantasies of cloned replacement children supported the work of life. The increased birthrates after wars seem to affirm this assumption at a global level. But, to the extent that the fantasy implies a refusal to mourn, our wish to replace a dead child remains within the regime of violence. Ultimately, it robs the murdered child of its own unique death and the replacement child of a unique life of its own. While this theft occurs primarily in collective or individual fantasies, it has concrete psychic and often somatic effects.

Substituting for a traumatic loss, the replacement child carries the legacy of a traumatic family history, if not a traumatic collective history. Many of the children born after histories of violence, war and genocide may, as Anisfeld and Richards show, collectively embody the fate of replacement children: "a child born to Holocaust survivors replaces not simply a specific dead child or ancestor, but all those who have perished" (3). Here, the replacement children are the recipients of a transgenerational transmission of the trauma of the Holocaust. They are haunted by a death or even millions of deaths they have never directly experienced. The experience of death comes to them second hand, so to speak, through its effect on their mother or father. We may ask how this is possible? How can a parent's emotion or fantasy, especially if it is unconscious, be transmitted to a child? How does unconscious "communication" work? The testimony of many replacement children reveals that they pick up on small cues, often hard to understand. Most commonly, the emotion or experiences behind such cues remain unspoken if not inaccessible to language. The child, however, nonetheless gains an indirect experience of a parent's psychic life. Often this experience comes in the form of moods or emotions, taking on many shapes, including grief or anxiety, hypervigilance or numbness, emotional unavailability or uncontrolled rage. A child may be haunted by a parent's sudden absences and experience the feeling that the parent goes elsewhere to a place from which the child remains excluded. Or it may take in the weight of a parent's recurring grief and depression and feel responsible without understanding it. Analyzing the fantasies of replacement children, Vamik Volkan speaks of "deposit representations," that is, representations of self or others deposited into the child's developing self-representation by traumatized parents.[2] It is in form of such representations that trauma is transmitted to the next generation and that replacement children are made to carry the legacy of a parental or generational distortion of mourning after traumatic histories.

In a healthy psychological and cultural environment, parents commonly try to shield their children from pain. In the case of traumatic histories, however, this function breaks down. Rather than serving as a protective shield against trauma for their children, traumatized parents transmit their own trauma transgenerationally in the form of what Masud Khan calls "cumulative trauma."[3] A replacement child himself, Anisfeld describes how he was reminded of the children his own father lost in the holocaust "not because they were ever spoken about but because of his father's periodic 'absences' or dream-like escapes from the present into the past. These fugue states of his father's became Anisfeld's psychic reality."[4] In *Children of the Holocaust and Their Children's Children*, Virag argues that replacement children grow up in "unconscious identification with the persecuted or exterminated members of the family. [. . .] The symptoms, the play activity, the dreams, and fantasies of the children made it very clear that they knew about the family 'secrets.'" Rather than being properly mourned, the lost child has, in the parents' fantasy, been magically restored to life by a replacement child. As a result of this distorted mourning and its pseudo-resolution, the child who has been put in the place of someone else is likely to be haunted by identity trouble. Often such identity trouble manifests itself in the form of a pseudo-identity or, as Winnicott calls it, a false self. Anisfeld and Richards point to the high frequency of identity disturbances in Jewish children of the post-War generation. Similar phenomena can be observed in children born in the aftermath of histories of violence such as colonialism, slavery, war or genocide more generally. It can also be observed among children of perpetrators who carry their parents' psychic legacy and, often, unconscious guilt and shame.

If we move the focus back to the fantasy of cloned replacement children, the question arises how such a fantasy might not only affect the process of mourning for the lost child, but also the relationship to the child from the very beginning. Being a genetic replica with a deceivingly identical physical appearance makes the cloned child exceedingly vulnerable to the fantasy that it could literally replace a lost child. This is why the desire for a cloned replacement child is often invoked to describe the potential cultural capital of the cloning of humans. But wouldn't parents inevitably stop relating to their child on the basis of his or her own unique and irreplaceable individuality? Wouldn't they mourn each individual child's loss less if his or her clone were already in place? And with children becoming ultimately more expendable, wouldn't this perhaps even increase parental willingness to sacrifice them for pending or future wars? Historically, the unwillingness of mothers to sacrifice their sons or bear children destined to die in a war has generated some of the most powerful movements of women's resistance against war. Would this change if children were deemed replaceable? Would we slowly become accustomed to considering children as precious, yet replaceable and indeed technologically improvable objects subordinate to the more encompassing logic of a waste consumer culture that needs its war machines and the concomitant militarism of the mind to serve the accumulation of ever more profit?

Moreover, the possibility of cloning replacement children would affect not only the real and fantasized relationship of parents to their children, but also the relationship of the children to their parents as well as the fantasized replacement child. What are the parental deposit representations that would become part of their child's self? Since the fantasy of cloned children would become part of the cultural politics of reproduction, we may assume that deposit representations would affect both the original child and the replacement child. How do we imagine children to relate to their imagined cloned replacement children and, vice versa, cloned replacement children to their originals? Moreover, would there be laws that devise an ethics and regulate the practice of cloning? Would the cloning of children be restricted to parents who lost a child? And, if not, would the haunting of children by the specter of possible new doubles become a culturally and technologically feasible reality?

Until recently, humans have been leery of doubles, because too much sameness in the wrong place felt uncanny. Wouldn't we expect anyone who meets an identical twin they have never seen or a clone in the street to react in a state of shock? Such doubles used to belong in gothic novels. Yet, something has changed in the age of simulacra, something that troubles the boundaries between original and copy. The age of technological reproduction, replication and seriality deeply affects our psychic disposition toward techniques of doubling. Popular culture is fascinated with doubles, impersonators and fakes. People love clones of Elvis as if they were proof of the King's legendary immortality. Elvis is, in fact, an interesting case. Haunted all his life by the death of his identical twin, he seeks and finds twin doubles in other singers. "As a twinless twin, his twin brother being stillborn, he 'twinned' himself to singers and performers such as Big Mama Thornton, LaVern Baker [. . .] Nat King Kole [. . .] who were African American; but also to singers who were not African American such as Mario Lanza [. . .] and Bob Dylan," says Peter Nazareth in "Elvis as Anthology." Interestingly, Elvis also seems to have managed to create his own imaginary twins in impersonators that carry part of his imaginary legacy for generations to come.

Yet, when the idea of cloning replacement children emerges as a feasible repro-ductive technology, things begin to weigh more heavily. At least from our current psychological disposition, we can easily imagine that children will be haunted by future clones who inhabit their psychic life from its inception. Moreover, we can just as easily imagine that the children they are supposed to replace will forever haunt these clones who bear the legacy of a death that is not really experienced as a death, because it has been denied before it happened. This is a psychic paradox not unlike the paradoxes D. W. Winnicott identifies as common phenomena in the transitional space of fantasies. It is as though death both happened and did not happen. The replacement clone is successor to a lost "original." But the original is, genetically, the survivor while the successor is psychically meant to replace it. Replacement clones thus literally embody a living death. The trauma of death lies at the very origin of a birth that is never a complete birth, because life has been lived before its inception. The logic of an uncanny, anticipated future, a future anterior, marks those shadow lives that are paradoxically supposed to prevent a death that has already happened. Another's half-death thus always foreshadows the half-life of a cloned double. Humans turn into beings without origin or end, hovering like Beckett's unnamable—a psychic clone if there ever was one—in a virtual space of endless replications. Yet, endless replications may paradoxically prevent psychological birth. Or, as the unnamable puts it: "You'll never be born again, what am I saying, you'll never have been born" (Beckett 128). No wonder then, that the unnamable consistently rejects his own attempted self-representations as mere deposit representations, put into him against his will by others, or inversely put into others as deposit representations of his own impossible self. In Beckett, the paradoxical effect of a cloned self emerges from philosophically radicalized boundary confusions between self and other as they become evident in statements such as: "He speaks of me, as if I were he, as if I were not he . . ." (163) or "I'll put myself in him, I'll say he is I" (159). Among contemporary writers, Beckett may be the one who captures the psychic life of clones most succinctly and this despite the fact that Beckett's texts do not overtly deal with fantasies of cloning. Rather, they deal with fantasies of involuntary psychic replication and seriality. But, with his figuration of this psychic dilemma, Beckett may have anticipated the condition of subjectivity and subjection in the age of human biotechnological reproduction.

As Laurence Tribe argues, cloning human beings may constitute "a fundamental threat to the concept and the reality of the human person as a unique and intrinsically valuable entity, conscious of its own being and responsible for its own choices" (223). And, as Leon Kass states, the prospect of human cloning takes "a major step toward making a human being simply another one of the manmade things," diminishing their singularity by transforming them into a generic kind of being. The fantasy that children and humans more generally become replicable, replaceable and exchangeable radicalizes the logic of substitution already inherent in industrialization and capitalism. Psychologically, this logic is based on a powerful defense against mortality if not a phantasm of immortality. Even if it were never implemented, the fantasy of cloned replacement humans as such already shifts the boundaries of the human in the cultural imaginary because it erases the boundary between original and copy. Do we then, as Benjamin did for the work of art, culturally witness the loss of the child's aura, that is, the idea of its uniqueness, authenticity and irreplaceable value? Cloned children may become placeholders of a dead child whose loss is denied or, worse perhaps, narcissistic doubles of a single parent and placeholder of this parent's fantasized immortality. As Laurence Tribe states, "The clone is the ideal emblem: the ultimate single-parent child" (227). Is this the most recent expression of a culture of narcissism with its omnipotent claims on immortality? In narcissistic spirals of phantasmatic asexual self-replication, those seeking immortality through the survival of their genes end up preventing their "replicas" from finding their own bounded lives.

I am well aware that I am speaking from within my own situated and culturally constructed subject position, perhaps even from within an essentializing notion of human nature. I do not think, however, that cultural worries about what the cloning of humans would do to the boundaries and values we attribute to human lives are exclusively tied to notions of Western humanism. But perhaps I'm simply old-fashioned if the fantasy of cloned replacement children violates my sense of human beings as defined within the boundaries between life and death. I admit I tend to hold on to things, particularly things that are vanishing in global corporate and increasingly militarized cultures. Perhaps my sense of impropriety or even queasiness stems from the powerful cultural enforcement of boundaries that mark, in Mary Douglas' terms, the vexed line between purity and danger. I may be constructing yet another problematic divide between the human and its others. Or my reaction may be fed by a psychological disposition toward cultural pessimism that makes me vulnerable to apocalyptic fantasies. Some may even say I'm buying into a conservative ecology of fear. On the other hand, I could all too easily master utopian fantasies of a free society of happy clones. It would be great fun to write a "Manifesto for Clones," honoring the joyfully experimental spirit of Donna's "Manifesto for Cyborgs" that, when I heard it in San Diego in 1983, made me want to stay in the U.S. and write my own paper on cyborgs. Thinking of Shulamith Firestone, I can even see myself writing a science fiction story that steps out of the epistemologies and cultures of feeling attached to those old-fashioned humans still hung up on the messy business of sexual reproduction. Finally, I can imagine how, in a culture where cloned children were the order of the day, the value and meaning of life and death would radically change. Yet, this is precisely my point. Do the fantasies about cloning tell us something about the value of life and death in *today*'s cultural imaginary and are we mindful of the ways they will affect our future *uses* of new gene-technologies?

I also continue to wonder about the psycho-political implications of fantasies of cloning humans in our time and age. I am struck by the unbridled flourishing of phantasms of technologically produced immortality—cloning, cryonics, AI, genetic enhancement, to mention just a few—at a time when the work of death, war and genocide looms as large as ever. I also wonder about the role of such fantasies in a society that becomes increasingly infatuated with what Baudrillard and others call "social cloning" (25). In *The Vital Illusion*, Baudrillard opens his reflections with the assertion: "The question of cloning is the question of immortality" (3). Yet, he proceeds to argue that the phantasm of immortality follows a paradoxical deadly logic that resembles a collective suicide as an effect of "the inclination to sacrifice the entire species to limitless experimentation" (17). And he asks, "Have we come, via an unexpected detour, to the same point at which an animal species, when they reach a critical saturation point, automatically switch over to a kind of collective suicide?" (19). Baudrillard describes this suicidal drive as an effect of a new kind of colonialism, a biocolonialism so to speak, that follows the colonial legacy of imperial annexation and domination: "The impulse to annex nature, animals, other races and cultures—to put them universally under jurisdiction—is in effect everywhere" (23). Baudrillard begs the question of a jurisdiction based on the genetic definition of the human: "Does a species have rights to its own genome and to its own eventual genetic transformation?" (22). What kind of mindset does the arrogation of these rights presuppose? The association of the new biocolonialism with a colonial logic according to which nature, other peoples and species, and now even bodies and genes can be invaded, owned and manipulated at will is one aspect of the dynamic. The other is a form of internal colonization within nations, societies and cultures, including the colonization of psychic space. Baudrillard describes the latter as a form of social cloning:

Through school systems, media, culture, and mass information, singular beings become identical copies of one another. It is this kind of cloning—social cloning,

the industrial reproduction of things and people—that makes possible the biological conception of the genome and of genetic cloning, which only further sanctions
the cloning of human conduct and human cognition. (25)

Even if Baudrillard's vision of singular beings becoming identical copies of one
another is pointedly overstated, the argument that the pervasive "social cloning" in
late capitalist global cultures prepares the ground for a mindset in which genetic
cloning lends itself to phantasms of human self-replication is well taken.

In "Cloning cultures: the social injustices of sameness," Philomena Essed and
David Goldberg propose to revisit current debates on cloning from an encompassing
perspective that includes the "cultural cloning of preferred types." In this vein, they
explore socio-cultural fabric that generates the desire to clone, reminding us of the
fact that the cultural preference for one's own kind is historically bound up with histories of war, violence and oppression and therefore raises questions about humanity, humanness and humaneness. In tracing the desires of those who volunteer as
guinea pigs for cloning, they also name the desire that lies at the heart of my reflections on replacement children: the difficulty to cope with loss and the wish to have
their deceased loved ones back. Yet, like Baudrillard, they emphasize the paradox at
the heart of this wish: "Ironically, the extreme implications of an unqualified culture
of cloning reproduce the very prospects of stasis and death to which it considers
itself threatened by the proliferation and incorporation of the different" (1080). I
include the fantasy of cloning humans among the phantasms of immortality that
proliferate in contemporary global cultures and media. Yet death seems to haunt
these phantasms with a vengeance. Carrying this logic to the extreme, Baudrillard even
subsumes it under the notion of a social fabric generated by a pervasive death drive.

As it tries to undo mortality, the fantasy of a replacement child also dispenses
with the sense of a singular and unique human life. It figures death as reversible—a
wish we know from fairy tales, religious fantasies and contemporary science fiction.
It also holds out the politically and psychologically suspect lure of narcissistic self-
replication within a technologically assisted production of homogeneity. Perhaps
most pertinently, I cannot help but see those fantasies in light of the current wars
and mass killings as well as the relentlessly progressing destruction of the resources
of our planet. I wonder if phantasms of immortality are not a reaction formation
against a pervasive species anxiety linked to the knowledge that we are threateningly
close to destroying our own species and the planet. This is why the cultural fantasies
of replacement children that emerge after histories of violence, war and genocide
become a touchstone to explore the psychic economy within which fantasies of
cloning replacement children are operating. As I reiterated throughout this paper,
the siblings fantasized as replacements for killed war children belong to a psychic
economy of trauma and refused mourning. They belong to a psychic economy of

manic defense. They carry the burden of a traumatic legacy and the identity trouble that comes with it. Could it be that the fantasy of the cloned replacement child plays a similar role in today's cultural imaginary? Does it, along with other related phantasms of immortality, operate as a manic defense that allows us to remain blind to the work of death we perform on a daily basis in the new histories of trauma we create as we speak?

Notes

1. Qtd. in Elshtain 183.

2. Consult Ainsfield and Richards 7.

3. Consult Ainsfield and Richards 8.

4. Consult Ainsfield and Richards 8.

Works Cited

Anisfeld, Leon, and Arnold D. Richards. "The Replacement Child: Variations on a Theme in Individual and Collective History and Psychoanalysis," Manuscript.

Baudrillard, Jean. *The Vital Illusion.* New York: Columbia UP, 2000.

Beckett, Samuel. *The Unnamable.* New York: Grove, 1958.

Brock, Dan W. "Cloning Human Beings: An Assessment of the Ethical Issues Pro and Con." *Clones and Clones: Facts and Fantasies about Human Cloning.* Eds. Martha C. Nussbaum and Cass R. Sunstein. New York: Norton, 1998.

Elshtain, Jean Bethke. "To Clone or Not to Clone." *Clones and Clones: Facts and Fantasies about Human Cloning.* Eds. Martha C. Nussbaum and Cass R. Sunstein. New York: Norton, 1998.

Epstein, Richard A. "A Rush to Caution: Cloning Human Beings." *Clones and Clones: Facts and Fantasies about Human Cloning.* Eds. Martha C. Nussbaum and Cass R. Sunstein. New York: Norton, 1998.

Essed, Philomena, and David Theo Goldberg. "Cloning Cultures: The Social Injustices of Sameness." *Ethnic and Racial Studies* 25 (Nov. 2002):1066–1082.

National Bioethics Advisory Commission. "Religious Perspectives." *Clones and Clones: Facts and Fantasies about Human Cloning.* Eds. Martha C. Nussbaum and Cass R. Sunstein. New York: Norton, 1998.

Nazareth, Peter. "Topics in Popular Culture: Elvis as Anthology." Course Description, Available online.

Phillips, Adam. "Sameness is All." *Clones and Clones: Facts and Fantasies about Human Cloning.* Eds. Martha C. Nussbaum and Cass R. Sunstein. New York: Norton, 1998.

Tribe, Laurence. "On Not Banning Cloning for the Wrong Reasons." *Clones and Clones: Facts and Fantasies about Human Cloning.* Eds. Martha C. Nussbaum and Cass R. Sunstein. New York: Norton, 1998.

Virag, T. "Children of the Holocaust and Their Children's Children: Working Through Current Trauma in the Psychotherapeutic Process." *Dynamic Psychotherapy* 2.1: 47–60.

Part Two: Cultural Cloning

Cloning, Cultures, and the Social Injustices of Homogeneities

Philomena Essed and
David Theo Goldberg[1]

Human cloning is a troubling notion, the suggestion of which triggers images of cold laboratories and gruesome Nazi experiments. But human cloning does not have to be horrible, its advocates claim. In an article about the "cloning mission," New York Times journalist Margaret Talbot comments that individuals and couples eager to serve as guinea pigs for cloning purposes "will tell you that they realize cloning does not produce a copy of the original person, but something more than a later-born identical twin, and yet say that they would want to do it anyway. They'd want to do it so that they could know in advance about their unborn children, so that they wouldn't have to take their chances of sexual reproduction, so they could perpetuate their own genes or so they could hope against hope to get somebody very, very much like somebody they had lost" (43). Putting aside our own moral objections against cloning, for the sake of the argument let us listen seriously to these wishes. These voices express a desire for ultimate control of nature, most notably, regarding self-determination with respect to the genetic composition of offspring. The desire to subject nature to the hands of human beings is not new. It has been central to the project of modernization, granting to human beings virtually limitless domination over "things," including animals. In that process, human bodies too have been objectified and increasingly subjected to manipulation in order to fit images of beauty or perfection. Cosmetic surgery is a case in point.

Here we find an overriding concern with human bodies made to order. The Platonic possibility of a baby just like us, no unexpected surprises, no physical or character traits hidden from view, yet to be discovered. Indeed, no procreation. Perfect reproductive efficiency and sterile social reproducibility. The dream of simply ordering exactly the type of child—and by extension social order—deemed desirable, and more of the same if pleased with the result. This dream, not that far from what is being made technically possible, says something not only about the cloning of human beings, but also about the social context in which a fantasy like this could emerge in the first place. In this discussion piece, we wish to draw attention to the socio-cultural fabric enabling the desire and drive to clone.

Who would be cloned, one might rightfully ask, if bio-medical factories were to take over from sexual reproduction? Thinking about cloning is saturated with references to the biological. For example, web searches reference only the biological or ethical issues emerging from the biological considerations. Thus, cloning is widely considered to be no more than a biological discourse. Radical biological cloning—the cloning of human beings—has been awaited anxiously now for some time, the technological inevitability prompting the tension between socio-scientific celebration and ethico-religious palpitation. Even plant seed and animal cloning can at least be said to be *for* human purpose, perhaps more assertively to be preparatory conceptually if not technologically to human cloning. The almost exclusive fixation on the biotechnology of cloning around the world concerns the ethics of human cloning followed distantly by concerns over the propriety of genetically engineered food products. Broadly, the ethical objections to human cloning concern intervention in nature; aiming for perfect bodies (implications of imperfect sameness—racism, eugenics, sexism, ableism, ageism, hetero-normativity); and the danger to the sustainability of humankind (bio-diversity).

While the discursive focus has been on the biological side of cloning, few have paid attention to the social and cultural contexts that make cloning possible, that have rendered it thinkable. By cloning in this broader sense, we understand the systemic reproduction of likeness. This is a phenomenon deeply engrained in the organization of contemporary culture, in social life generally, and in the racial, gendered and class structures of society, in particular.

In light of this, one can imagine "who" will be cloned. It seems not unlikely that the *biological* cloning of human beings will inevitably implicate the cloning of preferred *types* of human beings: male, white, able-bodied, heterosexual, highly intelligent, to be placed in economically privileged habitats. One can also imagine the cloning of nonwhite, able-bodied, good-natured, caring, docile, moderately smart but not too intelligent bodies to do the service work those more privileged seem to demand more and more. Whereas biological cloning is still, for the most part, a fiction waiting to be realized, the *cultural cloning* of preferred types to inhabit segregated spaces is everyday practice, especially but far from only among social elites. The notion of *cultural cloning*, initially used to problematize the systemic reproduction of white, masculine homogeneity in high status positions (Essed, "Cloning"), brings into focus another side of exclusion. Yet, same-kind preference reproducing white (Euro) masculine privileges in terms of race, ethnicity, gender, or profession is not countered with the same force of indignation as we find in the case of the suggestion of biological cloning.

Longing for a clone of a loved one is not simply or indeed principally a desire for a biological clone. In picturing cloned duplicates of loved ones, those contemplating cloning must necessarily also imagine same-kind personality traits, identities, life histories, in short, a socio-cultural context for the would-be-clone to inhabit. One might more properly think of biological cloning as instrumental to—making materially possible—the deeper desire for these forms of social sameness. While public conscience, national governments and international NGOs are denouncing the biological cloning of human beings, we want to insist here that cloning as a practice is not a new phenomenon, and not even a phenomenon that is generally rejected. Quite the contrary. The very context prompting the desire to clone human beings biologically is framed in historically rooted systems of preference for real or imagined replica and homogeneities. Cloning, in this sense, is properly *bio-social* reproduction, and not simply or strictly or primarily a biological phenomenon. We are offering here a framework for thinking about a set of concerns long passed over largely in silence. We will draw substantially from decades of insightful and important critical research on difference, discrimination and the struggles for equality. At the same time, our focus is different. We believe that critical research can gain from exploring the function and manifestations of normative preference for likeness and how these are instrumental in reproducing systems of social injustice.

There are good reasons to problematize normative preference for homogeneity, whether the "normative" is the result of explicit choice or of hegemonic consensus. The glass ceiling phenomenon is a case in point. The number of critical publications on (intertwined) processes of exclusion along racial, ethnic, gender, sexual, class, and other structural demarcations is abundant. As a result, we have come to a much better understanding of the relation between inequality and difference. In focusing on likeness, our aim is not to discount or disqualify established models of difference and social exclusion, but to build on their critical modes (Essed and Goldberg, *Theories*). We have also witnessed decades of policies regarding an inclusive work place, ranging across affirmative action in the US, equity policies in Canada, equal opportunity in the UK, and positive action in some European countries. But according to the weekly magazine *Newsweek,* problematizing the exclusive whiteness of the highest European echelons remains silenced.[2] Thirty years of feminism and race critical literature notwithstanding, the (culturally contextualized) privileging of white men and the social delimitation and denigration of women and people of color in the world have not been erased. Consider, as one instance among many, the radio discussion between Fox television host Chris Wallace and New York morning talk show host Don Imus that, when Sarah Palin would appear on Wallace's program, she would "sit in his lap." Furthermore, in spite of improvements in facilities for people with physical challenges, disabilities are generally perceived as indicative of a less than full human life (Reinders).

A new paradigm?

Converging discriminations *against* particular groups also reveal presumptive normative preferences *for* clones of imagined perfections of the same type and profile. We are concerned to problematize the *context* that makes it so "evident" that certain criteria will be taken into and "others" kept out of consideration in the cloning process, just as we are concerned to shine a critical spotlight on the forms of inequality resulting from privileging those, or those criteria marking one, as same.

In speaking about context, we are raising questions concerning the cultural assumptions about humanity, humanness, and humaneness, but also concerning preference for a certain kind of human. The deeper concern, therefore, is to engage in questioning what it means to be human, and implicitly what the normative commitment to humanism effects. This engagement reveals that the preference for one's own kind, whether at the micro level of the family or at the macro level of the nation, implies to varying degrees the dehumanizing of all others who are then seen as less deserving of human dignity and respect. By drawing attention to the socio-cultural fabric enabling cloning cultures, we aim in this discussion piece to re-direct focus from identity and difference to the social injustices and inequalities embedded silently in the reproduction of sameness and the privileging of likeness. Ultimately, we see that the work focusing on identity and difference would be complemented by that focused on likeness. Here, we are concerned to raise the question.

The effects of preference for homogeneity, whether intended or unintended, have been shown to be manifestations of all kinds of debilitating exclusions: racism, genderism, able-bodiedness, and so on. What we are claiming is new, because newly revealing, is the sustained critical focus on likeness for which we are calling. It follows from this shift that the cloning debate, with its focus on biological cloning of the human race, is only a symptom of a whole set of other social malaises, of which we should be critically aware. For instance, the drive to insist on difference that we have witnessed in social theorizing and some aspects of popular culture over the past two decades is predicated on the underlying assumption that the values of homogeneity represent the prevailing social norm. Questioning the normativity of likeness (equalness) implies that the need to exaggerate the right to be different (the difference debate) is problematized by the same token. Commitments to discourses of difference are dialectically tied to the (embedded or underlying) socio-cultural investment in sameness.

Cultural cloning is predicated on the taken-for-granted desirability of certain types, the-often-unconscious tendency to comply with normative standards, the easiness with the familiar and the subsequent rejection of those who are perceived as deviant.

In this sense, cultural cloning is enormously widespread if not a universal phenomenon, descriptively considered. It is neither confined to Western cultures nor to
dominant groups. Non-dominant groups or communities too can be essentialist in
choosing for their own kind, whether or not as a reaction against exclusion. We are
mostly interested here in cultural cloning as reproducing gender and racial inequalities. Preferences for homogeneity, whether gendered or racially indexed, are historically part and parcel of the social fabric of modern societies. Race as an ordering
principle has been interwoven in the very nature of and in the making of modernity
(Goldberg, *Racial State*). The same holds true for gender, where modern manhood
required the construction of dominant rational, emotionally suppressed identities
and the imitation of these images of manhood over generations (Seidler). At the
same time, a critique of cultural cloning goes much beyond the injustices of reproducing homogenous circles of privilege along lines of race and gender. Preference for
sameness is embedded in our allegiance to copy cultures, mass productions, consumerism and the promise of eternal growth (Schwartz; Klein). Cultural cloning, we
are suggesting, is underpinned by a culture of cloning.

The Scope of Cloning Cultures
Cloning culture in this broader sense accordingly has come to saturate politics (profiles of acceptable political figures), law (flattened notions of equality), education
(profiled standards of merit and ability), management (normative embodied profiles
of organizational orderings), aesthetics (somatic norm images, cosmetic surgery),
the military (uniforms, depersonalization), and processes of production and reproduction (advertising, mass production). However, not all standardizations, copies, replications, mass productions or equations can or ought to be treated in the same way.
They serve different purposes, and have different implications.

We are seeking here accordingly to link three socio-political debates: The first concerns a relatively new problem, at least in the bio-technological sense—the biological cloning of human beings. The second concerns the phenomenon of reproducing
homogeneities. We believe that a critical account of systems of preference for
likeness—from kinship to nation, from aesthetics to production and consuming—can
be revealed as contributing to the reproduction of systems of social distinction and
privilege. This introduces the third debate, which has to do with an old, yet unresolved,
global problem: (attributed) social differences and systemic inequalities. Social
distinctions refer here to those of "race," ethnicity, gender, and other ordering
processes. The related concepts of "cultural cloning" and "cultures of cloning," when
considered critically in their relation, shed a different light on issues of injustice and
inequality. We believe that a focus on what we call "cloning cultures (as uniting both
concerns) has the potential to shift the debates on social injustices and inequalities
by opening up issues almost never attended. It will surface dimensions of social

injustice that, for the most part, have remained hidden from view or under-emphasized. In addressing how the hegemony of normative models and systems of likeness disadvantage groups, this critical focus calls attention to new and overlooked grounds and highlights (relatively) unexplored processes of injustice.

We agree that there is no question that people's experiences and identities are multidimensional, not reducible to only one interest or category (Goldberg, *Racist Culture*; Essed, *Diversity*). At the same time, the range of literature on categorizing and standardizing suggests that people tend to seek a certain degree of sameness, in the sense of familiarity, similarity, identicality in their surroundings so as more easily to cope socially. In getting to know new situations and new people, we search for what looks and sounds familiar in order to establish a common ground from which to proceed. Sameness, repetition, and predictability render social circumstance more manageable, more comfortable, more readily negotiable. But there seems to be something specific about the ways of likeness in the context of modernity, where homogeneities and more of the same help to define the conception, shape, and reach of what counts as progress and growth.

Crucial Concerns of Cloning Cultures

Human histories have been replete with violations of nature and of health in the name of progress, and the projection of normative models for bodies in the name of civilization. In other words, over the course of history, economic, social, and cultural preferences have paved the way for human cloning to emerge as a pressing set of social commitments. The ease with which biological cloning has been taken up in contemporary thinking has been made possible by the widespread acceptance of the normative assumption of cultural homogeneity throughout much of mainstream modern thinking. In short, it is not that the interest in cloning has belatedly given rise to the preference for likeliness. Rather, the longstanding drives and demands for more of the same have made possible the very conceivability of cloning as a supposed ideal worthy of pursuit. The ethical concerns about biological cloning, by extension, arise only in the context of social reproducibility and propriety. It is these broad social(ly manifest) dispositions to reproduce likeness that we reference as *cloning cultures*.

Familiarity, shared taste and style, common values, and recognizable surroundings provide a certain degree of comfort, which no doubt are central elements of what it is to be a social being. In one sense, at least, any cultural reproduction can be seen as a form of cloning. We are careful, however, not to equate reproduction as such with cloning culture. To speak of "cloning culture" presupposes a society where productivity and efficiency occupy a prized position on the list of values (little time and energy wasted on the tensions and trials of difference and distinction), where one can expect a consumptive demand for certain types of commodities, including most notably children (think, for instance, of the ethno-national fantasies and fashions around adoption), according to what, aesthetically, is considered the fashion of the day. These societal dimensions are best referenced, we want to suggest, in terms of the principal concepts constitutive of cloning culture, which we delineate as *kinhood, productivism, consumerism,* and *aestheticism.* Each of these dimensions manifests through gender, racial, ethno-national and socio-economic dynamics. These dimensions also factor into understanding globalization for it is through the standardization of each dimension in their interactive relation with the others that global penetration is exercised.

Kinhood and associated familial identifications are relevant in a study of cloning cultures because of the tendency to prioritize larger collective identifications (notably race, gender, and nationality) while reducing those perceived as "other" to one-dimensional and so static prototypical images of identity. In the revolutionary period of US history, the prevailing politics of identity reinforced the preferred state of human life—whiteness, heteronormative masculinity, and ruling classes—in and through centering on those human variations perceived as problematic in their distinctiveness, primarily race, gender, and social class (Wiley).

Today, so-called colorblindness proclaims homogeneity (only one race, the human race), but in practice the "race" of "others" is as visible as it is disturbing in the eyes of the dominant group even as they perhaps see themselves as losing a (firm) grip on power (Goldberg, *Racial State*). In Europe, a growing sense of "we-Europeans" goes hand in hand with the resurgence of Neo-nazi groups, the increasing respectability of ultra-nationalist parties, and the more and more openly expressed assertion that immigrants are a threat to the cultural heritage of established residents. While problematizing others, in particular Muslims, for their "backward" or "threatening" cultures, the implicit message is a preference for cultural homogenization. Stereotypical in-group and out-group conceptions essentialistically defined, refined, and grounded in normative preference for traits of the dominant group, are reinforced through the very denial of preference for sameness of a certain kind when racial equality is the formal ideology. Cases in point are the unnamed preference for the comfort, safety, familiarity, and privilege associated with whiteness (Roediger). Conversely, Black Nationalisms and ethnic fundamentalisms are implicated in cultural cloning, as these discursive formations express preference for those seen as the same "race," religion or culture, in reaction and conflicted resistance to racisms and globalization.

Fitting the group norm by displaying prototypical behavior is a way of being accepted into a certain race, class, or community and a mechanism of cloning through culture. At the same time, the normative principle of merit regulates access to resources. The industrial and, more recently, information revolutions have increased competitive pressures to reward according to efficiency and systems of fashioned merit, inevitably to be measured by the use of standardized tests (Zwick). The idea that merit (for the most part technically defined as IQ) plus effort can be measured in a culturally neutral way has come under attack. It has been shown repeatedly that the myth of merit has served the cloned reproducibility of masculine-dominated, elite cultures. Becoming and succeeding as a business leader in Europe is largely a function of a prestigious education, wealthy families, and sustained networks. This seems strongly counter to what one would be tempted to believe in the wake of a century of women's emancipation, transformative social movements, and structural change. Nevertheless, business elites remain resiliently homogenous (masculine, middle to higher social classes, white) even while women have increasingly democratized higher education along gender lines. Critiques of prevailing ideas of rewarded credit according to certain prototypes of merit, the inherent privileging of cognitive intelligence and competence established on fixed terms, and the principle that only the "most deserving" can gain admission or promotion have had little substantive effect on eroding the persistence, pernicious effects of monoculturalism.

The concept of family has been commercialized to fit the needs of global productivism and consumerism and the cloning of taste and behavior according to class and spending power. In the age of mass production and consumption, the McDonald's "family restaurant" exemplifies the global cloning of a US prototype of family nourished by a certain culture of eating. This fast food franchise, quintessentially a product of late modernity, represents "all that is efficient, calculated, predictable and over which we can exercise control" (Gabriel 100). But it also reproduces a profile of desired (if far from healthily desirable) nutrition, of body types, and of "spending" fun time with a narrowly idealized sense of the family.

In disaggregating the analytic elements concerning cloning cultures in these examples, then, we focus accordingly on three interactive constitutive considerations: productivism, consumerism, and aestheticism.

a. *Productivism* concerns the widespread cultural commitment to being productive and efficient, in material or non-material ways, as a goal in itself. The production of goods in factories has over-flooded the market with uniform mass-products virtually indistinguishable from one another. The introduction of brand marks and logos distinguish privileged circles signified by a particular highly priced brand family from the anonymous masses. But imitations, theft of brand names, and literal cloning of brand products have emerged as a prevailing trend, expanding circles of consumption as they throw into question, while at the same time mimicking, systems of prevailing privilege. IBM clones are a well-known example, if now from an already bygone era (Klein). In terms of quality or design, it is often difficult even to distinguish the original from the many inexpensive clones. Productivism sustains the focus on quantity, timemanagement, and cost-benefit analysis. And it involves the profiling of the perfect worker in terms of productivity and notions of competence for different occupations. Those who do not fit the productivity profile along lines of gender, race, first-third world situatedness, or educated-illiterate are likely to be marginalized, for example, by way of surveillance and disciplining through the criminal justice system. Plagiarism, understood as the cloning of someone else's work, is fueled by the drive to get ahead on these terms.

b. *Consumerism,* relatedly, concerns the age of homogenizing shopping malls and shared products revealing, as they reproduce, assumptions of shared identity and belonging along lines of class, ethnoracial formations, and gender. Examples include the likes of The Body Shop, IKEA furniture, warehouse shopping at US mega stores such as Costco, and food consumption at family restaurants like McDonald's or Pizza Hut, or indeed Mövenpick, Hard Rock Café, and Starbucks coffee.. These modes of consumptive recreation and recreational consumption fashion identity formation: you belong to the class or peers of what and where you eat (Bell and Valentine), or how and where you exercise, whether and where, for instance, you play basketball or golf. As many have pointed out, consumerism has implications for exploitation of nature for the purpose of mass production with disastrous consequences for the environment, health, and the gap between rich and poor. It presupposes the creation of markets by creating needs: from dishwashers to brands of shampoo, from mobile phones to cosmetics for men. Other instances of cultural cloning as/through consumption include the universalizing of cultural taste through the mass consumption as well as the global proliferation of technological products such as Microsoft and Macintosh.

c. *Aestheticism:* Tastes are shaped by and reproduced through the impress of the tastes of others in one's own group and by the advertising power of mass media. Around the globe, cosmetic surgery has become a medico-cultural fixture (Gilman). Ideals of perfect bodies are rationalized in terms of universal standards of beauty to be emulated (for instance, the cosmetic industry, the exercise industry, fashion, and health fads) . . . The reduction of ethics to the aesthetics of the care for the already raced and gendered self reveals some of the complex processes at work in cloning cultures.

We conceive of these dimensions not as static, but as general placeholders for complex and interactive processes. We regard consumerism accordingly not as basic, but as the intersection point of the mutually constitutive and overlapping relationships between all three dimensions. For example, uniforms pertain to consumerism as well as to aesthetics and labor and productive practices, revealing features of each. Uniforms are about certain modes of fashion, of what people choose to wear or through which to express themselves. But they also mark one kind of productive activity or class from another, such as who occupies what position in the stratification of a society while perhaps denying that such stratification exists or persists (consider, for instance, school uniforms). And they represent standards of beauty and acceptability, normative dispositions to regard what is acceptable in a society and what is not.

Toward a Definition

We are conceiving of cloning cultures, then, as the reproduction of systems of likeness shaped by real or imagined kinhood in dynamic relation to modes of productivism, consumerism and aestheticism. Cloning through cultures is producing *more of the same at the same time* as well as *more of the same across time.*

Cloning is the imitation of a model with the intended result of potentially limitless copies of the same item. Such copying does not, of course, preclude variations on the theme. Indeed, often such variations are deemed desirable, but the logic of variation is both that it is predicated on an original model and serves to replicate and so reproduce identifiable and (at least implicitly) valued qualities of the original in its variation. Nevertheless, referring to likeness does not imply that it is a transparent notion. Cross-cutting and shaping the tendency to create sameness through cloning is that the original clone should be worked upon and improved to a status of perfection.

Cloning accordingly presupposes the initial fashioning or at least imagining of a supermodel. The idea of a supermodel is clearly visible in the fashion industry and in cosmetic surgery, thus embedding Platonic ideals of beauty and perfection. But it is a notion with considerably wider resonance. Consider, for instance, the role of prototypes in product design, or more pressing (because closer to what we are driving at) of "role models" especially with respect to children's socialization. Sameness according to a model of perfection reinstates the underlying hierarchy of humanity, revealing that its definition is always contrasted with the different and excluded, the deviant and excommunicated.

By cloning (as a quality *of*) culture, we mean the reproduction of these cultures through the processes of kinhood, productivism, consumerism, and aestheticism. These processes in turn embed those of socialization, education, mass media, and mass production. The debates on multiculturalism amounted to a critique of exclusion, a plea to reproduce other cultures rather than only the dominant one, but not a questioning of the assumption that cultures (of sameness) need to be maintained or reproduced. What for, and why? The mere fact of a culture is not sufficient reason for its maintenance or reproduction. Besides the reproduction *of* cultures, there is also the reproduction *through* cultures of models, procedures, modes of thought, and ways of being, from generation to generation.

The critical project we are proposing thus offers the potential to develop a comprehensive, critical vocabulary and grammar for addressing the pressing and emerging socio-cultural (including biological) concerns of our times. The lexicon of cloning culture includes the conceptual likes of replication and familiarity, networking and regularity, simulation and regulation, typification and stereotyping, copying and facsimiles (Schwartz), emulation and adaptation (Tilly).

Transforming interdisciplinarities: more relevant than ever

To summarize, we return to the opening paragraph of this essay. What do those who volunteer as guinea pigs for cloning want? They talk about control, when outcomes are otherwise uncertain or perceived as unsafe. They seek familiarity, they express self-love, desire for the same-kind. They express difficulty in coping with loss, they want their deceased loved ones back. If biological cloning is a microcosm, cloning culture is a macrocosm, likewise locked (in) between the logics and contradictions of individuality and belonging, choice and conformity, consensus and tolerance, security and limitless growth, social inequality and safety, punishing bodies in pursuit of eternal lives, manipulating nature while fabricating natural ties in making more of the same. Ironically, the extreme implications of an unqualified culture of cloning reproduce the very prospects of stasis and death to which it considers itself threatened by the proliferation and incorporation of the different.

What, do we want then with the concept of cloning cultures? Preliminary collection of ideas about cloning cultures suggests that we are dealing with a systemic and complex set of social issues. Once we employ the critical notion that societies have reproduced themselves through taking for granted the preference for sameness, examples can be found everywhere, as are counter-moves, for example, the insistence on being, or on the right to be, different and preferences for counter-standard expressions and articulations. The concept of cloning cultures problematizes the preference for likeness, including the pursuit of unique perfection both across and within difference, which then is invoked as a model for cloning. This is a genuinely novel way of approaching the question of the systemic reproduction of systems of inequality and injustice. We are suggesting that the concept of cloning cultures exhibits considerable potential for pulling together a range of compelling issues in thinking about contemporary social problems.

By way of conclusion, a word on the imperative of a research agenda that reflects in its nature as well as in its institutional arrangements the limits of emulating preference for trodden patterns and hierarchies of sameness. The fact that the culture of cloning broadly construed embeds both social and biological dynamics, indeed, in mutually constitutive fashion, automatically conjures the possibility of productive exchanges between genetic engineers, genome scientists, and critical geographers working on agribusiness, as well as anthropologists, sociologists, and humanists concerned with the socio-cultural assumptions, implications, and representations of these bodies of work. Interdisciplinarity and joint productions demand viable institutional arrangements to promote these inter- and transdisciplinary discussions and research programs and the products they are most likely to generate. We suggest therefore that disciplinarity and disciplinarization are both product and replicative of cloning culture, and that the kind of critical analysis of the range of phenomena falling under its conceptual and logical domains demands a vigorous and vibrant, but also self-critical commitment to interdisciplinary practices.

Notes

1. This article is an abbreviated and revised version of an earlier publication. Essed, Philomena and Goldberg, David. "Cloning Cultures: The Social Injustices of Sameness." *Ethnic and Racial Studies* 25, No. 6 (2002): 1066–1082.

2. See special report on Race in the Boardroom, 18 Feb. 2002.

Works Consulted

Appiah, Kwame A. "Racisms." *Anatomy of Racism*. Ed. David T. Goldberg. Minneapolis: U of Minneapolis P, 1990.

Bell, David, and Gill Valentine. *Consuming Geographies: We Are What We Eat*. London: Routledge, 1997.

Essed, Philomena. *Diversity: Gender, Color and Culture*. Amherst: U of Massachusetts P, 1996.

———. "Cloning Cultural Homogeneity While Talking Diversity: Old Wine in New Bottles in Dutch Work Organizations?" *Transforming Anthropology* 11.1 (2002): in press.

Essed, Philomena, and David Theo Goldberg, eds. *Race Critical Theories. Text and Context*. Oxford: Blackwell, 2002.

Gabriel, John. *Racism, Culture, Markets*. London: Routledge, 1994.

Gilman, Sander. *Making the Body Beautiful*. Princeton: Princeton UP, 1999.

Goldberg, David Theo. *Racist Culture*. Oxford: Blackwell, 1993.

———. *The Racial State*. Oxford: Blackwell, 2002.

Klein, Naomi. *No Logo*. New York: Picador, 1999.

Reinders, H. *The Gift of Friendship: Profound Disability, Theological Anthropology, and Ethics*. Grand Rapids, MI: Eerdmans, 2008.

Roediger, David. "Whiteness and Ethnicity in the History of 'White Ethnics' in the United States." *Race Critical Theories*. Eds. Philomena Essed and David Theo Goldberg. Oxford, UK: Blackwell, 2001.

Scheff, Thomas. "Emotions and Identity: A Theory of Ethnic Nationalism." *Social Theory and the Politics of Identity*. Ed. Craig Calhoun. Oxford, UK: Blackwell, 1994.

Schwartz, Hillel. *The Culture of Copy. Striking Likeness, Unreasonable Facsimiles*. New York: Zone, 1996.

Seidler, Victor J. *Not Man Enough: Embodying Masculinities*. London: Sage, 1997.

Shell, Marc. *Children of the Earth: Literature, Politics, and Nationhood*. New York: Oxford UP, 1993.

Talbot, Margaret. "A Desire to Duplicate." *New York Times Magazine* 4 Feb. 2001.

Tilly, Charles. *Durable Inequality*. Berkeley: U of California P, 1998.

Wiley, Norman. "The Politics of Identity in American History." *Social Theory and the Politics of Identity*. Ed. Craig Calhoun. Oxford, UK: Blackwell, 1994.

Zwick, Rebecca. *Fair Game? The Use of Standardized Admissions Tests in Higher Education*. New York: RoutledgeFalmer, 2002.

Thamyris/Intersecting No. 25 (2012) 111–126

The Pursuit of Perfection

Ross D. Parke,
Christine Ward Gailey,
Scott Coltrane, and
M. Robin DiMatteo

In this century, the routes to parenthood promise to be increasingly diverse. New reproductive technologies (NRT) are expanding ways in which individuals become parents. Recent changes in technology assisted childbearing include *in vitro* fertilization (IVF) and intracytoplasmic sperm injection (ICSI), techniques involving genetic donation such as sperm or egg donations and the utilization of surrogate mothers. Djerassi observed that, just as "technology's gift to women (and men) during the latter half of the 20th century was contraception, the first 50 years of the new millennium may well be considered the decade of conception" (53).

The spread of reproductive technologies throughout the world (Golombok "Parenting"; Golombok "New") has sparked debates among philosophers, scientists, physicians and policy makers about regulation of the use of these new techniques, the safety of these procedures, the ethical and moral implications of their use and inequalities associated with access to these new routes to parenthood as a function of social class, sexual orientation and ethnicity. The current dialogue about these issues is less about the historically troubling doctrine of eugenics and more about the ways in which the democratization of access to these medical advances can be achieved. As a group of scholars involved in research on family processes and ideologies of health and medicine, we wish to raise what we consider to be deep ethical issues surrounding the search for perfectibility through new reproductive technologies. As we will argue, the newly discovered ability to manipulate, select and, in the end, design offspring with desired traits and characteristics taps into a deeply-seated cultural value, namely our preoccupation with the pursuit of perfection in many spheres of life. We explore the generalization of this pursuit from the removal of facial wrinkles and the reduction of fatty thighs to the application of this notion of perfection to the design of infants and, by extension, to our definition of the "perfect" family. Underlying our examination of these issues is the question: Is the pursuit of perfectibility the route to a better, more just society?

The Cultural Pervasiveness of the Pursuit of Perfection: From Botox and Steroids to Designer Babies

First, let us explore the pervasiveness of this pursuit of perfection. This is not an isolated issue that is restricted to NRT, but part of a cultural endorsement of a value of individual betterment. While, in the modern era, the pursuit of this goal has been intimately linked with progress in science and medicine, historically, values of initiative, industry and ingenuity were the major routes—at least in the United States—to the achievement of upward mobility—a commonly accepted avenue of enhanced perfection or well-being. However, as Michael Sandel notes in his provocative *Atlantic Monthly* article "The case against perfection,"

> The predicament is that our newfound genetic knowledge may also enable us to manipulate our own nature—to enhance our muscles, memories and moods; to choose sex, height, and other genetic traits of our children to make ourselves "better than well." (52)

Like the inhabitants of Garrison Keilor's imaginary Lake Wobegon, where "all the women are strong, all the men are good looking and all the children are above average," we are increasingly obsessed with striving for perfection.

Our daily newspapers are rife with stories of performance enhancing drugs, not just for human athletes such as baseball players and Tour de France cyclists but even equine Kentucky Derby contenders. And efforts to achieve a culturally defined ideal of personal beauty through the use of surgery, drugs or creams has resulted in a billion dollar cosmetic enhancement industry. Although the advances in designer baby medical technology receive fewer headlines, the ethical and moral dilemmas that these possibilities raise are much more serious than baseball, cycling, horse racing or face lifts.

A new set of prenatal assessment techniques have developed that include not only amniocentesis and ultrasound but, more recently, preimplanation genetic diagnosis (PGD) in which one cell of a recently formed eight-cell embryo is removed and genetically evaluated (Spar). Initially, these prenatal tools were used to detect genetic abnormalities such as Down Syndrome or Spina Bifida that, in turn, would provide parents the opportunity to terminate the pregnancy rather than risk the birth of a handicapped infant. However, these techniques are used not only to detect

genetic abnormalities, but also to detect a variety of other fetal characteristics including the sex of the developing fetus. This may, in turn, open up the re-introduction of
a form of infanticide through selective aborting of fetuses that are of the undesired
sex. In fact, in some countries such as China and India, where boys are more highly
valued than girls, selection on the basis of gender is already common. In China, for
example, in 2000 there were 117 boys born for every 100 girls (Dugger; Hudson and
den Boer).

Even in the United States, the ability to screen for gender early in the pregnancy
through PGD increased the demand for this "fertility" service, although most of the
consumers were not infertile, just curious and motivated to choose their infant's
gender (Spar). The present reality is not far removed from the imagined future
depicted in the movie Gattaca, where parents routinely screened embryos for sex,
height, immunity to disease and even I.Q. (Sandel 53). Advertisers are willing to pay
$50,000 for an egg with the desired characteristics. Some Ivy League newspapers
ran ads seeking "an egg from a woman who was at least five feet ten inches tall and
athletic, had no major family medical problems, and had a combined SAT score of
1400 and above" (Sandel 59; Weaver et al.). And one can cruise the internet, not
only for cheap books, but also for a vast array of eggs offered by fashion models or
for sperm for sale by struggling medical interns eager to sell their reproductive wares
for $10,000 and up! The commercial market in eggs and sperm is no longer
restricted to East Coast newspapers or exotic web sites. On a recent plane trip, we
encountered this advertisement in American Way, an in-flight magazine. The ad from
the Genetics and IVF Institute reads: "We offer approximately 100 fully screened
donors immediately available for matching and utilization by our patients. These
donors include many Doctoral Donors in advanced degree programs and numerous
other egg donors with special accomplishments, talents or ethnicity" (Genetics and IVF).
As one newspaper writer recently observed, "Egg donor technology has gone as
mainstream as selling cereal" (Rubin). Clearly, the search for perfection in terms of
"designer infants" is becoming pervasive if not commonplace.

What moral and ethical issues does this pursuit of perfection raise? And is there
a concern that it is not only designer babies but also designer families that are
implicitly being encouraged by the differential access to these new reproduction
technologies? Sandel examined the problems with genetic engineering for humans
and argued that the key problem is one of hubris, the arrogance of thinking one can
control creation, as well as the intolerance of diversity that the pursuit of what is
assumed to be perfection implies. For us, the ethical issues include the underlying
ideologies of race, class, gender, and sexuality that shape the assumptions made in
the development and organization of services and in the definition and promotion of
desire.

Commercial Perfection

The market for reproductive perfectibility is the service provider's dream. The customers have a deeply felt desire, even desperation for the product—a baby—and they are willing to pay for bodily intervention over long periods of time to achieve their desires. As Debora Spar, author of *The Baby Business* points out,

> Many infertile couples become consumed with the desire to conceive, willing to do whatever it takes to create a child of their own. For most of these would-be parents, the economic value of their desire, the price of a child, is literally inestimable. At a personal level, of course, such unmet demand is tragic: millions of people are fervently seeking to purchase what everyone around them, it seems, gets for free. At a commercial level, however, it is exceedingly attractive. For who wouldn't want to sell in a market of millions, each of whom is desperate to buy? In 2004 more than one million Americans underwent some from of fertility treatment, participating in a nearly $3 billion industry. (2–3)

Moreover, the process of obtaining the product includes a range of paid services that may or not be dependent on decision-making by health insurance providers. As Charis Cussins points out, providers deploy a range of definitions of success for the range of procedures available: fertilization or implantation or, more rarely, a solitary fetus, or even more rarely, pregnancy to term of a healthy infant and live mother. The marketing rests on avoidance of controversy and thus overwhelming emphasis on married couples, the depth of the customers' wallets, and the relationship between the limits of the customers' desire/patience/physical tolerance and the ramifying number of alternative procedures.

Put bluntly, the perfection achieved is in marketing: perhaps only plastic surgery as an industry can boast such a match between societally promoted ideology and product lines. However, the marketing itself is more successful than the achievement of successful pregnancy and birth. For example, in 2003, only 35 percent of all IVF cycles performed in the United States resulted in a live birth (Wright, et al.) and the rate drops dramatically as women get older, from 43 percent for women under 35 to about 14 percent for women who are 41 or older (Wright, et al.). Moreover, these procedures are by no means risk free. In addition to hormonal side effects and the risks associated with surgery for egg retrieval, multiple pregnancy involving twins, triplets or even more offspring increases the risk of prematurity as well as the possibility of birth defects and/or developmental delays (Jackson, et al.; Kurinczuk). In spite of the limited success rates and associated risks, marketing has been more successful in promoting the positive possible outcomes than in publicizing the downside of these new advances. Moreover, where marketing rules development, reduction of diversity is inevitable. And this reduction is clearly evident in the differential access to these technologies by different groups in our society.

Restrictions to Access: Another Case of Class, Race and Age Discrimination

Access to the new reproductive technologies is restricted by class, ethnicity and education. The total cost incurred for successful delivery after successful IVF can be U.S.$55,000 for the first cycle to $73,000 by the sixth cycle. Obstetrical and peri-natal costs are considerably higher for twins and triplets than for singletons.[1] Many insurers and public health systems do not cover or only partially cover these proce-dures, making IVF and related therapies available only to those with the ability to pay. Not only are costs prohibitive for most working class couples in the United States; but also insurance coverage varies by state with little federal coverage or oversight. For example, IVF is fully covered in some states (Massachusetts), partially covered in other states (Florida) and up to the free market in other states (California, North Dakota) (Spar 212). By contrast, some countries such as Israel, Great Britain, and Denmark make NRTs available—regardless of income while others (Egypt, South Africa) provide no insurance coverage for IVF interventions (Spar). Government and insurance related support depends largely on whether or not infertility is treated as a medical problem. If it is viewed as a medical issue, it will be covered like any other medical problem such as a heart bypass or hip replacement. "If infertility is seen as fate, a decision, or bad luck, then states stay out of the market and prices flutter upward" (Spar 213). For example, in the United States, the costs of *in vitro* fertilization are high whether the procedure involves using a woman's own eggs ($12,500–$25,000) or donor eggs ($20,000–$35,000). Insurance will often cover only part of the cost of the procedures and sometimes it will not cover these costs at all.[2] Clearly, these costs are likely to limit access to these techniques with the result that homogeneity in class and race is virtually guaranteed. This is merely another reflection of the differential access to health and medical support in the United States as a function of social class and ethnicity. In short, NRT represented a middle class and generally white enterprise and, by implication, is limiting the repro-ductive rights of less wealthy and non-white individuals. The average user of IVF serv-ices in the United States is white, college educated with an average income well above national medians. As Paulson and Sachs argue, this situation is a reflection of our capitalist system.

> In a system that uses money as an evaluation of what things are worth it is hard not to wonder whether we are evolving into a culture that pays hard cash for every-thing good, and pities the poor individual who can't participate because she doesn't have the means. Whether the prize is a deluxe Caribbean Cruise, a heart transplant, a Porsche or a late-life baby, you have to put your money where your mouth is. And this clearly puts a restriction on such luxuries. If you don't come from wealth, achieve wealth or have wealth thrust upon you, you're out of the game. (252)

There is another form of discrimination that has received less attention than the economic barriers associated with race and class, namely the exploitation of the young (and often poor) in the service of providing for older (and often rich) recipients. Paulson and Sachs framed it as "society's bargain: young, poor women help older rich women" (251). Users of NRT are often older women and/or couples who have turned to these procedures after encountering infertility problems. On the other hand, the providers—egg donors, sperm donors, or surrogate mothers—are often younger. In effect, we have another division based on age between the recipients and providers. It is not unwarranted to recall Margaret Atwood's *The Handmaid's Tale* in which one class of women service another—higher—class of women by providing eggs as well as a uterus. Although we have not institutionalized the form of reproductive slavery that Atwood imagined, the unintended parallels are more than a little unnerving and raise serious questions about income-based access to health services in general and to reproductive assistance in particular.

Beyond Perfect Babies: The Quest for Perfect Families
With the advent of the new reproductive technologies, there is a renewed interest in how we define the term "family." Every society and historical era invents and legitimates a particular version of the family in terms of the identity of members, their rights and responsibilities toward each other and their children (Coltrane and Collins). This issue has, of course, emerged in recent years as a result of the new family forms that have arisen in cases of divorced and stepparent families, same sex parent families and adoption. The variations and deviations from our traditional ideas of a family as two heterosexual parents who conceive and raise their natural biological children reminds us that the concept of the family is, in fact, a "cultural invention" and an "ideological code" (Smith). Just as the concept of perfection was useful in our discussion of new trends in the technological design of "perfect" babies, it can be fruitfully introduced here as well. Many of the problems faced by families "conceived" by NRT flow from their deviation from a culturally scripted portrait of a "perfect family" as a two-parent nuclear family unit, that naturally produces a child.[3]

In fact, family formation through the use of some form of new reproductive technology violates this culturally-defined "perfect family" format in a variety of ways. First, one partner or both may be infertile, which in itself is stigmatized and a violation of the expectation that reproductive capability is "normal." Second, in some cases a single, i.e., unmarried man or woman may be the contracting party, a further deviation from the cultural script that a married couple household is the proper social context for reproduction and child rearing. Third, same sex couples—either lesbian or gay—may be the ones who use alternative routes to parenthood. Again, this violates cultural norms concerning the appropriate composition of the parenting unit. This bias has, in fact, little empirical support since research clearly documents that same sex couples are not only adequate parents, but their children are also well adjusted in terms of mental health (Golombok *Parenting: What*; Patterson). Fourth, with assisted reproduction, there are a number of contributors who co-operatively participate to complete the reproductive cycle and produce an offspring (Parke "Parenting"). In the most extreme case, an infertile couple could use a donor egg, donor sperm, and a surrogate to carry "their" fetus. In this hypothetical scenario, there are five individuals who are potential members of the family—the two donors, the surrogate and the contracting couple. This set of possible parents clearly violates our notion of the "perfect family" form.

We argue that many of the current debates about the rights and responsibilities of each of the individual contributors to the infant production scenario flow from disagreements about the nature of the concept of family in general and of their acceptance or rejection of the culturally endorsed definition of a "perfect family." On one side of this debate, a restrictive definition of family and resulting family boundaries suggest that the contracting couple and their technologically reproduced child should be viewed as the family unit; all other players could simply be viewed as paid contributors of either biological material—in the case of egg and sperm donors—or as providers of biological/physical services—in the case of surrogates. None of these players would have any claims in terms of physical access to the child that was produced or any financial, emotional or social obligations to the child. By endorsing this restrictive definition of "family," the NRT family can, in part, achieve the "perfect family" form by the social presentation of a family arrangement (mother, father and child) to the outside world that is consistent with the perfect family ideal. By excluding the other players, the social untidiness and possible embarrassment associated with these other individuals who have no culturally scripted roles in this NTR family can be avoided and the perfect family myth can be maintained. This public presentation of a restricted family form, however, comes at a price paid by the other players whose rights to social contact with either the contracting parents or the child that they jointly produced are severely restricted or even eliminated. On the other end of the debate continuum is the definition of NRT produced families as "expanded family forms" with porous boundaries that not only permit, but also encourage the development of social relationships among and between various contributors, but especially between the child and the non-child rearing contributors, e.g., egg and sperm donors, and surrogates. This set of family arrangements, of course, violates the "perfect family" form but, as we will argue, variations on this expanded family form need to be carefully considered and may, in fact, be a new "ideal" family form that may benefit not only the non-custodial players, but also may have potentially positive outcomes for the contracting couple and the child as well.

As we show below, the issues are not clear-cut in terms of either rights or responsibilities of various contributors to these new technologically assisted births or the rights and responsibilities of the contracting parents and children. In fact, it is probably more profitable to view possible variation in the amount and type of relationships between the contracting family and non-family members as a continuum rather than a simple dichotomy between family and non-family member categories.

The Rights of Parents, Children and Biological Contributors and the Protection of the "Perfect Family" Form

The right of parents (especially fathers) to define their family form and their family boundaries is long-standing and firmly established in our legal heritage. However, as new family forms have evolved, new legal guidelines have been developed to deal with new complications in cases, for example, of divorce and adoption (Fine and Harvey; Gailey). Similarly, legal guidelines are gradually emerging to deal with the rights, responsibilities and obligations of the various contributors to NRT assisted births (Rothman; Schwartz; Verny).

Although child rights have become increasingly recognized, parental rights generally supersede child-based considerations. This argument is rooted in a long-standing historical assumption that children are viewed as property and only as mature adults do they possess rights that equal parental prerogatives. As Murray argues:

> the idea that a child is the property of its biological parents is out of favor, but not dead, either in our laws or our customs . . . even though the concept of child as property is based on faulty evidence and truncated ethics. (59)

A more contemporary version of this perspective argues that parents—in their greater wisdom—will take children's best interests into account. Murray refers to this as the "parent as steward" model and argues that it is clearly more attractive than the property ownership model of parent-child relationships. Based on this view, it is argued that parents have a right to manage the amount of information and the timing of disclosure of data to children about their origins (egg, sperm donor, surrogate). The degree of disclosure varies across types of families. Withholding of information is highest in the case of sperm donor insemination families (Golombok "Parenting and Contemporary") which, in part, is due to the stigma associated with donor insemination, acknowledgement of the father's fertility problems, uncertainty about the best time and method of telling the child, and lack of information to give about the genetic father (Golombok "Parenting and Contemporary" 352). By contrast, lesbian donor insemination families and single mothers are more likely to disclose than heterosexual families (Golombok "Parenting and Contemporary"). Although parental decisions to limit children's access to knowledge about their origins is justified on a number of grounds, according to the theme of our essay, the underlying concept that unites the various arguments for withholding information about their origins and the cooperative nature of their production is the parental desire to preserve the public presentation of their "perfect family" ideal, both for themselves and their child. On the parent side, public disclosure or awareness may undermine the marital relationship by causing embarrassment or shame due to public disclosure of their single or joint infertility. In turn, this marital strife could have negative effects on the child (Cummings and Davies; Parke, Kim, et al.). Second, the possibility of social contact between the "social" (contracting) parents and the donor/surrogate agents could present further opportunities for public disclosure of their route to parenthood and further violate the restrictive and culturally defined "perfect" family form. Moreover, the potential disruption of family routines by the need to include or accommodate other "expanded" family members is a further argument for endorsing the restricted definition of family boundaries. Evidence from intracultural inquiries in the United States of African-American and Latino families suggest that these concerns about the involvement of extra-familial social players in the lives of nuclear family members are misplaced and unjustified. For example, many African-American and Latino families develop extensive networks of kin and fictive kin who play a role in family life and in the socialization of children (Baca-Zinn and Wells; Parke and Buriel 3: Taylor). Similarly, an abundance of cross-cultural evidence suggests that shared responsibility for child rearing with members of the community is the rule rather than the exception (Harkness and Super). And the social-emotional and economic support provided by these non-family social networks is beneficial to both adults and children (Coleman; Cochran and Niego; Stack). In short, the imagined violation of the ideal of a "perfect" family often prevents families from embracing more fluid social boundaries that may, in fact, be valuable.

On the child side, parents justify their lack of disclosure to children about their origins on the grounds of avoiding misunderstanding and confusion due to children's inability to comprehend issues surrounding reproduction and especially the biological and social nuances of the new reproductive technologies. Perhaps more central to our argument is that, once a child understands the fact that multiple players were involved in their production, the child's conception of the "perfect family" form is undermined. Therefore, in order to preserve the myth of the "perfect family" for their child, parents fail to disclose this information to their child. Parental secrecy may be motivated by a desire to protect the child from the stigmatization associated with living in a non-conforming family form. A further concern is that this knowledge on the part of the child may weaken children's ties to their parents by the realization that their social or functional parents are not their biological parents. By undermining the quality of the parent-child relationship, the child's development may be undermined. Closely related is the concern that the introduction of others (donors, surrogate) within the social boundaries of the family may create ambiguity and confusion for the child and/or may further undermine the closeness of the bonds between the "social parents" and the child. Again, the extant evidence suggests that these fears are largely unfounded. Children are, in fact, capable from early in life of forming multiple social ties, not only with parents but also with non-family members as well (Thompson 3). For example, recent work on the effects of child care suggests that children are not only capable of forming close ties to non-family caregivers, but also this does not undermine the quality of their relationships with their primary caregivers (Clarke-Stewart and Allhusen; Rankin). Although we have focused on parental rights and parental management of information about the child's reproductive origins, it is imperative that the child's rights be considered as well. Although this issue is complicated by the relative immaturity of the child, there is evidence that children begin to understand the causal nature of the reproductive process by ages seven or eight and gradually develop a relatively accurate comprehension of the process by ages 11 or 12 (Bernstein and Cowan). Moreover, there are books available for young children (seven years and up) such as Schaffer's *How babies and families are made (there is more than one way)* that explain the new reproductive technologies in a simple, but accessible way to children. Therefore, while parents need to be sensitive to the age-related limitations of their children, there are means of communicating the central "facts" about their child's origins that are age appropriate.

Why is this important? The first reason concerns the value of knowledge of the biological contributors for the child's future health decisions. As we increase our knowledge about the genetic bases of disease, children who are armed with an awareness of their genetic ties will clearly be advantaged. Some have argued (Bauman) that a child has a right to information about the donor, especially if evidence of a genetic illness is present. A second concern is the right of children to know their genetic history as part of their identity formation process. Although less concrete than the health issues, this identity formation issue may be just important or more so for the developing child—in this case for their mental rather than their physical health. Finally, based on related work on open vs. closed adoptions, it is clear that disclosure rather than secrecy is better for children's emotional adjustment (Grotevant and McRoy). In spite of the fact that nondisclosure is the rule in NRT families, in one study of parents who did inform their children, the majority (57%) reported good feelings about the disclosure (Rumball and Adair). As NRT procedures become more widely used and accepted, it is likely that the curtain of secrecy will gradually fall, just as it has in the case of adoptive families.

Together these lines of evidence are consistent with the view that the development of multiple relationships with non-family members is not harmful for children, but normative in many cultures and potentially beneficial for the developing child. Entertainment of a new or, at least, a more expanded definition of the "perfect family" would be welcome and potentially helpful for both the social parents and their NRT assisted offspring as well as for the other partners in this cooperative reproductive process.

In light of this evidence, we propose that an alternative model of parent-child relationships is needed. In contrast to the property or steward models (Murray), a more humane model that is more consistent with our understanding of children's capacity to play an active role in their own socialization is the mutual influence/marital rights model (Murray; Maccoby). This model recognizes the rights of all individuals within the family, including women and children and views decisions about definitions of family boundaries and the consequences of these decisions to be mutually generated by both parents and child rather than unilaterally by the parents. The central advance implied by this model is the acceptance of children's rights to be both fully knowledgeable about their own biological as well as social origins and to be a partner in constructing the definition of their family and articulating the boundaries that grant or deny membership to various reproductive players.

Conclusions and Challenges

In this essay, we have argued that the quest for perfection raises serious moral and ethical issues for our utilization and regulation of the new reproductive technologies. Not only does this quest result in the perpetuation of equalities across class, racial and ethnic lines, but also it opens the possibility of misuse of these strategies for purposes beyond the fulfillment of the desire to reproduce and form a family. Of major concern is the frivolous use of these strategies for gender selection and, more ominously, selection of infant attributes—both physical and intellectual. This search for the perfect baby is part of a wider cultural preoccupation with both personal perfection as well as hyper management of children's lives to ensure later occupational, educational and social success (Elkind). There has been some retreat from this agenda as exemplified by recent calls for a less pressured childhood (Hirsh-Pasek and Golinkoff). The other implication of NRT is the re-visitation of our definition of family when multiple players may be involved in the collaborative reproductive process. Not only does this new collaborative route to parenthood remind us that the family is a cultural invention, but also new challenges arise in determining the rights and responsibilities of the cooperating reproductive participants. We urge entertainment of the advantages that a more extended definition of family boundaries holds both for adults and the children who are the products of these NRT procedures. Successful management of these new technologies, including their wider availability regardless of class, race, age or sexual orientation, could yield new family forms that could be models for more meaningful rearing of children. These advances will continue. Our challenge is to recognize and humanely manage the ethical and moral challenges that these new frontiers of reproductive science present and, at the same time, to seize the opportunities that these advances offer for redefining the nature of families.

Acknowledgements

Work on this chapter was supported by a Ford Foundation grant "Cloning Cultures: The Social Injustices of Sameness" to Emory Elliott and Piya Chatterjee, co-directors of the project at the Center for Ideas and Society, University of California, Riverside. The authors were scholars in residence as the Family and Kinship Systems working cluster during the spring quarter 2004 at the Center for Ideas and Society. The material presented in this chapter was jointly developed by this group during this period. We extend special thanks to graduate students Katrina Paxton (History, University of California, Riverside) and Christopher Schmitt (Sociology, University of California, Riverside) for their contributions to our weekly dialogue during our residency. We thank the members of the staff of the Center for their support and Piya Chatterjee, University of California, Riverside, Philomena Essed, Antioch University, U.S.A. and the Equal Treatment Commission, The Netherlands, for their intellectual guidance during our stay at the Center.

Notes

1. See Center for Disease Control and Prevention U.S. (2000).

2. See American Society for Reproductive Medicine.

3. For a related discussion of adoption as subverting American kinship ideology, see Gailey.

Works Cited

Baca-Zinn, M., and B. Wells. "Diversity Within Latino Families: New Lessons for Family Social Science." *Handbook of Family Diversity.* Eds. D. H. Demo, K. R. Allen, and M. A. Fine. New York: Oxford UP, 2000. 252–273.

Bauman, J. H. "Discovering Donors: Legal Rights to Access Information About Anonymous Sperm Donors Given to Children of Artificial Insemination. Johnson v. Superior Court of Los Angeles County." *Golden Gate University Law Review* 31 (2001): 193–217.

Bernstein, A., and P. A. Cowan. "Children's Concepts of How People Get Babies." *Child Development* 46 (1975): 77–91.

Clarke-Stewart, K. A., and V. Allhusen. *What We Know About Child Care.* Cambridge, MA: Harvard UP, 2005.

Cochran, M., and S. Niego. "Parenting and Social Networks." *Handbook of Parenting.* Ed. M. Bornstein. 2nd ed. Mahwah, NJ: Erlbaum, 2002. 123–147.

Coleman, J. S. "Social Capital in the Creation of Human Capital." *American Journal of Sociology* 94 (1988): 95–120.

Coltrane, S., and R. Collins. *Sociology of Marriage and the Family: Gender, Love and Property.* 5th ed. Belmont, CA: Wadsworth/ITP, 2001.

Cummings, M., and P. Davies. *Children and Marital Conflict.* New York: Guilford, 1994.

Cussins, C. "Producing Reproduction: Techniques of Normalization and Naturalization in Infertility Clinics." *Reproducing Reproduction.* Eds. S. Franklin and H. Ragone. Philadelphia: U of Pennsylvania P, 1998.

Djerassi, C. "Sex in an Age of Mechanical Reproduction." *Science* 285 (1999): 53.

Dugger, C. W. "Modern Asia's Anomaly: The Girls Who Don't Get Born." *New York Times* 6 May 2001.

Elkind, D. *The Hurried Child.* Cambridge, MA: Perseus, 2001.

Fine, M. A. and J. H. Harvey, eds. *Handbook of Divorce and Relationship Dissolution.* Mahwah, NJ: Erlbaum, 2006.

Gailey, C. W. "Adoptive Families in the United States." *Families and Society.* Ed. S. Coltrane. Belmont, CA: Thompson/Wadsworth, 2004. 277–289.

Genetics and IVF. Advertisement. *American Way Magazine.* 1 May 2006: 92.

Golombok, S. "New Family Forms." *Families Count: Effects on Child and Adolescent Development.* Eds. A. Clarke-Stewart and J. Dunn. New York: Cambridge UP, 2006. 273–298.

———. "Parenting and Contemporary Reproductive Technologies." *Handbook of Parenting.* Ed. M. Bornstein. 2nd ed. Mahwah, NJ: Erlbaum, 2002. 339–361.

———. *Parenting: What Really Counts.* London: Routledge, 2000. "Gay Fathers," *The Role of the Father in Child Development.* 4th ed. Ed. M. E. Lamb. New York: Wiley, 2004. 397–416.

Grotevant, H. D., and R. G. McRoy. *Openness in Adoption: Connecting Families of Birth and Adoption.* Thousand Oaks, CA: Sage, 1998.

Harkness, S., and C. Super. "Shared Child Care in East Africa: Sociocultural Origins and Developmental Consequents." *Child Care in Context: Cross-cultural Perspectives.* Eds. M. E. Lamb, K. J. Sternberg, C. P. Hwang, and A. G. Broberg. Hillsdale, NJ: Erlbaum, 1992. 441–459.

Hirsh-Pasek, K., and R. Golinkoff. *Einstein Never Used Flash Cards.* New York: Rodale, 2004.

Hudson, V. M., and A. M. den Boer. *Bare Branches: Security Implications of Asia's Surplus Male Population.* Cambridge, MA: MIT P, 2004.

Jackson, R. A., K. A. Gibson, Y. W. Wu, and M. S. Croughan. "Perinatal Outcomes in Singletons Following In vitro Fertilization: A Meta-Analysis." *Obstetrics & Gynecology* 103 (2004): 551–563.

Kurinczuk, J. J. "Safety Issues in Assisted Reproductive Technology." *Human Reproduction* 18 (2003): 925–931.

Maccoby, E. E. "The Role of Parents in the Socialization of Children: An Historical Overview." *Developmental Psychology* 25 (1992): 1006–1010.

Murray, T. H. *The Worth of a Child.* Berkeley: U of California P, 1996.

Parke, R D. "Parenting in the New Millennium: Prospects, Promises and Pitfalls." *Retrospect and Prospect in the Psychological Study of Families.* Eds. J. P McHale and W. S. Grolnick. Mahwah, NJ: Erlbaum, 2002: 65–93.

Parke, R. D., and R. Buriel. "Socialization in the Family: Ethnic and Ecological Perspectives." *Handbook of Child Psychology.* Series eds. W. Damon and R. M. Lerner. Vol. ed. N. Eisenberg. 6th ed. Vol. 3. New York: Wiley, 2006. 429–504.

Parke, R. D., M. Kim, M. Flyr, D. J. McDowell, D. S. Simpkins, C. M. Killian, and M. Wild. "Managing Marital Conflict: Links with Children's Peer Relationships." *Child Development and Interparental Conflict.* Eds. J. Grych and F. Fincham. New York: Cambridge UP, 2001: 291–314.

Patterson, C. "Gay Fathers." *The Role of the Father in Child Development.* Ed. M. E. Lamb. 4th ed. New York: Wiley, 2004. 397–416.

Paulson, R. J., and J. Sachs. *Rewinding Your Biological Clock: Motherhood Late in Life.* San Francisco: Freeman, 1999.

Rankin, J. L. *Parenting Experts: Their Advice, Their Research & Getting It Right.* New York: Praeger, 2005.

Rothman, B. Katz. *The Book of Life: A Personal and Ethical Guide to Race, Normality and the Implications of the Human Genome Project.* Boston: Beacon, 2002.

Rubin, B. M. "The Incredible, Sellable Egg: What Was Once a Personal Journey has Become a Booming Business for Donors and Recruiters." *Chicago Tribune* 4 March 2007.

Rumball, A., and V. Adair. "Telling the Story: Parents' Scripts for Donor Offspring." *Human Reproduction* 14 (1999): 1392–1399.

Sandel, M. J. "The Case Against Perfection." *Atlantic Monthly* April 2004: 51–62.

Schaffer, P. *How Babies & Families Are Made (There is More Than One Way).* Berkeley, CA: Tabor Sarah, 1988.

Schwartz, L. L. "A Nightmare for King Solomon: The New Reproductive Technologies." *Journal of Family Psychology* 17 (2003): 229–237.

Smith, D. "The Standard North American Family: SNAF as an Ideological Code." *Journal of Family Issues* 14 (1993): 50–65.

Spar, D.L. *The Baby Business.* Cambridge, MA: Harvard Business School P, 2006.

Stack, C. *All Our Kin.* New York: Harper and Row, 1974.

Taylor, R. L. "Diversity Within African-American Families." *Handbook of Family Diversity.* Eds. D. H. Demo, K. R. Allen, and M. A. Fine. New York, Oxford UP, 2000. 232–251.

Thompson, R. A. "The Development of the Person, Social Understanding, Relationships, Conscience, Self." *Handbook of Child Psychology.* Series eds. W. Damon and R. M. Lerner. Vol. ed. N. Eisenberg. 6th ed. Vol. 3. New York: Wiley, 2006. 24–98.

Verny, T. R. "The Stork in the Lab: Biological, Psychological, Ethical, Social and Legal Aspects of Third Party Conceptions." *Pre- and Perinatal Psychology Journal* 9 (1994): 57–84.

Weaver, S. E., A. J. Umana-Taylor, J. D. Hans, and S. E. Malia. "Challenges Family Scholars Face in Studying Family Diversity: A Focus on Latino Families, Stepfamilies, and Reproductive Technology." *Journal of Family Issues* 22 (2001): 922–939.

Wright, V. C., J. Chang, G. Jeng, and M. Macaluso. "Assisted Reproductive Technology Surveillance—United States, 2003." *MMWR Surveillance Summaries* 55 (2006): 1–22.

Cloning the Physician

Philomena Essed[1]

After decades of advising international law firms, major financial service institutions, and other multinational conglomerates on organizational development and diversity issues, I've developed keenly astute antennae for detecting the kind of subtle issues that aren't addressed by typical diversity protocols. The uniformity of these offices and the senior managers in them were disturbing. Each one felt exactly the same as the next: impressionist style artwork on the walls, deep mahogany furniture arranged in identical fashion, and one family photo placed at the upper-right corner of the desk. By the time I was introduced to the last executive I was convinced that this company had a complex, systemic problem, but it was not the problem the firm had called me to address.
— Klein 1

This excerpt from Freada Kapor Klein's ground-breaking study *Giving Notice* succinctly typifies the kind problem addressed in this chapter. It is about preference for *likeness*, in particular in view of maintaining (imagined) homogeneity in high status positions. By preference for likeness, I mean constructed or claimed homogeneity while identifying individuals as like-minded, like-looking, like family, like "us," like clones of the appreciated "types." As Klein comments about the upper echelons of corporate USA: "they perceive talent only if it comes in familiar packaging—that is, looking and acting exactly as they do" (18). "Cloning," in a cultural sense, is a well-established practice for securing privilege. Among top managers, the wish to clone super managers like themselves does not even seem to raise any eyebrows. One anecdotic example can be found in the words of Mr. Henny de Ruiter, president-commissioner of Ahold[2] and the most powerful corporate hot shot in the Netherlands. In an interview for a business magazine, in late September 2003, de Ruiter proclaims his admiration for two other hot shots, much like him heavy with commissioners' posts, saying: "They should be cloned, but regretfully that is not possible" (Dinther 33). Within weeks after this interview, one of the "should be cloned" candidates would become de Ruiter's successor as Ahold president-commissioner. Interesting detail: Journalists quoted sources qualifying the Ruiter as a "yes-man"—"he never says no" (Dinther 30, 32) and his successor Karel Vuursteen as a man who "just does not know how to say no" (Boogaarts 8).

Preference for more of the same type points to *cultural cloning.* This seems an apt concept to refer to gate keeping in top positions where (combinations of) racial, gender, ethnic, age and other systemic discrimination *against* particular groups is also indicative of normative preferences *for* combinations of (perceived) masculinity, whiteness, European-ness, able-bodied-ness and related markers (Essed, "Cloning Cultural Homogeneity"). In this context, cultural cloning is a process of control, of preservation, of (constructed) likeness *in view of maintaining privilege and status.*

Let me give an example by way of introducing the notion of cloning in a cultural sense analytically. In his book *Diploma of Whiteness: Race and Social Policy in Brazil, 1917–1945,* author Jerry Dávila recounts an anecdote about the Minister of Education and Health who served during the late 1930s. He had called upon a group of anthropologists and national intellectuals to advise him about the physiognomy of the body of the "future Brazilian man": "Not the vulgar type, but the best example of the race" (21). His concern about the Brazilian "race" had been aroused by the artist whom he had commissioned to sculpt the statue of "the future Brazilian man." The statue, meant to be placed at the entrance of the Ministry of Education and Health building, did not match the sensibility of this new and modern design. The artist had come up with a representation that "looked racially degenerate rather than virile and Aryan" (21) as the minister had imagined Brazilians would evolve. The minister's dismay was a function of his belief that the modernization of Brazilian society implied that Brazilians would come to look more like clones of the hegemonic model of perfection: white, blond haired, blue eyed. Yet, the "future Brazilian man" could not be seen only in terms of "race." This idealized body represented a racialized perception of progress—Europeanization and "genetically" uplifting (whitening)—as much as it represented a gendered perception of modernization—the triumph of masculinity. At the same time, this perfectly healthy body was to project progress in terms of physical and mental capacity—as ultimate control over the disabling imperfections of nature—and as eternally "young"—progress as the defeat of the disabling signs of aging. Indeed, the epitome of progress was a male body beaming with Aryan masculinity.

Because body images gain meaning in a cultural context, it seems fair to suggest that the desire for Brazilian clones of this perfectly white European male body meant also for Brazilian education. It involves emulating the modernization package the

Aryan male body is perceived to represent, including modes of economic and techno-logical development, racial ideologies, bodily aesthetics, and other ideological values, norms, images, and practices.

I intend to problematize the homogeneities of cultural cloning and the gate-keeping practices it entails. In light of this, professional profiles are interesting because they express norms, values, and images of competence, and the way in which these are anchored in racial, gender, national, ethnic, structures and in local and situational processes.

In order to offer more than a theoretical exercise, I apply the concept of cultural cloning to one specific high status position: the profession of physician. The choice for this profile is foremost pragmatic, assuming that most readers have at least some everyday experience with medical practices or with the health sector in general. Most of us know from our daily lives about the limited time slots available to see a doctor, the objectification of our bodies, the rigid boundaries between different spe-cializations catering to different parts of the body, or the absolute authority physi-cians exert over nurses (Rosenstein, Russell, et al.).

"The physician" in a (post)modern work environment

The medical field is shaped by paradigmatic underpinnings of Western science, including the commercialization of health and bodies, the medicalization and, increasingly, the bio-medicalization of our lives (Clark, Mamo, et al.). In a constantly changing world of health care and in a world where "new products are the lifeblood of the marketplace," the drive to create and to maintain superior competitive advan-tage is perceived as imperative (Spevak 32). Competencies deemed relevant to develop superior medical skills are racially and culturally charged, including among other things intelligence, rationality, emotional detachment, high ambition, high competitive drive, and a workaholic mentality prioritizing work above family. This pack-age of requirements and behaviors is likely to be attributed more generously to those perceived closer to the value systems and cultural contexts from which the elevation of these competencies emerge: (post)modern societies, whiteness, European-ness, masculinity, middle class cultural habitat, Western science habitat. In light of this, a critique of particular modes of cultural cloning (for instance, through everyday racism) must be read against the background of the *total* framework of historical and societal forces supporting the cultural cloning of normative profiles of physicians and of other top positions for that matter. Conversely, it must be seen that the quest for (racial, ethnic, gender) workplace diversity would call for a disruption of the myth of maintain-ing (claimed or projected) similarity. This probably explains why diversity require-ments are easily read as having to deal with "something extra," because they are not the same and not like the familiar business as usual (Essed, "Cloning Cultural Homogeneity").

While physicians (and other high status professionals) are expected to be highly competitive, to prioritize work above family, to objectify patients, to work against the clock, to repress emotion and the ability to place oneself in the shoes of others, these very working codes and conditions are conducive to generating insensitivity, condescension, impatience to listen, irritation, and disregard for the feelings of others. The demands of the physician's work presume that the working environment, colleagues and nurses, cooperate. It is *expected* that they be tolerant of disruptive behavior. In U.S. surveys, it has been found that disruptive behavior by physicians is rampant, while fueling the shortage of nurses. They leave the institution for fear of retaliation, because they believe nothing ever changes, for lack of administrative support, or because of physicians' lack of awareness or unwillingness to change (Pfifferling; Rosenstein, Russel, et al.). Disruptive behavior includes a range of every-day humiliations: physical abuse, condescension, insults, disrespect, yelling, berating patients, and abusive anger—the kind of behavior that fluently channels into modes of everyday racism, sexism, patronizing of economically or educationally disadvantaged people, and a dismissive attitude toward critique. The survey does not make any explicit racial or gender qualifications, but indirectly there are a few indicators. It turns out that, when humiliating behavior is categorized by specialty, general surgery ranks number one, followed by cardiology, cardiovascular surgery, and neurology, areas strongly shaped by Western principles of hard sciences, dominated by masculine values.

How does this relate to cultural cloning? Arguably, profiles are not static, but many physicians are reluctant to change their behavior, even when confronted with critical data, says one research report . . . Instead, "they rationalize why the data either doesn't apply to them or is just wrong" (Marco 30). Defensiveness also points to anxieties, a sense of uneasiness among physicians about the rapidly changing technology and the new demands of the Information Revolution. But many doctors are reluctant to face the emotional toll their work takes on them. They find it hard to talk about anxieties, concerns about inadequacies or mental problems they experience, for fear of losing face among peers (West). There is anger about the (postmodern) ways of managed care, which have changed the relationship with patients and financial arrangements (Bottles). It has been found that one of the most pressing concerns of physicians today is time pressure and that an increasing number are unhappy with their jobs (Williams and Skinner). Other sources agree that, in many medical organizations, the culture of pacesetting and commanding leadership styles have created a crisis of leadership (Goleman, Boyatzis, et al.).

Medical organizations, like other (bureaucratic) organizations in market economies, operate in a competitive market. Management in view of competitive advantage implies, among other things, the homogenizing of practices, rules, procedures, tasks and profiles, and in that sense, cloning as replication in the name of efficiency. Once a particular mode, product or model has been tested and found to work for the defined purposes, it can be patented in order to be multiplied and applied until replaced by an improved version—think of medication, medical instruments, healing techniques and so on, or closer to home, the computers and software we all work with. In the age of globalization, medical institutes and their physicians operate in a field with mega high stakes, in complex conglomerations of corporate interests. Western countries protect their hold on the medical industry, among other things, with enormous financial investments in (bio)technology and pharmaceutics, and with patents preventing the vast majority of the world, mostly people of color, from access to (producing) cheap products and medicine (Scheper-Hughes). Various feminist scholars in the area of science, technology and the environment have called the pursuit of ultimate control over creation in all its forms, the relentless exploitation of earth's resources, quintessential symptoms of the triumph of Western masculine values underlying the process of modernization (Shiva; Kirk).

Western science has been successful in sowing and reaping physicians with the right disposition, the willingness to accept and internalize as "necessary in the name of progress" even the most cruel and dehumanizing demands of cloning culture. Medical science has a long history of harboring racist, sexist, socially elitist, assumptions, for instance involving human, often painful, experimentation in which imperialist, Eurocentric, and patriarchal goals have been inflicted on Others—Jews, the poor, blacks, African Americans, women of color and so on, with no regard for ethics (Mwaria). The power that comes with Western medical authority is precious, highly rewarded financially and in terms of social status, the preservation of which requires that membership in this group remains limited and highly guarded. With a few examples, I illustrate how mundane gender, racial and other taken-for-granted cultural imaginaries and everyday practices define this high status position by privileging those perceived as representing whiteness and masculinity, and by seeking homogeneity. Homogenizing means that a limited number of cultural and physical attributes are selected to serve as primary markers defining who belongs and who does not, who can qualify as a physician and who cannot (really). Thus, otherwise complex human beings are reduced to traits representing the normative image of their profession, thereby suggesting that no other than these normative traits fit best the requirements for the profession. Examples are selected from the Dutch context, but the issue at hand does not necessarily apply only to the Netherlands.

Homogenizing through cultural cloning

It has been found that "men are selected for managerial positions because they are perceived, especially by male selectors, to be more reliable, committed and predictable, free from conflicting loyalties between home and work" (Collison and Hearn). Likewise, the ideal construct of the competent medical specialist is deeply imbued with masculine values. Maya Keizer, a Dutch expert in the area of gender and health care, pictures the medical specialist as follows:

He (sic) is totally available for his job but not necessarily as accessible to patients. He is very conscious of his authority over nurses, junior doctors and trainees. He is rational and detached, and takes pride in heroic individual successes. He sees patients as objects rather than as human beings.

The cultural process of "cloning the physician" is facilitated in at least the following two ways: (a) through the dominance of masculine, European norms and values in medical cultures, and (b) by relating interpretations of medical competence to these norms and values. There is also an embodied dimension to cultural cloning: the white male body speaks to perceivers' sense of whiteness, and (Dutch) masculinity. Therefore, (middle class) white men will be attributed more generously than others traits qualifying them as medically competent. Others (non-whites, non-males) may have to prove more vigorously that they master the qualifying criteria in spite of their different bodies.

The highest *cloning quality* can be found among surgeons—over 96% of which are (white) men. The tenacity of cultural cloning in this profession becomes even clearer when considering that the percentage of white males decreased only 4% over a period of four to five centuries! In the 16th century, all surgeons were white men. Today, even the more "feminine" directions are still male dominated: Of pediatricians, generally perceived as the specialization with the lowest status among physicians, (only) 60% are white men. Gynecologists and family doctors rate over 70% (Keizer).

The medical specialist is a protected profession; salaries are kept high, in private practices three times as high as in university hospitals. Opportunity hoarding operates through the creation of permanent supply shortages: there are caps on the number of medical students allowed to register per year and there are high barriers against allowing into Dutch medical practice refugees who have been physicians in their home countries (Couwenbergh).

In what follows, I briefly highlight three modes of sustaining sameness:

1. Overrepresentation of masculine mentors

Cultural cloning among medical specialists does not begin at the hospital entrance. When physicians, as parents, socialize their sons (or sometimes their daughters) to follow in their footsteps, cultural cloning is pre-structured in the homes. Many male surgeons in the Netherlands are sons of surgeons. This is not the case for the few women surgeons, most if not all of whom had to create their own paths. Cloning is also shaped by the medical sciences. Ninety-eight percent of the full professors in medical faculties are (white) men, thus maintaining a cultural climate conducive to reinforcing existing Western, masculine values and practices.

2. Everyday racism as a mode for (white) students to identify with whiteness (or the dominant culture)

Cultural cloning operates through everyday (gendered) racism: recurring incidents of being ignored, put down, rejected, often events that seem trivial as such but in accumulation gradually undermine self-confidence, trigger constant alertness, while causing stress, depression or high blood pressure. For the purpose of this volume, I pay closer attention to this instrument of cultural cloning. I have selected a few experiences of Rosa N., a black woman, about the period when she was a medical student. More of her story has been published elsewhere (Essed, Understanding).

She recalls a class situation where the professor, a surgeon, freely expresses contempt for immigrants, racist comments meant to elicit laughter. He speaks to whiteness (in this case white Dutch-ness) thus advantaging those who identify as such:

> We were in a surgery class. It was taught by a plastic surgeon (. . .) who told us about an industrial accident in a food processing plant, where a Turk working on a cutting machine had sliced open his hand. He even started the story with: the stupid Turk (. . .). Stupid, his hand is not a can! He said: "(. . .) I didn't really have much confidence, but still, I wanted to save the man's hand, because, you know what it costs the Dutch government if that man loses his hand! (. . .) He gets unemployment benefits. (. . .)." So, the surgeon had to save the man's hand.
>
> He showed us another series of slides about how he'd operated on the hand. It looked really weird (. . .). Eventually the hand started to die anyway. It looked really terrible. (. . .) The surgeon left the hand alone until it was completely black, like a hand of coal. (. . .) The hand was amputated, after all.
>
> And then he showed the next picture. Someone's heel gone, "that's another stupid foreigner in a factory," he says. He talks about there being so many accidents (. . .), but only with foreigners. (. . .) But he (doesn't add) that it's foreigners who do this kind of work and that they are the highest risk group for having an accident (. . .).

While the professor speaks to Dutch whiteness when he ridicules immigrants, students respond in recognition of white bonding. They laugh along. Nobody objects to the racist comments:

> The students thought it was real funny. They don't really give it much thought, because it arouses a kind of hilarity when it's told that way. (. . .) Then everyone laughs about it. But I find such humor out of place, actually.

Whiteness as a mode for bonding is further strengthened when the consensus, tolerance of racism, puts critics of racism on the spot. Moreover, those who refuse to tolerate racism are often pathologized for being oversensitive. Rosa N. is the only one in class who raises objections in public (a few white students support her later, but in private):

> I waited until the man was finished. The lights went on, I told him he shouldn't make remarks like that again because they are offensive, and I chose that attitude because I thought: I must not become uncontrolled, agitated or aggressive.
>
> Now at my work (her internship), they find me oversensitive (. . .), probably because I just can't let certain things pass. And I can absolutely not do that. I do not want to and I will not. So I always respond (against racism), because I just can't keep quiet.

Everyday racist discourse as a matter of joking is one mechanism to reconfirm the norm of whiteness or white Dutch-ness—in this case white middle class Dutchness, because calling the immigrants stupid also reinforces their lower status as factory workers. By the same token, the professor could have resorted to sexist innuendos. Male managers—another masculine world—frequently use racist and sexist jokes to break the ice when they present and as a way of emphasizing their professionalism, competence, rational self-images, total confidence, detachment, and control (Cockburn, *Space*). Similar styles occur in classrooms heavily imbued with masculine whiteness, such as large MBA classes, where teachers who intimidate and cajole students, often receive highly positive feedback. Is it relevant to mention that the resulting atmosphere of "we" and "us-hood"—emphasizing shared sameness—often makes it difficult for individual white or male students to disconnect from (a mixture of) racialized and gendered pressures to embrace attributed sameness for fear of repercussions. Indeed, the few students who agreed with Rosa N. expressed their support only off the record.

The story of Rosa N., a woman of Surinamese background, was published in 1991. Ten years later, in 2001, a journalistic inquiry among medical students of Iranian background—a refugee group with a substantial percentage of highly educated members including physicians in re-training—indicates that tactics of humiliation, including shouting and the use of abusive words still serve to put ethnic students in their place (Slutzky). One medical (male) student of Iranian background comments that some professors are intolerant of the fact that he speaks Dutch with an accent. Rather than asking him to repeat his question, he has had professors shout back: "I do not understand a damn word of what you are saying." The student comments that, after a couple of put downs, you just stop asking any more questions. Another Iranian medical student, a woman, comments that some professors address non-Dutch students with a hostile tone in their voices. There is also a comment about one of the professors who examines student's lab results. On his rounds past the test tables, he visits the table of the Iranian woman, the only woman of color, invariably last. The fact that she has to wait longer than anybody else symbolizes the perceived distance between the image her body is seen to represent and the normative image of the physician (in training).

3. Preference for masculine and white (Dutch) cultural values in rewarding performance

Medical culture is not very hospitable to expressions of emotion, and least when it concerns the physicians themselves. Only a minority of doctors seem open to "understand their own feelings and use these reflexively, not least to understand more of what may be happening within the patient; if, that is, they remain open to the patient, rather than becoming emotionally withdrawn and defensive" (West 301). Those who distance themselves from their own emotional lives, often white men, learn to be suspicious of their spontaneity (Seidler). As a result, there will be rejection if not pathologizing of compassion, instead of recognizing empathy as a humane expression of medical competence. Rosa N. gives an example when she talks about interactions with colleagues in the hospital:

> Recently there was a patient who had responded unexpectedly well to treatment, after we had almost given up on her. (. . .) I wanted to show that to one of the superiors. So I said: "come along, you gotta see this!" That's my enthusiasm (. . .). When I noticed his whispering with the others I felt he's talking about me because (. . .) they feel I am too emotionally involved, they don't like that. You have to be detached (. . .) when making a report. That is the general trend in Holland. You may not display any emotion.

Cultural cloning, choosing automatically for likeness, for the familiar paths in the name of competence, effectiveness and efficiency while preserving privilege, works even better when there is little time to reflect, when pressures to perform are high, and where there is a premium on quantitative output (number of patients, operations, and so on). At the same time, there are also doctors who behave like the rational "know it all" authority in order to mask emotional difficulties such as fear of inadequacy. The reluctance on the part of many doctors to consider or reflect upon the emotional dimensions of their professional practice has been linked to increasing unhappiness, alcoholism and stress (West).

Internalizing or challenging cultural cloning?

Today Rosa N. would not have had more women professors, but she would have had more female company among the students—40% of student surgeons are women, 60% are men. All students, men and women, majorities and ethnic minorities, are expected to internalize and accept values based in masculine and Western experiences if they want to be respected and rewarded as (future) physicians. In a study on women in health professions, two Dutch researchers, women, both surgeons, found that the small percentage of women among surgeons just want to be surgeons, not women or men. This radical reductionism—a one dimensional sense of identity—fits the picture of fragmented rather than holistic approaches to patients as well. Interviewed about their study, the authors firmly subscribe to masculine values commenting that surgery is too demanding a profession to combine with family life or child care. The surgeon has to be available 24/7 which is difficult for men-husband-father surgeons—let alone women-wife-mother surgeons. They agree that a good surgeon feels emotionally detached from his work. They reject the (feminine) value of empathy with patients as human beings (Keulemans).

In Eastern European countries, women dominate numerically, but their advantage in numbers is offset by lower status and payment compared to the relatively small numbers of male physicians. In that respect, privilege continues to be cloned along masculine lines. There is a substantial increase of women physicians in various Western European countries and North America, but masculine values continue to dominate the cultures of medicine (Riska). In all fairness, it should be mentioned that the inclusion of more women has not gone unnoticed altogether either. It has been found that Dutch women physicians give less medication, thereby also providing more effective treatment. They are less inclined to engage in heroic surgery (Keizer), or in unnecessary surgery. They devote more time to social dimensions of health problems. With many women doctors opting for part-time jobs, often shared with a colleague, this might have a positive effect, in particular on younger (women) doctors who want to balance family and work. These and other indications of the effects of female gender optimistically suggest that more diversity might chip away at systems of cultural cloning along (white) male gender lines.

In the meantime, most doctors continue their practice as usual while some, often women, take over neglected, mostly psychological dimensions. Men more often than women lack emotional intelligence and social competence, or do not consider emotional care to be relevant. It has been found that women family doctors assume a larger share of psychosocial work. Gender-socialized as caregivers, they are more open to holistic medication, illnesses placed in a larger context of family and other social relations (Keizer). Patients, in particular highly educated women, feel more comfortable with women. Many women have been able to develop better communication skills than men. At the same time, cultural cloning continues to work against alternative practices. The number of women medical specialists and family doctors is increasing, but medical cultures have remained largely masculine. Going against the wheels of cultural cloning comes with a price. Clearly, not all physicians (want to) fit the characteristic of "detached" and "objectifying" as readily as the normative profile requires them to. But the time slots available to "see" patients are not conducive to holistic and emphatic approaches to health care. A widely-spreading problem among family doctors is burn out—This is an area of medical practice from which men are now retreating (down to 77%) and women are entering.

Conclusions

With the concept of cultural cloning, I have problematized the relationship between dominant value systems and the skewed embodiments of high power positions. This critique is not new, but what is distinctive about the suggestions I have made in this paper is to insist that racism cannot be countered without questioning and re-assessing the larger package of norms, values and practices cloning cultures stands for, while transforming (some of) its fundamental characteristics.

Our universities are part and parcel of shaping and cloning the physician proto-type. Increasingly, education has to meet the demands of the commodification of time in the pursuit of ever higher levels of productivity. The corporate model is about managing standardized packages. We can question who this models serves. The assessment, accountability, corporate-derived and increasingly market-driven culture of higher education, has privileged quantity (number of students, publications, grants received) and pushed reflectivity and quality (time for students, time for authentic research) away from the center to the margins of higher education. The current emphasis on knowledge production—the more publications the better, even when many have less and less time to read—needs to give way to other aspects, particu-larly the pursuit of wisdom (in using knowledge and information). The old quest for wisdom is more relevant than ever, given the (mass) destructive capacity of (techno-logical) knowledge and the lack of progress in finding solutions to durable injustices, despite the mountains of publications that have been produced.

In questioning some of the underlying values of our culture, I seek to encourage reflective elaboration on the meaning and implications of cultural cloning. What is it that we are reproducing with the cultural cloning of high status positions along lines of perceived homogeneities? I have tentatively and analytically applied the concept of cultural cloning to the profile of "the physician." The analysis highlighted how cloning operates through everyday racism, the privileging of masculine whiteness (Dutch-ness), but also as expressed in other problems emerging from and within cloning culture. Preference for more of something similar means investing in the continuation of the best and the worst characteristics of current high status positions including the best and the worst of the social environments in which these positions are embedded. There is no question that modern medical science has been beneficial to large groups of people. But there is also another side. If dominant modes of exercis-ing medical power and authority include tolerance for patronizing humor, derogatory remarks, fierce competition rather than collaboration, the erosion of a caring disposi-tion, the commodification of lives and bodies, and hence, the dehumanization of humankind, could it be that the dominance of whiteness and of masculine values hampers humane and wise decision-making over societal problems and the future of humankind?

Notes

1. This is an abbreviated and revised version of an earlier publication (Essed, "Gendered Preferences").

2. Dutch originated mega-holding specializing in food and food related services and operating in many countries across the world. In 2003, Ahold was negatively in the news for investigation into budget fraud and excessive CEO salary. As a consequence, President-Commisioner de Ruiter had to resign.

Works Cited

Boogaarts, R. "Karel Vuursteen moet Ahold in de gaten houden." *FEMBusiness* 39 (27 Sept. 2003): 8.

Bottles, K. "Why Are Physicians So Angry?" *Physician Executive* 26 (2000): 44–48.

Clark, A. E. L., L. Mamo, et al. "Biomedicalization: Technoscientific Transformations of Health, Illness, and U.S. Biomedicine." *American Sociological Review* 68 (April 2003): 161–194.

Cockburn, C. *In the Way of Women: Men's Resistance to Sex Equality in Organizations*. London: Macmillan, 1991.

———. *The Space Between Us: Negotiating Gender and National Identities in Conflict*. London: Zed, 1998.

Collins, P. H. *Fighting Words: Black Women and the Search for Justice*. Minneapolis: U of Minnesota P, 1998.

Collison, D. L., and J. Hearn. "Breaking the Silence: On Men, Masculinities and Managements." *Men as Managers, Managers as Men: Critical Perspectives on Men, Masculinities and Managements*. Eds. D. L. Collison and J. Hearn. London: Sage, 1996. 1–24.

Couwenbergh, M. "Buitenlandse arts behandeld als vreemd wezen [Foreign Physician Treated as Alien]." *Contrast* 18 January 2001.

Crenshaw, K. "Mapping the Margins: Intersectionality, Identity Politics, and Violence Against Women of Color." *Stanford Law Review* 43 (1991): 1241–1299.

Dávila, Jerry. *Diploma of Whiteness: Race and Social Policy in Brazil, 1917–1945*. Durham, NC: Duke UP, 2003.

Dinther, M. "De val van een jaknikker." *FEMBusiness* 38 (20 Sept. 2003): 30–33.

Essed, Philomena. "Cloning Cultural Homogeneity While Talking Diversity: Old Wine in New Bottles in Dutch Work Organizations." *Transforming Anthropology* (2002).

———. "Gendered Preferences in Racialized Spaces: Cloning the Physician." *Racialization: Studies in Theory and Practice*. Eds. John Solomos and Karim Murji. Oxford: Oxford UP, 2004. 229–249.

———. "Multi-Identifications and Transformations: Reaching Beyond Racial and Ethnic Reductionisms." *Social Identities* 7 (2001): 493–509.

———. *Understanding Everyday Racism: An Interdisciplinary Theory*. Newbury Park: Sage, 1991.

Essed, Philomena, and David T. Goldberg. "Cloning Cultures: The Social Injustices of Sameness." *Ethnic and Racial Studies* 25 (2002): 1066–1082.

———. "Cloning Cultures." Paper presented at WISER. Witwatersrand Univeristy. Johannesburg, South Africa. 29 July 2003.

Gilman, S. L. *Making the Body Beautiful: A Cultural History of Aesthetic Surgery*. Princeton, NJ: Princeton UP, 1999.

Goldberg, David T. *Racist Culture, Philosophy and the Politics of Meaning*. Oxford: Blackwell, 1993.

———. *The Racial State*. Malden, MA: Blackwell, 2001.

Goldberg, David T., and J. Solomos, eds. *A Companion to Racial and Ethnic Studies*. Oxford: Blackwell, 2002.

Goleman, D. *Emotional Intelligence*. New York: Bantam, 1995.

Goleman, D., R. Boyatzis, et al. *Primal Leadership: Realizing the Power of Emotional Intelligence*. Boston: Harvard Business School P, 2002.

Keizer, M. *Acht stellingen over gender en professionaliteit [Eight Theses about Gender and Professionality]: Gender en professionals in de gezondheidszorg [healthcare]*. Den Haag: Raad voor de Volksgezondheid & Zorg (RVZ), 2000.

Keulemans, M. "Bent ú dokter Mulder! [Are You Doctor Mulder?]" Interview with Ella de Jong and Mimi Mulder. *Folia* 55 (2002): 8–9.

Kirk, G. "Women Resist Ecological Destruction." *A Diplomacy of the Oppressed: New Directions in International Feminism*. Ed. G. Ashworth. London: Zed, 1995. 69–89.

Klein, Freada Kapor. "About the New York Headquarters of a Corporation." *Giving Notice*. San Francisco: Jossey Boss, 2008.

Lane, R. *The Loss of Happiness in Market Democracies*. New Haven: Yale UP, 2001.

Marco, A. P. "Why Doctors are Afraid of Numbers." *The Physician Executive* (May–June 2002): 30.

Markus, M. "Cultural Pluralism and the Subversion of the 'Taken for Granted' World." *Race Critical Theories: Text and Context*. Eds.

Philomena Essed and David T. Goldberg. Oxford, UK: Blackwell, 2002. 494–408.

Mwaria, C. "Biomedical Ethics, Gender and Ethnicity: Implications for Black Feminist Anthropology." *Black Feminist Anthropology: Theory, Politics, Praxis, and Poetics*. Ed. I. McClaurin. New Brunswisk, NJ: Rutgers UP, 2001. 187–210.

Oommen, T. K. *Citizenship, Nationality and Ethnicity*. London: Polity, 1997.

Pfifferling, J.-H. "The Disruptive Physician." *Physician Executive* 25 (1999): 56–61.

Riska, E. *Medical Careers and Feminist Agendas: American, Scandinavian and Russian Women Physicians*. Hawthorne, NY: Aldine de Gruyter, 2001.

Root, M., ed. *The Multiracial Experience: Racial Borders as the New Frontiers*. Thousand Oaks, CA: Sage, 1996.

Rosenstein, A.H., H. Russell, et al. "Disruptive Physician Behavior Contributes to Nursing Shortage." *The Physician Executive* Nov.–Dec. 2002): 8–22.

Scheper-Hughes, N. "The Global Traffic in Human Organs." *Current Anthropology* 41.2 (2000): 191–224. http://www.journals.uchicago.edu/CA/journal/issues/v41n2/002001/002001.html.

Seidler, V. J. *Man Enough: Embodying Masculinities*. London: Sage, 1997.

Sennett, R. *The Corrosion of Character*. New York: Norton, 1998.

Shiva, V. *Staying Alive: Women Ecology and Development*. London: Zed, 1989.

Slutzky, M. "Sommige docenten hebben de pest aan buitenlanders [Some Teachers Hate Foreigners]." *Contrast* 18 Jan. 2001: 5.

Spevak, C. "The Competitive Advantage: Strategic Thinking for Physician Leader." *The Physician Executive* Jan.–Feb. 2003: 32.

Tilly, C. *Durable Inequality*. Berkeley: U of California P, 1998.

Werbner, P., and T. Modood, eds. *Debating Cultural Hybridity: Multi-cultural Identities and the Politics of Anti-racism*. London: Zed, 1997.

West, L. "Doctors on an Edge: A Cultural Psychology of Learning and Health." *Biographical Methods and Professional Practice: An International Perspective*. Eds. P. Chamberlayne, J. Bornat, and U. Apitzsch. Bristol, UK: Policy, 2004. 299–311.

Williams, E. S., and A. C. Skinner. "Outcomes of Physician Job Satisfaction: A Narrative Review, Implications and Directions for Future Research." *Health Care Management Review* 28 (2003): 199–140.

Young, I. M. *Justice and the Politics of Difference*. Princeton, NJ: Princeton UP, 1990.

Young, J. *The Exclusive Society: Social Exclusion, Crime and Difference in Late Modernity*. London: Sage, 1999.

Yuval-Davis, N. *Gender and Nation*. London: Sage, 1997.

Cloning Disappearance, Consuming Fakes

Ackbar Abbas

Writing in 1988, a year before the fall of the Berlin Wall, Guy Debord noted in an off-handed but prescient way the joint emergence of globalization and the fake. "Today," he remarked, ". . . the tendency to replace the real with the artificial is ubiquitous." This is all the more worrying in that "what is false creates taste, and reinforces itself by knowingly eliminating any possible reference to the authentic. And what is genuine is *reconstructed* as quickly as possible, to resemble the false." What Debord is saying in other words is that a taste of the false creates a taste *for* the false, which is why "the globalization of the false was also the falsification of the globe" (*Comments* 10, 50, 51). Examples abound, and they include the replacement of the Marly Horses in Place de la Concorde and the Roman statues in the doorway of Saint-Trophime in Arles, by plastic replicas, and fakes of the Terracotta army being passed off as the real thing by the Chinese authorities to visiting diplomats.

For Debord, the explanation for such a strange proclivity is a mutation in the form of the spectacle: from the 'diffuse' and 'concentrated' forms found in earlier capitalist and authoritarian societies respectively, to a recent merger of the two forms into the "integrated spectacle" that characterizes global society. What is the "integrated spectacle"? If what integrates global society are information networks, then another word for integrated spectacle might be—information. Moreover, because of the speed with which it moves, information does not necessarily take on a visual form. This is tantamount to saying that the integrated spectacle confronts us with something of a paradox: it is a spectacle that is no longer spectacular, a spectacle that has reversed itself in that it is more covert than overt, a spectacle that is *secret*. Hence Debord could write: "Secrecy dominates this world, and first and foremost as the secret of domination" (*Comments* 60). And again: "The spectacle has brought the secret to victory, and must be more and more controlled by *specialists in secrecy* . . ." (*Comments* 60).

Placing this moment of the integrated spectacle would require quite a radical revision of the earlier theory of the spectacle. In his influential book *The Society of the Spectacle* published in 1968, Debord had postulated two critical historical shifts in ethical and social life. The first involved a "downgrading of *being* into *having*," when what you have becomes more important than what you are, the moment of "the acquisitive society"; the second involved "a generalized shift from *having* to appearing," when what you appear to have is more important than what you actually have, the moment of the spectacle (*Society* 16). Today, we will have to postulate a third shift: from appearing to *disappearing*, a shift to the non-spectacular form of the spectacle, to its secret informational form. One indication that such a shift has already taken place is a general blurring of differences that ushers in the age of the clone. A specific instance of this is what Debord describes as "a parodic end of the division of labor" that can be observed at all levels of social ad cultural life: "A financier can be a singer, a lawyer, a police spy, a broker can parade his literary tastes, an actor can be president, a chef can philosophise on cookery techniques as if they were landmarks in universal history. Anyone can join the spectacle . . ." (*Comments* 10).

Like the integrated spectacle, cultural cloning too, it seems to me, has to be situated in this shift from a problematics of appearance to a problematics of disappearance. Cultural cloning can no longer be thought of simply as one culture plagiarizing another, with the culpable and shameless all on one side and the long-suffering and blameless on the other. Moreover, it is not simply a matter of "influence", ending up with one culture taking on the appearance of another—the "westernization" thesis. Cultural cloning is less a matter of the dissimulation of appearance than the simulation of disappearance. As such it may well be part of the genetic code of global culture itself, seen for example when a hi-tech company like Xerox could boast in a cheeky advertisement: "Xerox never produces anything original." What we will need to address therefore are the unprecedented challenges to ethics, aesthetics, and politics that a problematics of disappearance poses, with cloning as both its cause and effect. I propose to do this through a brief case study of the fake.

Unlike the simulacrum (the perfect copy, a dream of technology more familiar to us in films like Bladerunner and Matrix, and in the writings of Jean Baudrillard, than in everyday life), the fake exists in the ordinary social world of economic transactions. First sold in all the "night markets" of the developing world, today fake goods are also found in malls and shopping centers; most recently, the customer buys them on the Internet, where all of the world's major currencies and credit cards are accepted. The trade in fakes contributes quite significantly to the creation of a "shadow economy", though there are understandably no exact figures: the shadow economy has no CEOs, no management boards, no archive, no statistics, no accountants. In spite of this, the fake today has an important and paradoxical role to play: we can think of it as a social, cultural, and economic response, at a local and apparently trivial level, to the process of globalization and the uneven relations such processes have engendered.

This is not to say however that we should romanticize the fake or overlook the many obvious objections to it. Some have argued that morally speaking, the fake is a form of cheating. Economically speaking, it is a form of theft. From an aesthetic point of view, the objection is that the fake is never as well made as the genuine article. Its social value too is highly dubious, as it can be seen, at best, to be a form of pretension; at worst, as in the case of fake Viagra and fake milk powder, it has led to moments of intense embarrassment and to infant deaths. The list can be easily extended and in fact many of these objections are undeniably valid. The danger though is that indignation may make us lose sight of the structural and historical features of the fake, and the paradoxical role it plays in the context of globalization.

Moralism will not take us very far in the analysis of the fake because the moral issues are hardly straightforward. Take the example of the US who is now leading the world in the moral condemnation of fakes and the defense of intellectual property rights. This was not always so, as in the nineteenth century, the US was one of the chief violators of intellectual property rights, as China is today. American publishers reprinted Charles Dickens' novels, and refused to pay him royalties, just as China is doing today with the reproduction of software and designer tools. Those who protest the loudest against intellectual property rights violations are those who stand to lose most by them: morality follows economics. Or take the case of the big brand-name companies with their highly publicized campaigns against fakes. Do fakes hurt the big brands and reduce their profits, as these companies claim, or do they provide free advertizing, and so increase their profits? The answer may well be a toss-up suggesting that the real issues are elsewhere: you protest loudly and indignantly against the fake in order to send the message that your product is real and authentic and valuable; just as in the university, "plagiarism" is loudly condemned as the cardinal sin, more often than not by those who are least original. Instead of moralism, we must learn to see the fake as an *anthropological object*, a symptom of our time that enables a comparative study of cultures and societies in a global age. Even if we succeed in suppressing the symptom (through law, for example), we have not changed the *conditions* that gave rise to the symptom in first place. In so far as the fake points to unresolved problems in the world today, it should be analyzed, not dismissed. What I shall attempt to provide now is a preliminary historical analysis that might help us situate a problematic practice in a problematic space—the space of the integrated spectacle and disappearance.

For the student of such a space, the fake has a unique value, largely because the question of the fake never involves just the fake alone. It forces us to re-assess all the objects and processes around it, including legal systems, politics, the global market, and technology. This point is beautifully made in Orson Welles' great film *F for Fake* (Criterion Collection, 1973). We are introduced to Elmyr de Hory, one of the most talented forgers of all time, whose works signed with the names of famous artists were once in all the great art museums of the world. Elmyr turned to forgery to demonstrate the ignorance and pretence of the art experts and museums that rejected his original work, because they are only impressed by big names. Welles goes on to show that the forger is not an isolated figure and that behind the forger is a whole series of other figures that make him possible. The series includes ironically the art expert, whom Elmyr wryly observes is "god's gift to the forger," because without the expert who authenticates, the forger would never have succeeded so well with his deception: the knowledgeable expert is in ignorant collusion with the faker. The series continues with Elmyr's biographer, Clifford Irving, whose book, *Fake!* not only made Elmyr into a folk hero but also gave Irving the inspiration to try faking himself. He published a bogus "authorized" biography of Howard Hughes, forcing the reclusive Hughes to issue a public denial. Then there is Welles himself, a great filmmaker and actor, for whom filmmaking and acting are no more than forms of fakery. The series goes on, and does not stop even with the artist, with Picasso, the most famous artist of our time. One of the most insightful moments into the nature of faking comes when an art dealer brings some Picassos to show Picasso. "Fake!" Picasso said of the first painting; "fake" he said of the second and again of the third. At this point the art dealer felt he had to protest. "But Pablo," he said, "I saw you painting that last one with my own eyes!" To which Picasso's reply was: "I can paint fake Picassos as well as anybody."

Fakes of art-works have had a long history, but the fakes that concern us are more mundane. They are copies not of art-works but of the everyday commodity; or to be more precise, of the *global commodity*—all those brand-name products destined to colonize the world's subconscious. A large part of the value of such commodities is created by advertisements, i.e., by information and new media. Just as the global media circulates information about the latest commodities for Asian consumers to buy, so the global media brings information about these goods for counterfeiters to copy. The conditions that make the global commodity desirable are the same ones that make the fake possible. Both belong to the same history, the history of information; both belong to the moment when information is the most important commodity. This suggests a related point, namely, that the production of fakes appears when cities are just about to enter the world economy and become exposed to media representations of global commodities. Beijing, Shanghai, Guangzhou, and Shenzhen are just the best-known examples of Chinese cities at this point of development after China's entry into the WTO. Fake production ceases or diminishes when a city or nation becomes more integrated into the global establishment, at which point strict copyright laws begin to be passed, partly as a result of pressure from global companies. Hong Kong is an example of a city at this stage, where fakes are now less common. Here again the fake functions as a historical maker.

However, if cloning today as suggested earlier is a question of cloning disappearance, then it may be much too naïve to believe that faking as such will come to an end with the advent of globalization and the passing of a few laws; what will end will only be the more obvious modes of faking. It fact there are already signs that faking is endemic to global processes themselves and not just a temporary aberration. Take the Swiss watch industry, the most global of global enterprises, and its relation to faking. When high-grade Chinese fake watches are made, the practice is to use actual unfinished Swiss movements or *ebauches* and provide cases to house them. Amazingly enough, this is also the standard practice of the majority of Swiss watch companies, very few of which produce their own 'in house' movement. Even more fantastic is the way in which some second or third tier Swiss manufacturers are now copying the designs of fake Chinese watches: the original as a faking of the fake. Against standard preconceptions, fakes do not just come from China and the Third World; in more sophisticated form, and protected under a veneer of legitimation, fakes can be found in the most established and integrated places.

The critical point to grasp is the following: the problem of the contemporary fake is not how close the fake is to the original, but how close the original is to the fake. In the first scenario, it is still a matter of cloning appearances. It is a scenario that does not disturb us very much because even though it might be difficult to distinguish between fake and original, the categories of fake and original are still reassuringly in place, and the original is still the standard by which the fake is judged. In the second scenario, when faking is no longer confined to the fake, when it is not only the usual suspects who practice it, it is these categories and standards themselves that disappear and everything dissolves into general confusion and easy reversibility. This is the scenario of cloning disappearance.

When cloning is a matter of cloning disappearance not appearance, new issues and confusions begin to emerge for the consumer. One sign of the fake used to be that it was cheap. Now you could be paying a small fortune for an object and still have no guarantee you would end up with something not fake. This does not mean however that there is now no relation between cost and value: there is, only that the relation is a perverse one. It follows a strange logic: objects are not costly because they are valuable; they are valuable because they are costly. This is a point that Thorstein Veblen had noted already in his pioneering analysis of consumption, conspicuous or otherwise; and interestingly enough, he made his most provocative observations when his analysis turned to the question of the fake. The fake he writes "may be so close an imitation as to defy any but the closest scrutiny; and yet as soon as the counterfeit is detected, its aesthetic value, its commercial value as well, declines precipitately. [. . .] It loses caste aesthetically because it falls to a lower pecuniary grade" (169). In other words, the fake is not *perceived* to be different; it is *conceived* to be different. The other side of the coin is that when one buys something that one can think of as not fake, like designer t-shirts, one pays dearly for the assurance. In this regard, there is a cautionary tale (possibly apocryphal) told about Giorgio Armani that is highly appropriate. On a trip to China, the story goes, Giorgio Armani was shown a fake Armani T-shirt by one of his aides, who expected from the great designer an outburst of moral indignation. Instead, Armani examined the t-shirt carefully and simply said, "Very nice. Copy it."

What the fake shows very clearly is not only that a large part of what we consume is information, but also that this information is inseparable from ignorance; and in today's world of advanced design and hi-tech products, ignorance is endemic, which explains why faking is everywhere. As Walter Benjamin observed, it is when the consumer is ignorant about how objects are produced that "taste" becomes important, filling in for knowledge. The consumer, Benjamin wrote around 1938, "is not usually knowledgeable when he appears as a buyer [. . .] The more industry progresses, the more perfect are the imitations which it throws on the market [. . .] In the same measure as the expertness of a customer declines, the importance of taste increases—both for him and for the manufacturer" (105).

The consumption of fakes also raises a number of socio-political issues, but in a typically ambiguous way. There is to begin with the global division of labor. Many commodities today are designed in one place, usually a "developed" country, and manufactured in another, usually a "developing" country. It has been argued, over-optimistically in my view, that such an arrangement is actually beneficial to all concerned, an instance of the advantages of globalization. Not only do manufacturing countries receive much needed foreign investments and benefits from technological transfers, the argument goes; in the long run they could also develop their own designs. What is clear though is that in the meanwhile, the global division of labor has cast the cities in developing countries in the role of workhorses or production units. Moreover, they are allowed to produce, but not to consume, as many of the commodities labeled "Made in China" are only sold in the USA or Europe and are not available for sale in China itself. It is at this juncture that the fake enters to reverse the order of things. It produces objects labeled "Made in Italy" or "Made in France", the design centers of the world, and offers them for sale in China, at the fraction of the cost of "the real thing." Thus the fake obtains economic advantages and effects its own version of "technology transfer"—not in the long term, but right now. It profits and learns through copying, and in its own way gestures toward leveling the difference between developed and developing countries, albeit through a ruse. Ziauddin Sardar speaks of the fake as a form of resistance against exclusion from the global order of commodity consumption, and even as a form of "gentle subversion" against globalization itself: "Slight Malay bodies," he writes, "clad in fake designer jeans, fake T-shirts, wrists adorned with fake designer watches, clutching fake designer bags and cloned mobile phones look as if they have wandered straight out of Beverly Hills for the pittance the get-up costs them. They are *in*-cluded, fashion and fancy, not *ex*-cluded, marginalized onlookers. In the international politics of self and style, they are fully empowered. And the transformation can be accomplished within the ambience and precincts of living history" (89).

It seems to me that Sardar's argument about consuming fakes as a means of subverting globalization is in its own way as over-optimistic as arguments about the advantages of globalization. When something is faked, global order is not disturbed; in fact, the fake confirms rather than subverts the global division of labor, made worse now by the fact that it is developing countries that condemn *themselves* to the (fake) production of first-world designs. The fake is not capable of being politically subversive of the global order because there is a passive quality to the fake that makes it work as symptom but not as subversion. As symptom, it gives us, in its own shabby and damaged way, a negative side of globalization that is usually well hidden under a rhetoric of co-operation and collaboration. That is its value: what we might call the counter-value of the counterfeit.

It is when we turn to a globalizing China, which is what I propose to do now, that the full complexity of the political, economic and aesthetic issues raised by the fake fully emerges. In Beijing, the Hung Qiao Mall where fake goods are retailed stands next to the historic Temple of Heaven where Chinese Emperors used to make offerings to the Gods for good harvests: side by side with the Temple of Heaven stands the Temple of Fake Heaven, an emblem perhaps of China today, and its historical complexity and contradictions. It is much too simplistic to say that China tolerates fakes because it has no respect for international law and intellectual property rights. In the past, socialist idealism might have been tolerant of fakes because of its belief in egalitarianism and communitarianism. If "private property is theft", then in a sense fakes are a form of egalitarianism, the sharing even of intellectual property. But then, during the socialist era lasting, say, into the 1970's, there was no fake production to speak of in China. It is in the era of market reform, when fake production is in fact more and more criminalized, that we see its golden age. The explanation of this paradox is that strange thing, the socialist market economy (which is the form globalization in China takes), where older social attitudes like egalitarianism jostle with the new. The official line today is that "egalitarianism" is a "feudal" hangover, but it is this residual egalitarianism that allows the faker to operate without a bad conscience, and authorities to be a little too casual about copyright laws. However, it should also be noted that in the socialist market economy, emerging together with the fake and in contradiction to it, is a new sense of private property, and of the value of privacy in general: the discreet charm of the bourgeoisie. Every couple now wants its own private space and its own private means of transport. It is this new social attitude as much as anything else that has resulted in the greatest building boom in Chinese history, and the sight of cities choked with traffic. The point is that the fake, which first world countries lament, and the building boom and motorcar sales, which they applaud, emerge together in the socialist market economy. They are the contradictory aspects of a contradictory, transitional historical moment.

How we might ask can a solution to the problem of the fake be found, where the cure is not more lethal from the disease? One suggestion is to do so not by developing stricter and more punitive legislation, but by developing design cultures. The fake, precisely because it is the antithesis of design culture, can provide some hints on how to proceed. In the first place, it is not true that fakes need to be legislated against because they are lawless and transgressive. In fact, the contrary is the case. Fakes are rule-bound and conservative; they have too much respect and reverence for the global objects they imitate: hence they cannot transform the object or invent a new object. The fact that they can reproduce these objects to perfection shows how thoroughly they have studied and understood them; fakes are as it were the eternal *understudies* of the global commodity, never actors on the world stage. They can clone appearances, but they cannot falsify enough. This is a distinction that Welles' *F for Fake* was implicitly trying to draw by putting the artist/filmmaker next to the faker: the artist falsifies, the faker merely clones—an important difference in spite of a certain family resemblance between them. The fake relates to a global environment by allowing itself to be seduced by it and becoming like it; but such an environment not only seduces, it also betrays and reduces to servitude. This suggests that the first law of design culture is: more important than understanding the object is the ability to change it.

This brings us to another lesson that the fake has in store for design culture, which comes when the faker is confronted by an object that for whatever reason is impossible to clone—perhaps because it is too complex as in certain kinds of watch movements, or perhaps because the raw materials are not available, as in certain kinds of fashion design. Under such circumstances, the faker is forced to improvise, to make do; and sometimes, with luck and talent, such initiatives succeed in coming up with startling solutions. At such moments the faker practices a kind of design that could be called *poor design*. Poor design is not bad design, nor do only those without money practice it; rather poor design means making the best use of limited resources, working with what is at hand, and looking out for new possibilities. Most of all it means no longer looking at oneself obsessively in the crazed mirror of globalization. It means exiting the spectacle and affirming one's own historical experiences. Perhaps it was the "poor design" in the fake Chinese t-shirt and the fake Chinese watches that so impressed Armani and the Swiss watch manufacturers.

Works Cited

Benjamin, Walter. *Charles Baudelaire*. Trans. Harry Zohn. New York: Verso; NLB, 1997.

Debord, Guy. *Comments on the Society of the Spectacle*. Trans. Malcolm Imrie. New York: Verso, 1990.

———. *The Society of the Spectacle*. Trans. Donald Nicholson-Smith. New York: Zone, 1994.

Sardar, Ziauddin. *The Consumption of Kuala Lumpur*. London: Reaktion, 2000.

Veblen, Thorstein. *The Theory of the Leisure Class*. New York: Penguin, 1994.

Part Three: Replicating and Marketing Faith

Marketing Religion

Eileen Luhr

There is nothing unusual about a crowded baseball stadium on a summer night in the United States. But the 37,000 people—plus the 12,000-person overflow crowd seated in the parking lot—that packed into Anaheim Stadium in Orange County, California on August 16, 1997 were not watching America's pastime; rather, they were attending the Harvest Crusade, an annual evangelical revival meeting. The four-day event featured not only an updated version of old-time fire-and-brimstone sermons urging believers to recommit, but also it aimed to bring the "unchurched" to God. In the months preceding the Crusade, organizers saturated southern California with flyers, posters, and bumper stickers heralding it, and urging attendees to bring non-Christian acquaintances to the event (Rivenburg). On this particular night, the Crusade took what a spokesman for the event called "an MTV approach to evangelism" as it tried to appeal to local high school and college students with a bill featuring Christian rock 'n' roll bands Audio Adrenaline, Big Tent Revival, and The Kry (McGraw, "Harvest"). As the event's youth ministry coordinator explained, the kids "arrived for the music, but we want them to leave with the message of Jesus ringing in their ears. . . All those songs and riffs are just an avenue for them to come out and hear God's word." Bob Herdman, a member of Audio Adrenaline, agreed suggesting, "You can have fun and discover Christ at the same time. We're just a regular rock band—except we use our God-given gifts to explore our faith and inspire others to do the same" (Phan). At the end of the evening, 5,000 people attested to the Crusade's effectiveness by responding to the nightly "altar call," when evangelist preacher Greg Laurie—in a sermon translated into Spanish, Korean, Chinese, Japanese, Vietnamese, and sign language—invited participants to come onto the field and dedicate their lives to Jesus (Harvest Crusades, "Past").

This chapter examines how evangelicals adapted to and politicized the landscape of Orange County—the most exalted consumer exurb in post-liberal America—as they sought to shield children and adolescents from non-normative behaviors and lifestyles. Events such as the Harvest Crusade exemplified the suburbanization of American evangelicalism and the "Christianization" of popular culture—twin pillars of the conservative shift in national politics during the Reagan, Bush, and Clinton eras. In contrast to the discourses of the old Christian Right, which maintained a dogmatic resistance to youth culture, this new "rock" evangelicalism embraced contemporary youth styles to broaden the effect of its proselytizing efforts. These efforts, in turn, abetted the hegemonic conservative politics of the late 20th century. The suburbanized evangelicalism developed in Orange County, California provides an opportunity to explore the uses of consumerism to market conservative religious beliefs and "traditional family values." Once perfected, these "new methods" could be transplanted to other suburban and exurban areas.

The Crusade Template

To some nonbelievers, events such as the Harvest Crusade were an example of an isolated Christian subculture known only to its adherents. Others used such events to reject evangelicalism as crassly commercial (McDannell 222–223). Yet the importance of the Harvest Crusade rests neither in its invisibility to nonbelievers nor in its commodification of religion. Rather, the Crusade demonstrated how religious conservatives mastered the cultural formulas of consumerism as they adjusted their witnessing practices to a suburban landscape where civic life increasingly occurred in commercially owned spaces.

Event organizers prided themselves in their ability to suture current cultural styles to religious content. Beneath the crusade's relaxed atmosphere—the ballpark, the contemporary music, and casual dress—there remained a very conservative message about self-reliance, personal responsibility, and obedience to authority. These themes, in turn, echoed many of the arguments put forward by Christian conservatives in grassroots political campaigns undertaken during the 1990s. But just as the Crusade should not be dismissed for its embrace of consumerism or its illegibility to secularists, it also cannot be simply categorized as an offshoot of the Christian Right. Rather, in its calls for the protection of the economic and cultural prerogatives of the white family in the post-liberal era, the Harvest Crusade represented the emergence of a cultural activism that was, in fact, more innovative than the better-known political protests among conservative Christians.

Earlier in the 20th century, conservative Protestants were linked to the small towns of the Old South and Great Plains and were outnumbered by urban majorities in the Northeast and Midwest. However, as a result of the migrations of the postwar era, many conservative Christians resided in the politically, culturally, and demographically dominant suburbs, especially in what Republican political strategist Kevin Phillips called the "sunbelt" in the American South and West (38–39). The fast-growing suburbs soon began to skew Republican: while the suburban vote in 1960—33 percent of the electorate—slightly favored Republicans, by 1988, the suburban vote—by then 48 percent of the electorate—favored Republicans over Democrats, 28 percent to 20 percent (Schneider 35). The nation's growing number of megachurches—usually defined as nonsectarian Protestant churches with over 2,000 members—became sought-after allies in tight political campaigns in which candidates sought to seek out voters concerned with "traditional values." The Harvest Crusade, produced through the coordinated efforts of several large churches across the county, provided a venue for reaching "values" voters.

The concern over "family values" continued a longer-running theme in American politics over the status of the white middle-class home. Whether it was anti-communism, federal subsidies for home mortgages, law and order, anti-feminism, or culture wars, the key to conservative ideological politics during the second half of the 20th century was the protection of white middle-class interests. White evangelicals found that their concerns about the influence of popular culture on children meshed perfectly with other late-century conservative movements—based on "gut-level issues" including the taxpayer and anti-busing revolts as well as the anti-gay and anti-feminist movements—that purported to defend the sanctity of the home[1]. As historian Matthew Lassiter has argued, the partisanship of suburban voters mattered less than their "populist identifications" as "homeowners, taxpayers, and schoolparents."[2] Yet while recent case studies have examined the political culture of conservative movements, less has been written about how the cultural politics of events such as the Harvest Crusade sought to promote the prerogatives of white middle-class suburbanites. Through culture, conservatives created what literary critic Lauren Berlant has called the "national sentimentality" of the late 20th century, which was defined by "a politics that abjures politics, made on behalf of a private life protected from the harsh realities of power" (11). Using this logic, conservatives maintained that the protection of the white middle class entailed not only home values, but also values in the home. Cultural activities such as the Harvest Crusade were integral to this process of domestic sanctification because they provided a consumer-based method for reproducing the normative "family" image—white, Christian, middle class, and heterosexual—across the suburban landscape.

An expanded understanding of political action better captures how cultural events such as the Harvest Crusade intersected with faith-based protests and campaigns to protect normative values and traditional authority. During the "culture wars" of the 20th century, gay rights, abortion rights, and Christian conservatives contributed to an increased politicization of public and semi-public spaces. Activists sought access to public spaces through ballot initiatives, civic hearings, court battles, and protests.

Events such as the Harvest Crusade, however, reveal how evangelicals sought to reclaim both space and culture for "Christian" beliefs in response to threats against "the family" represented in Orange County by gay activism, abortion clinics, and youth alienation.

Popular culture was an appealing way to intervene in American public life because evangelicals emphasized the importance of changing hearts (a cultural issue) rather than votes (a political issue). As Paul Apostolidis has explained in his analysis of James Dobson's "Focus on the Family" radio program, the political significance of the Christian conservative culture rested not only in its direct relationship to political activism, but also "in its expression, reinforcement, and contestation of contemporary, social-structural relations of power" (6). Within this logic, respect for traditional authority obviated the need for government welfare programs by replacing them with "family values." This moral solution to American social problems was well suited to the political outlook of a decade of economic restructuring and government retreat from the safety net programs established during the New Deal and the Great Society. Pointing to the problems among teenagers in the United States—not just kids in the cities, but those in the *suburbs* too—Christians declared that society had lost its values, and it was their duty to help the nation recover its Judeo-Christian sensibilities. Events such as the Harvest Crusade served as a starting point for restoring these values to suburbia.

Protecting Normative Values in Local Politics

The conservative evangelicals of Orange County were well-positioned to become innovators in religious, political, and cultural activism in the late 20th century. Since the Second Great Awakening, American revivals have tended to thrive in areas that feature mobile populations with respectable but slightly precarious social positions.[3] The Harvest Crusade followed in this tradition, as it primarily addressed itself to a white, middle-class audience—or those aspiring to that status. As historian Lisa McGirr has shown, the area had already proven receptive to conservative political beliefs, as the grassroots activism of Orange County's fiscal and normative conservatives portended a national conservative ascendance. In the 1990s, Orange County remained, in the words of one political operative, "the Republican womb of the state of California" (Peterson).

Despite the appearance of white evangelical dominance in Orange County political and cultural life, Orange County underwent dramatic changes during the late 20th century that challenged the area's reputation as a bastion of white homeowners. Cities such as Santa Ana and Westminster became known for their Spanish-speaking and Vietnamese populations. With the end of the Cold War looming, the area's economy began to transition from a manufacturing to an information- and service-based economy (Kling and Turner).

In addition to these racial and economic shifts, there were significant cultural changes in the county. Political scientists John Green, James L. Guth, and Kevin Hill note that "Christian Right activism occurred predominantly in rapidly growing—and relatively prosperous—suburban areas" where conservative Protestants confronted "direct challenges to their values" (85). In fact, modern evangelicalism thrived on confrontations with diversity. As sociologist Christian Smith has explained, American evangelicalism "is strong . . . because it is—or at least perceives itself to be— embattled with forces that seem to oppose or threaten it" (89). This was very much the case for Orange County's conservative evangelicals in the 1990s, as they under- took campaigns to banish either gay rights or abortion rights groups from the spaces of Orange County.

With their alternative vision of affluent whiteness, Orange County-based gay rights groups posed significant challenges to evangelical definitions about each facet of the phrase "family values": whiteness, middle-class respectability, and gender norms (especially masculinity). Conservatives viewed gay rights campaigns undertaken by ACT UP and the Gay Visibility League as an unwelcome disruption to the family-friendly sub- urban space. Evangelical Christians therefore mobilized to deny gays access to space: first, through an anti-gay rights initiative campaign in Irvine in 1989; second, through campaigns designed to deny gay rights groups access to local public spaces, as in the efforts to block the Gay Pride Parade; and third, through campaigns aimed at pressur- ing corporations to exclude gays from employee benefits as well as access to semi- public spaces such as Disneyland. While not every campaign against gay rights proved successful, anti-gay mobilization allowed evangelical activists to energize voters based on "quality of life" issues that focused on protecting the local community.

Women's health clinics that provided abortions similarly antagonized pro-life Christian conservatives, who viewed the clinics as an extension of the Left's cam- paign against children. To pro-life activists, abortion represented a threat to mother- hood as well as the family, as it threatened to upset social, biological, and religiously-ordained roles of men and women (Ginsburg 6–7). While marches on the National Mall received more attention, local action became a routinized and ritualized contest between pro-life and pro-choice sides. Local conservatives protested against abortion by holding vigils in public parks, staging protests outside clinics, and walk- ing picket lines on sidewalks outside private homes in residential neighborhoods. In 1989, Operation Rescue staged a "Holy Week of Rescue" that resulted in 771 arrests at southern California clinics (L. Smith). Like the anti-gay protesters, anti- abortion protesters supplemented their legislative efforts with direct action demon- strations that politicized local spaces and highlighted the competing understandings of femininity in the post-1960s era.

By laying claim to Orange County's public spaces, gay activists and abortion rights activists disrupted the heterosexual order that had been built into the county's environment. Christian conservatives responded by vilifying these groups as "special interests" that were anxious to gain access to children through education curriculum, government office, and consumer products. Through these actions, evangelicals were forced to make their own assumptions about "family values" and public laws, space, and culture more explicit. In each instance, local activists maintained that their actions were motivated by a desire to protect the family.

Witnessing Suburbia: A New Form of Cultural Activism

An analysis of Christian political intervention that ends at boycotts and picket lines misses the most important political innovations of the era, as it neglects the cultural work undertaken by institutions such as the megachurch and Christian retail store as well as large-scale revivals such as the Harvest Crusade. Unlike the anti-gay rights and anti-abortion campaigns, where grassroots activists organized and protested in the name of children and families, Christian consumerism addressed parents and children alike through popular culture. These items could be carried to all of the spaces of suburbia—including the store, car, school, highway, and home. And while no area surpassed Orange County in integrating consumer culture into public space, the structural similarities of suburbia guaranteed that the most effective cultural interventions would be replicated across the United States.

A number of cultural organizations and businesses catered to the area's conservative Christian population. Calvary Chapel owned a 50,000-watt radio station in Costa Mesa that featured preaching and spoken-word programs, and seven other religious stations dotted the radio dials of Los Angeles and Orange County in 1997 (McDougal; Brownfield). The cultural influence of evangelicalism extended to print media: the area boasted an independent Christian newspaper and a Christian phone directory. Believers could choose from a range of Christian coffeehouses and bookstores that dotted the area. The traffic in souls even spilled into rush hour, as thousands of believers seized upon freeway gridlock to witness to other drivers with *icthus* (fish) emblems, antenna balls, and Christian-themed bumper stickers—including many that advertised the annual Harvest Crusade.

Events such as the Harvest Crusade became the preferred method for simultaneously celebrating and protecting normative values and traditional authority in American exurbia. Crusade organizers were innovators when it came to adapting to the suburban spaces of Orange County as well as to the countercultural origins of late-20th century youth culture. While mirroring the themes of the explicitly "political" activism associated with this era, cultural activities such as the Harvest Crusade localized politics by inserting them into everyday contexts such as the home and neighborhood. The belief that inner-city pathologies had infected suburban harmony quite literally put the fear of God into some middle-class white parents. Adolescents were particularly vulnerable to social maladies such as single parenthood, drug use, and gang membership, so the Crusade's youth-focused message appeared at what seemed like a critical time for suburban parents. Their resourcefulness defied expectations of cultural backwardness among conservative believers and, in turn, created a more persuasive argument for their conservative worldview. The increased immediacy made it easier for Christians to view themselves as "citizen activists" who had been deputized to protect the local community. Rather than emphasizing a public culture of civic action, these evangelicals preferred to celebrate the private nature of families in public space. And while it celebrated the emotionally powerful categories of family and nation, the Crusade avoided mention of mundane ones such as government. The Harvest Crusade therefore offers a glimpse of what Christian conservatives believed civic life in a culture of "family values" would look like.

The Crusade conveyed its cultural message in three critical ways. First, while other conservative organizations condemned the events of the 1960s, the Harvest Crusade emphasized its roots in 1960s counterculture. The event and its organizers claimed to offer a counter-narrative—not a reaction—to the decade. Second, while the Harvest Crusade defended a conservative worldview, its methods were far from old-fashioned: rather than denouncing popular culture for its role in the decline of Western civilization, evangelicals tried to buttress conservative values by making consumer culture—ranging from bumper stickers to contemporary music to a ballpark atmosphere—a starting point for restoring biblical values to the suburbs. This approach allowed Crusade organizers to address young people directly rather than simply undertaking public campaigns in their names. Third, the Crusade was an important act of sacralization in which the spaces of suburban culture were claimed for Christ. Evangelicals believed that they had a special role to play in American society—a rhetorical tradition of American Protestantism dating from Puritanism. The Crusade offered evangelicals a chance to take a position of cultural leadership through which to model "family values."

The Harvest Crusade located its origins in the Jesus Movement of the 1960s, an era when thousands of countercultural youths were reintegrated into mainstream society through religious faith. Rather than downplay their connections to the Sixties, Harvest Crusade organizers staked their claim to the historical memory of Orange County by offering a smooth narration of religion's vital role in quelling youthful rebellion during the Vietnam era's days of rage. For the Harvest Crusade, the "unfinished revolution" of the 1960s was not in its campaigns against war or social injustice, but rather in the failure to claim more souls for Jesus. But there was still time. In this formulation, memories of the Great Refusal became a starting point to bring families together. Alluding to his earlier work among the youth who came of age during the Sixties, Chuck Smith attributed the interest in the early Crusades to a new generation: "These are the children of the Jesus People. It's happening to them just like it happened to their parents" (Weber, "Revival").

Crusade organizers were not afraid to harness countercultural impulses for religious purposes. While conservatives such as William Bennett criticized the counterculture of the late 1960s and early 1970s, the Crusade proudly showcased converts from secular music as trophies from the culture wars. In 1997, the Crusade invited singer Ritchie Furay, the former Buffalo Springfield singer who had performed at the Monterey Pop Festival in 1967, to sing the Neil Young-penned song "On the Way Home" at a night devoted to remembering the 30th anniversary of the "Summer of Love" (McGraw, "United"). Organizers saw no contradiction in re-purposing the LSD-laced summer of 1967 in Haight-Ashbury into a nostalgic call for spiritual renewal, showing that historical memory could be redeemed as well as souls. In the minds of the organizers, the dissidence witnessed during the decade was an eternal yearning for salvation rather than an earthly youth revolt. Any search for authenticity in the 1960s that had not led to Jesus had been (or would be, in the eternal sense) subsequently discredited. Referring to Furay's appearance at the Crusade, Greg Laurie told an interviewer, "The fulfillment of the ideals of the '60s—the peace, joy, and innocence of purpose—could not be found in drugs, sex, and rock 'n' roll." Underscoring Furay's song, Laurie stated that the ideals could only be reached "in coming home to God" (McGraw, "United"). In this version of events, the tumult of the 1960s—the Civil Rights movement, the student movement, the riots of 1965 and 1968, the Vietnam War, and the Great Society—receded in importance behind the effect of a great revival that brought order to a lost generation through religious belief.

Laurie's willingness to accept the accoutrements of youth culture gave him a tremendous advantage in addressing young people. Sinclair Lewis may have parodied ministers' attempts to appeal to youth in Elmer Gantry's promise that his church-sponsored youth group would "take the *wreck* out of recreation and make it re-creation," but Laurie capitalized on his own participation in that great symbol of generational revolt, "the Sixties," to establish credibility within the youth vernacular (Lewis 286). To Laurie, the youth of the 1960s and 1990s shared similar worlds. Laurie continued Calvary Chapel's tradition of suturing "countercultural" styles—casual dress, long hair, contemporary music—to a fundamentalist, Bible-believing religious message. Organizers hoped the religiously inspired youth culture of the Crusade would secure, rather than sever, family bonds and would induce self-discipline and self-control in suburban kids. The willingness to engage with popular culture was evident in Laurie's sermons at the crusade. Celebrity, fame, and Laurie's own youthful experimentation with drugs became the basis for cautionary parables about modern life. For example, Laurie mentioned rapper Tupac Shakur's death at the Los Angeles youth jam in 1996. Shakur was murdered, but Laurie nonetheless noted the sense of doom in his work, saying that Shakur often "sang of his hopeless and empty condition." Laurie also drew upon his early pre-conversion years, when he was both "in the world *and of* the world." He talked about his experimentation with drugs and confided,

> People get into drugs, drinking, sex, partying, even joining gangs because they are empty inside. Jesus says "I love you." He'll fill that void inside you. Before I became a Christian, I thought using drugs would make me more aware. Well, I was aware, but what I was aware of was how empty I was! (Harvest Crusades, "Live" 1996)

Returning to current cultural events, Laurie criticized the Smashing Pumpkins' song "Bullet with Butterfly Wings" for its lyrics ("Despite all my rage, I'm still just a rat in a cage/And I still believe that I cannot be saved"). He told the audience:

> But that is wrong! You can be saved! God can save you. Maybe you feel like a rat in a cage. Maybe you are out there right now, searching for answers. Christianity is not just some brand of toothpaste, you know! You have a choice! (Harvest Crusades, "Live")

Laurie's 1996 talk typified his Harvest Crusade sermons. Rather than prohibiting gang membership, sexual activity, and drug use through stern lecturing, the sermons stressed that teenagers were capable of making the right choices.

In addition to offering a counter narration of the counterculture and a direct appeal to young people, the Crusade provided white evangelicals with a chance to understand their everyday consumer habits as acts of sacralization. This, in turn, allowed evangelicals to claim a degree of cultural leadership in suburban society. In 1994, an evangelical commentator argued that Christians had to regulate their consumption of popular culture because:

> everything we do is a witness to what we believe. The clothes we wear, the cars we drive, the homework we do and the music we buy are all witnesses to our basic values. We tell other people what we believe by everything that we do. (Schultze 46–48)

The author emphasized the obligations and opportunities that consumer society posed for devout believers. The Great Commission, a directive symbolic of Christians' chosen status, required Christians to produce the best possible culture and to lead others by consuming the best. By this logic, even attending a concert became a form of "witnessing," since Christians were "telling others what music is worthwhile and of value" and "casting [their] cultural allegiance with particular groups, artists, or companies" (Schultze 46–48). Far from impeding devout belief, consumerism offered believers an effective means for reproducing their creed in others.

The sacralization of popular culture began well before Laurie delivered his sermon. The event replicated the "family-friendly" recreational atmosphere familiar to its middle-class audience: lively music, friendly ushers, crowd interaction, fireworks and even the JumboTron. At each turn, however, organizers reminded the crowd that their focus should remain fixed on the religious message (McDannell 222–223). The enthusiastically interactive nature of the Crusades was made clear in the Internet broadcasts created for people who were unable to attend the event. In 1996, 8,000 virtual concertgoers followed the Anaheim Crusade through a typed transcript and slide show (Gale). The broadcasters emphasized the crowd's enthusiasm during the early parts of the concert:

> 7:50 – The Kry has the crowd on its feet clapping and praising the Lord to "Let's Stand Together." The Stadium is now almost completely filled. This is the best attendance of any Harvest Crusade to date. Praise God! The boom camera pans in and captures close-ups of the musicians. . . The image is displayed on the big JumboTron. . . it's like being on stage! The Kry just reminded all of us that, all that is being said here, all that's being done here, it's all for the purpose of glorifying JESUS CHRIST!!! Praise God! (Harvest Crusades, "Live. . . Thursday, July 4th")

The transcript recounted all of the elements of a stadium concert: the excited crowd, the band with a big sound, and a camera crew to enliven the stage experience. However, the broadcasters and bands wanted their audience to remember that this was not mere consumerism: the band warned participants to keep God at the center of their experience. They were witnessing through the event, and the success of the event would be proportional to its spirit.

Evangelicals' desire to proselytize through consumer culture led them to Disneyland, the happiest place on earth. In 1996, Harvest Ministries held a one-day event at Disneyland offering a perfectly synergized blend of religion and consumerism. The organization's website captured evangelicals' use of consumer culture as a means for evangelism when it described the event as a day when "the good news of God's kingdom was proclaimed in the magic kingdom" (Harvest Crusades, "Disneyland"). Joined on stage by musicians such as The Kry and Lou Gramm, Laurie delivered his message from the Rivers of America on Tom Sawyer's Island to an estimated evening crowd of 12,000. In the previous week's church bulletin, Pastor Rick Myers had written about the significance of the event with great anticipation:

> One of the exciting things to do as a kid growing up was going to Disneyland. . . Truly, Disneyland was the happiest place on earth; a place where you could escape the real world. . . In the early years of Disneyland the tickets were sold in packets with each packet having a certain amount of letter tickets, A, B, C, D, and E. . . Of course, the best rides were the E ticket rides. . . . Well, here we are in May of 1996 and before us is an opportunity to have an E ticket day at Disneyland. Never before has any group gone into the Magic Kingdom with the express purpose to preach the gospel. So ask an unsaved family member or friend to Harvest Day at Disneyland,

and who knows they may have an E ticket ride into God's kingdom. On second thought, I think the E ticket stands for "Eternity!" And the happiest place on earth is in the heart of a new believer. (Harvest Crusades, "Disneyland")

Some might see the Disneyland event as evidence of secularization or even sacrilege: here was a perfect example of sacred beliefs being expressed in the consumer vernacular. Event organizers, however, viewed the event as a significant act of sacralization of both time and space. Clearly, the pastor was not a man who believed that consumer culture was intrinsically evil. By eagerly melding the cheerful atmosphere of the "magic kingdom" with the message of "God's kingdom"—and by skirting the negative connotation that the word "magic" denoted to some Christian believers—the Crusade had an opportunity to turn a one-day park pass into an eternal commitment. Rather than robbing religion of its meaning, organizers believed that they were adding import to what would otherwise be a fun—but spiritually empty—outing.

The Cultural Politics of the Harvest Crusade

Harvest Ministries, the organization that sponsored the Harvest Crusade, did not venture directly into electoral politics, but the organization's cultural politics endorsed a decidedly conservative view of society as it attempted to proselytize young people. Thus, the political significance of the Christian conservatives' culture rested not in its direct relationship to political activism, but rather in its support of the dominant conservatism of the era: first, in its preference for individual conversion over structural reform in achieving social change, the Crusade implicitly accepted neo-liberal economic themes; and second, in its call for the restoration of "traditional family values," the Crusade echoed the demands of normative conservatives.

In the first instance, the Harvest Crusade's message of self-reliance and individualism provided a justification for the era's dominant political and cultural ethos. This was, after all, a period when the Reagan, Bush, and Clinton administrations rolled back New Deal and Great Society programs aimed at achieving some measure of economic redistribution. The event consistently told concertgoers that the answers to society's problems rested in the renewed religious commitment of individuals. It is clear that Laurie believed that social change could only be achieved through individual conversion. In a 1993 letter to the editor, Laurie argued, "Throughout history, revivals have done more good for society than any moral reform or social campaign ever did." Laurie maintained that this was the case because the revivals have "dealt with changing the person before trying to change the person's environment. To do it the other way around is to place the proverbial cart before the horse" (Letter). A few weeks earlier, Laurie told the *Orange County Register*, "I'm striking at the root of the problem. Instead of dwelling on social issues I try to get to the heart of the matter by helping people establish a personal relationship with God" (Wagner).

In the second instance, the Harvest Crusade's message of family values, which reflected a white suburban cultural sensibility, echoed the calls of other conservatives in American society during the 1980s and 1990s. The Crusade's celebration of the emotionally powerful categories of family and nation—as well as its disdain for mundane categories such as government—proved to be an irresistible combination for conservative political operatives searching for audiences likely to yield a high percentage of GOP votes. In August 1992, concertgoers heard a pre-recorded message from President George Bush. One adviser explained Bush's desire to speak to the gathering: "It will be the Judeo-Christian, traditional family values coalition that gets Bush elected. And this is probably the largest Christian gathering in California each year" ("Bush"). With the family values debate raging on the national scene, Bush assured the crowd of where he stood on the issue: "There are four principles that inspire us: freedom, family, faith, and fellowship" (Horan). The four principles may have seemed harmless enough but, within a month, Bush presided over a Republican National Convention during which Pat Buchanan condemned the recent riots in Los Angeles and declared a "cultural war" that urged American voters to "take back our cities, take back our culture and take back our country" (2544). As Buchanan demonized the underclass of the inner city, Bush sentimentalized the middle-class suburban family. Of course, both speeches were aimed at the same audience: adults attending the Crusade could find comfort in the notion that, by attending the revival, they were reinforcing the bonds of family while infusing American suburbs with Christian witness.

The Crusade showed a consistent concern for the plight of the American nuclear family. Laurie's sermons on the topic were unmistakable jeremiads. At the Crusade's Fourth of July concert in 1996, Laurie urged:

With the breakdown of the society, crime on the street and the dissolution of the American family, we're going to have to turn back the clock. Only through changing people's hearts through God's promise are we going to get America back on track. (McGraw, "Join")

After Bush gave his speech in 1992, Laurie, a registered Republican, downplayed the political effect of Bush's message but nonetheless proceeded to echo the President's emphasis on the interconnection between religion, freedom, and family in his own sermon. Laurie told the *Orange County Register* that "The family can survive without the nation, but the nation can't survive without the family." Echoing Dan Quayle's recent condemnation of the "lawless social anarchy" exhibited in the Los Angeles riots, Laurie stated that many of the country's problems were "directly connected to the breakdown of the family" (Weber, "Crusade").

The national "breakdown of the family" had local implications. While much of the Harvest Crusade's message focused on reinforcing the bonds of individual family lives, organizers believed that the call for "family values" could have a larger social effect. In this part of its message, which was not addressed to youth, the Crusade called upon evangelicals to become "social parents" who would infuse American suburbs with Christian witness (Berlant 76). After all, parenthood—a social unit established by God—was clearly more critical than that of the earthly political activist.

Conclusion

Critical media accounts of the conservative movement often portray its impetus as negative, reactionary, or delusional—that is, as backlash or false consciousness— rather than as a social movement with a persuasive ideological core.[4] Yet the regulation of the home—a site that could unify nationalism, individualism, and values— provided the moral core of the conservative movement. The valorization of the middle- class white family required a connection between emotional themes such as nation, duty, authority, and tradition and economic themes of competitive individualism, anti- taxation, and anti-government (Hall). The suburban Christian conservatives of the late 20th century provided critical groundwork in this area, and they did so by embracing— rather than condemning—suburban cultural forms. Popular culture allowed believers to proselytize among young people and to offer models of "Christian" behavior expressed in contemporary vernacular. Revivals, in turn, became part of a broader infrastructure for locating conservative voters, as political operatives searched for cultural events that would mobilize a disproportionate percentage of conservative voters. The Christian revivalism of the 1990s therefore became a form of activism for Christ—a way of witnessing God's message to suburbia in its own idiom.

Notes

1. Richard Viguerie, *The Guardian* (New York) (1 Apr. 1981), cited in Davis 171.

2. Lassiter 7. For other case studies of middle-class political culture in the late 20th century, see Kruse; or Nicolaides.

3. For a general review of American revivalism, see McLoughlin.

4. For a discussion of this tendency, see Wiener.

Works cited

Apostolidis, Paul. *Stations of the Cross: Adorno and Christian Right Radio.* Durham, NC: Duke UP, 2000.

Berlant, Lauren. *The Queen of America Goes to Washington City: Essays on Sex and Citizenship.* Durham, NC: Duke UP, 1997.

Brownfield, Paul. "A Topic of Conversation." *Los Angeles Times* 25 Nov. 1997, Orange County ed.: F.

Buchanan, Patrick. "The Election is About Who We Are." *Congressional Quarterly Weekly Report* 22 Aug. 1992: 2544.

"Bush to Talk by Telephone Sunday with Crusade." *Orange County Register* 1 Aug. 1992: B.

Davis, Mike. *Prisoners of the American Dream: Politics and Economy in the History of the U.S. Working Class.* New York: Verso, 1986.

Gale, Elaine. "Crusade Uses Web to Let Believers Attend in Spirit." *Los Angeles Times* 23 July 1999, Orange County ed.: B.

Ginsburg, Faye D. *Contested Lives: The Abortion Debate in an American Community.* Berkeley: U of California P, 1984.

Green, John C., James L. Guth, and Kevin Hill. "Faith and Election: The Christian Right in Political Campaigns, 1978–1988." *Journal of Politics* 55 (Feb. 1993): 85.

Hall, Stuart. "The Great Moving Right Show." *The Politics of Thatcherism.* Eds. Stuart Hall, and Martin Jaques. London: Lawrence and Wishert, 1983. 29.

Harvest Crusades. "Harvest Night at Disneyland." (1996), 5 Apr. 2003 <http://web.archive.org/web/19970104175607/harvest.org/crusades/harvestnight.html>.

———. "Live at the Harvest Crusades." (1996), 26 Apr. 1999 <http://www.harvest.org/crusades/11_19.html>.

———. "Live at the Harvest Crusades: Thursday, July 4th." (1996), 26 Apr. 1999 <http://www.harvest.og/crusades/thu.html>.

———. "Past Crusades." (1997), 1 May 1999 <http://www.harvest.org/crusades/past/1997/body.htm>.

Horan, Andrew. "A Song in Their Hearts." *Orange County Register* 3 Aug. 1992: A.

Kling, Rob, and Clark Turner. "The Information Labor Force." *Postsuburban California: The Transformation of Orange County Since World War II.* Eds. Rob Kling, Spencer Olin, and Mark Foster. Los Angeles: U of California P, 1991. 92–141.

Kruse, Kevin M. *White Flight: Atlanta and the Making of Modern Conservatism.* Princeton, NJ: Princeton UP, 2005.

Lassiter, Matthew. *The Silent Majority: Suburban Politics in the Sunbelt South.* Princeton, NJ: Princeton UP, 2006.

Letter. *Los Angeles Times* 5 Sept. 1993, Orange County ed.: B.

Lewis, Sinclair. *Elmer Gantry.* New York: Harcourt, 1927. New York: New American Library, 1970.

McDannell, Colleen. *Material Christianity: Religion and Popular Culture in America.* New Haven, CT: Yale UP, 1995.

McDougal, Dennis. "'Building Highways in the Skyways': Old-Time Religion Meets High-Tech Media World." *Los Angeles Times* 9 Feb. 1985.

McGraw, Carol. "Harvest Crusade Begins Tonight." *Orange County Register* 14 Aug. 1997: B.

———. "Join in Praise: A Fire and Brimstone Night." *Orange County Register* 5 July 1996: B.

———. "United in Faith at Harvest Crusade." *Orange County Register* 15 Aug. 1997: A.

McLoughlin, William G., Jr. *Modern Revivalism: Charles Grandison Finney to Billy Graham.* New York: Ronald, 1959.

Nicolaides, Becky M. *My Blue Heaven: Life and Politics in the Working-Class Suburbs of Los Angeles, 1920–1965.* Chicago: U of Chicago P, 2002.

Peterson, Susan. "Irvine Gay-Rights Vote Might Have Broader Effect." *Orange County Register* 30 Oct. 1989: B.

Phan, Hieu Tran. "Message is Music to Their Ears." *Orange County Register* 17 Aug. 1997: B.

Phillips, Kevin. *The Emerging Republican Majority.* New Rochelle, NY: Arlington, 1969.

Rivenburg, Roy. "A Cool Crusader." *Los Angeles Times* 10 July 1994, Orange County ed.: E.

Schneider, William. "The Suburban Century Begins." *The Atlantic Monthly* July 1992: 35.

Schultze, Quentin J. "Witnessing with our Music." *CCM* Feb. 1994: 46–48.

Smith, Christian, with Michael Emerson, Sally Gallagher, Paul Kennedy, and David Sikkink. *American Evangelicalism: Embattled and Thriving.* Chicago: U of Chicago P, 1998.

Smith, Lynn. "Operation Rescue Plans More Protests." *Los Angeles Times* 22 Apr. 1989, Orange County ed.

Wagner, Venise. "Crusade Expecting Bountiful Harvest." *Orange County Register* 23 July 1993: B.

Wiener, Jon. "Working Class Republicans and 'False Consciousness.'" *Dissent* Spring 2005: 55–58.

Weber, Tracy. "Crusade Expected to Draw 90,000 to Anaheim Stadium." *Orange County Register* 31 July 1992: B.

———. "Revival Concert Offers Christianity as an Encore." *Orange County Register* 16 Aug. 1990: A.

Thamyris/Intersecting No. 25 (2012) 169–186

Civilizing Missions

Rebecca Kugel

"[T]o Labor in the midst of heathenism and where the errors of the
Romish Church prevail"
— Hall to Greene, 2 June 1841

Central to the interconnected projects of nation-state building and colonization that have preoccupied Western Europe since the 15th century were notions of "the civil." Subjects of empire, that is, the "Natives," who existed on every continent and island to which Europeans ventured, be it the Americas, Africa, Asia or the Pacific, were seen to be in the direst need both of Christianization and civilization. As embodiments of their nation-state's religious orthodoxy, but also as exemplars of its civil society, missionaries were thus absolutely critical to the colonial project. And since "Christianity" began dividing, zygote-like, into multiple denominations during these same centuries, and as different Christian traditions became associated with emerging nation-states (the Church of England and its arch-rival, the holy Catholic faith of Spain, are obvious examples of this association), missionaries hurried to save heathen souls from the wrong form of Christianity as well as from the clutches of the prince of darkness, a fact of some relevance to this study.

This essay probes one particular colonial encounter between Anglo-American missionaries and aboriginal peoples in the U.S./Canadian border region of the western Great Lakes in the early decades of the 19th century (1823–1850). The ramifications of this modest colonial encounter in a small, out-of-the-way corner of the empire are nevertheless significant and instructive. The global project of constructing the "civil" is revealed as an exercise in cultural cloning as missionaries sought, both consciously and unconsciously, to replicate their specific culture—its religion, language, political and educational institutions obviously but, often unconsciously, also its subtler cultural forms, gender roles and racial categorizations—onto the bodies and into the minds of Native peoples.

The cultural assault on Native peoples is fairly well recognized as a central component of the civilizing mission, but it is worth considering how completely interconnected the different elements of the missionary project were. They challenged every aspect of Native life though, paradoxically, missionaries themselves often did not recognize how deeply their civilizing/Christianizing projects would reach into the most mundane and intimate areas of daily Native life. This paper examines two broad interconnections, probing how missionary efforts to introduce their religion affected, first, Native political institutions and governance and, second, intruded into pre-existing tribal constructions of ethnic and national identity. In both instances, the consequences were unintended, but completely consistent with the replicating nature of the missionary enterprise. Indeed, the metaphor of cloning, of complete and exact duplication, is strikingly apt in describing the missionaries' expectations. Anglo-American missionaries anticipated the complete cultural and personal transformation of indigenous peoples, expectations they viewed as flowing naturally from their particular form of evangelical Protestantism, which emphasized the spiritual rebirth and personal transformation of the "saved" individual.

At the same time, it is critical to recognize that Native peoples found many of the missionaries' demands utterly incomprehensible, if not life-threatening and dangerous. To continue the cloning metaphor, the colonial project was never simply a process of replication onto willing and passive subjects; it was always contested. If indigenous peoples welcomed missionaries into their communities, they did so for their own reasons, which were only rarely concerned with having missionaries "tell them about God, Jesus Christ, and heaven" and extol the benefits of male-dominated market-oriented agriculture (Boutwell, "Diary" 19 June 1832).

Constructing the "Indian"
The missionaries' understandings of Native Americans were, not surprisingly, inaccurate and built on imagery and assumptions about North America's Native peoples that were old in Anglo-American culture by the 1830s. Native peoples were understood to be nomadic hunters who roamed aimlessly across a wilderness landscape eking out a living that was Hobbesian in its nastiness, shortness and brutality. Women, as Anglo-Americans endlessly liked to point out, were grossly oppressed in "the savage state." In an early report back to Boston headquarters, the missionaries described one Native people, the Ojibwes, in language that faithfully reproduced these assumptions. The Ojibwes were "extremely improvident people," they observed, who lacked plow agriculture and thus could cultivate only "small gardens," in contrast to large mono-crop fields. "[T]hey build no permanent houses but live in small temporary lodges," the missionaries intoned, "their food is of the coarsest kind" and their

clothing "wrought into garments in the rudest manner possible." The men were "extremely indolent" and nearly all "labor [was] performed by the women." Worst of all, "they have no idea of the value of property" (Hall and Boutwell, 1833).

Even more noteworthy than the repetition of the stereotype is the fact that the missionaries used the generic term "Indians" throughout this report, even though they knew the name of the indigenous people they were describing. This word usage was not innocent or coincidental. By the early 19th century, the construct of the "Indian" was so naturalized in Anglo- American discourse that the ABCFM missionaries rarely used tribal names. Although they maintained missions among such culturally diverse and geographically far-flung Native nations as the Cherokees in Georgia, Senecas in New York, Nez Perces in Idaho and Osages in Arkansas, they referred to them all as "Indians." On one very important level, then, the first form of cloning to which indigenous New World peoples were subjected involved replacing the diversity of their nationalities and cultures with the flattened and interchangeable and, as the 19th century progressed, increasingly racialized identity of the "Indian." That Anglo-Americans inherited this construct from their own colonial forebears serves as a reminder of the overlapping objectives of the multiple colonial projects visited upon North America and its peoples.

In ironic contrast to both the cultural sameness of the missionaries, and their intellectual constructs of generic "Indians," the indigenous peoples of the western Great Lakes were far from homogenous. In the 1830s, the region was home to Ojibwes, Odawas, Potawatomis, Menominis, Ho-chunks and Dakotas (the latter two called "Winnebagoes" and "Sioux" at the time), as well as eastern immigrant tribes, among them Oneidas, Stockbridges, Munsees, and Brothertons. Though many spoke Algonkian languages of varying degrees of mutual intelligibility, others spoke Siouan and Iroquoian languages. They were members of politically autonomous and politically fluid tribal nations. They lived in varying ecosystems and traded the differing products of those ecosystems with each other. They practiced religious ceremonies in different ways, accorded their leaders different forms of authority, reckoned kinship differently, dressed differently and wore their hair in different styles (Tanner 144). Indeed, according to one knowledgeable observer, "marked and peculiar differences" among Native nations were so obvious that it was easy to tell indigenous people's nationalities just by looking at them. The nation with whom the ABCFM would have most of its dealings called itself "The Spontaneously Created Beings," or "Anishinabeg." The other tribal peoples of the region identified them as "Ojibwes," a name that probably referred to the political visibility of one kin group, the Crane Clan.[1]

Constructing the "Frontier"

The missionaries who sought to bring God and civilization to the western Great Lakes were New Englanders. They were sponsored by the prestigious and well-funded

American Board of Commissioners for Foreign Missions (or ABCFM), a Boston-based umbrella organization of evangelical Protestants with a truly global presence of its own—it maintained missions in China, Lebanon and Hawaii as well as among a dozen Native American nations (Berkhofer 3). The global vision of their parent organization notwithstanding, the missionaries who departed for the Great Lakes were extremely parochial. All were members of the same religious denomination, a stern Calvinist Congregationalism; two of the four men had been educated at the same seminary. Culturally, they could truly be called Anglo-American; they were descended from English colonists who had arrived in New England in the 17th century. Two hundred years later, they still identified themselves by their towns of origin in Massachusetts, New Hampshire and Vermont and, while they could be nationalistic enough, their point of reference for societal perfection was still New England.[2] For instance, they praised a particular prairie in Wisconsin where hay "may be made with as little trouble as hay in New England," and complained that "[t]here are no New England taverns here, at which the traveler can rest . . . and find supplies for all his wants." Even the weather came in for comparison. One of their number, William T. Boutwell, likened the "pleasant" weather in Minnesota to "a real New England June day." New England's class hierarchy—where ministers still occupied the highest rungs of the social ladder regardless of their relative lack of material wealth—also shaped their definitions of what constituted the "civil." They arrived in the western Great Lakes believing their religious authority entitled them not only to membership in, but also to leadership of, the local social elite. Theirs was a Whiggish evangelism. They would remake the "perishing heathen" from the top down.[3]

Missionization efforts at "preaching Christ to the Indians" began in earnest in spring 1831. A small group of six, two married couples (of which only the men were actually regarded as missionaries) and two single men, embarked from New England for the fur trade town of LaPointe, on the southern shore of Lake Superior in present-day Wisconsin. It was an intensely self-conscious journey. These missionaries were keenly aware of themselves as figures acting in history, both religious and secular, performing momentous acts that would be memorialized in later times. They solemnly recorded their many firsts for posterity: they preached the first sermon ever heard, they built the first schoolhouse ever constructed, their party included the first white women in the western Great Lakes.[4]

But if the ABCFM missionaries saw themselves as part of a worldwide evangelizing effort, they were also heirs to specifically Anglo-American constructs of space and history. They described themselves in quintessentially American terms as "pioneers" journeying through an "unbroken wilderness." Native peoples, too, were reconfigured into the familiar trope of untouched primitives. The missionaries not only traveled "beyond the limits of civilization," but also they anticipated "Indians who are remote" and "but little effected by intercourse with white men." Such descriptions blithely ignored the 200 years of prior French and British colonization of the North American interior. Creating this imagined wilderness was a critical part of the process of replicating Anglo-American culture, in particular replicating its ways of knowing, and its sense of history and memory, onto a landscape that told another story. The process was not seamless, however, and the missionaries' many struggles to mesh their imaginary with the reality of the western Great Lakes reveal how the process of cultural cloning worked and how Native peoples contested it.[5]

The first reality that the missionaries reconstructed was their solitary journey into the "distant and dreary wilderness." In spite of the impression they left in their writings, they did not, in fact, travel alone. They made their journey in the company of over 70 people comprising the American Fur Company's brigade on its annual spring supply run. The head traders, or factors; their clerks; the voyageurs, the trade's crucial labor force; plus family members of everyone; made up the brigade as it wound its way through the rivers and lakes of the North American interior to the towns on the shores of Lakes Superior, Michigan and Huron. With names such as La Pointe and Sault Ste. Marie, these towns were obvious reminders that the region had been a French colony, a part of the province of Quebec, in fact, just as the fur trade itself indicated that the colony had long been enmeshed in a global and highly profitable mercantile system of exchange. Had the Reverends Sherman Hall or William T. Boutwell stopped to give it any thought, they would have realized that French Jesuit missionaries had been preaching the gospel in the Great Lakes region since Fathers Isaac Jogues and Charles Raymbault established the first mission at Sault Ste. Marie in the 1640s (about the same time the earliest of their own Puritan ancestors arrived in New England, incidentally). French missionaries had also constructed schools and there had even been the occasional French female settler among the colonists. Quite obviously, the New Englanders were not the first European-descended, racially-constructed "white" people in the Great Lakes region. Just as obviously, the indigenous peoples of the Great Lakes had long experience with Europeans.[6]

But the Reverends Hall and Boutwell did not stop to give it any thought, and they and their fellow missionaries were genuinely and repeatedly surprised to find evidence of a prior and lengthy European presence in their "boundless wilderness." Their journey to LaPointe first took them through two larger fur trade towns at Mackinac Island and Sault Ste. Marie (both in present-day Michigan) where the evidences of civilization were indeed striking. The missionaries remarked on the substantial frame houses of the prosperous head factors and commented wonderingly on their fine personal libraries and the number of newspapers to which they subscribed. They noted approvingly that these men had land under cultivation and kept domesticated livestock, conforming to Anglo-American concepts of proper land use. The social hierarchy of "gentlemen and common men" in fur trade society, analogous to their own understanding of "the minister, the school master, the blacksmith, [and] the shoe maker," was also reassuringly familiar. Their eventual destination, the fur trade town of LaPointe, was another surprise. Almost 130 years old in 1832, it supported a population of several hundred people. It "appeared like a small village," Sherman Hall conceded, noting it contained "houses, stores, barns and out buildings." There were even "40 or 50 acres of land under cultivation." All in all, the missionaries concluded, rather bewildered, that the frontier was "much more pleasant than we had anticipated."[7]

Wilderness towns might be a troubling contradiction, calling into question the missionaries' construction of civilization, but it was obvious that the Native peoples of the Great Lakes were not Christianized. Here the missionaries' understanding of civilization and Christianity as inseparably intertwined and mutually supporting institutions revealed its elastic intellectual strength. Although they could imagine civilizations that were not Christian in religion (they had the historic examples of ancient Greece and Rome as proof of this), they could not believe that any society, once Christianized, could exist without what they called "civilization." Civil society, as the missionaries imagined it, rested on market-oriented agriculture conducted on family farms privately owned by senior males. These household heads, while they performed farm labor themselves, more importantly controlled the labor of their subordinates—their wives, unmarried sons and daughters, and servants of both genders. While sons and arguably even male servants might eventually marry and acquire land of their own, the women of these families remained lifelong economic dependents, their work undervalued and confined to the household and barnyard. So inextricably were Protestant religion and patriarchal agriculture combined in the missionary imagination that they assumed Native peoples could only accept them together as a package. One of their number, Edmund F. Ely, captured the missionaries' confident expectations when he enthused, "When God converts them, they will flock to their homes and farms."[8]

Cloning Native Political Leadership

Having constructed a universalized vision of a wilderness frontier inhabited by universalized "Indians," the missionaries would collapse the cultures of distinct Native peoples, such as the Ojibwes, into yet another generic frame. Reflecting their prior experience in dealing with indigenous peoples in the United States and elsewhere, as well as Federal Indian policy that regarded Native-held territory as legally distinct and independent from American territory, the ABCFM governing board instructed its personnel to work within existing aboriginal political systems as they began missionary work. The need to work with the indigenous leadership of the communities they hoped to evangelize did not mean, however, that the missionaries understood tribal governance. Quite the contrary; the four missionaries brought to the Great Lakes a construct of Native political organization and leadership as flattened and generic as

their larger idea of the "Indian." Ironically, the origins of Anglo-American understandings of Native polities and governance owed much to the observations of some of the
missionaries' own Puritan ancestors, among them Roger Williams, a careful though
not altogether accurate observer of Native New England life. Over the two centuries
since Williams wrote in the 1630s, Anglo-Americans had refined their understanding
of Native governance to reflect both what they perceived as truth and what they
desired might be true.[9]

The attribute of Native leadership that most forcibly engaged and troubled Anglo-
Americans and their European forbearers as well was its lack of coercive authority,
particularly when compared to the ways they expected to see governmental authority
embodied and enacted. Native leaders did not possess greater wealth than most
other tribal members, nor could they forcibly compel the obedience of their people;
they did not monopolize the use of state violence by means of a legal system and
courts or a large standing military force. Although Native leaders employed a wide
range of sanctions, it was nevertheless true that they governed far differently than
either European monarchs or later Anglo-American democratic republicans. The idea
that Native leaders possessed little authority and could exert only minimal control
over their people was so embedded in Anglo-American cultural constructions of the
"Indian" that missionaries Hall and Boutwell had no trouble immediately situating
Ojibwe leadership within the trope. In their first report back to Boston in 1833, they
described the Ojibwe leader as one who "acts more as an adviser than as a king"
(Hall and Boutwell).

Having defined Native leadership in these sweeping terms, Anglo-Americans also
named tribal leaders and described a form of generic governmental structure they
believed was possessed by all Native peoples. The various leadership terms from
earlier centuries, such as "werowance," "sachem" and "sagamore," that had been
borrowed from Native languages and by their multiplicity alone suggested diverse
responsibilities and levels of authority, had been collapsed into yet another easily
replicated category. All Native leaders had become known by a single English-
language word, as "chiefs." Such men possessed attributes in common across tribal
lines. They rose to power in the same way, either obtaining "considerable influence"
or else "not much regard," depending on their personal abilities. While they were not
hereditary leaders, as Anglo-Americans noted self-consciously, neither were they
elected democratically. A chief governed with the assistance of "a council" of "his
men" with whom he "consulted" on important issues. This image of loose-knit forest
patriarchy allowed Anglo-Americans to position themselves between extremes of
governance, the hated monarchy on one hand and the equally unpalatable savage
chieftaincy on the other. It also reflected their view that Native women had no political
role or presence, except as passive witnesses to the deeds of males, a situation that
was almost always at odds with Native realities, but neatly supported the oft-asserted

Anglo-American belief that Native women were oppressed and degraded in indigenous societies.[10]

Because they focused on Native leaders' lack of European-style coercive power, Anglo-Americans paid little attention to the actual workings of power within Native societies. Their attempts to treat Ojibwe leaders according to their construct of a chief and his followers, rather than trying to learn about the actual leadership positions and dynamics, would ultimately undermine the entire missionary project. While the ABCFM missionaries reported serious difficulties with Ojibwe leaders in each village where they established missions, the experiences of Edmund F. Ely present a particularly vivid instance.

In 1836, Ely sought to expand his mission station at the Ojibwe village of Fond du Lac, in eastern Minnesota. He soon found himself embroiled in controversy when he insisted on conducting the negotiations for buying land upon which to enlarge the mission with a particular village political figure, Mang'osid. Ely considered Mang'osid to be the "Chief, appointed by government," a statement that neatly reveals the missionary's understanding of Ojibwe politics. Since the American government had recognized Mang'osid as the "chief," Ely expected him to display the political attributes of the Anglo-American construct of an "Indian chief." He furthermore expected the Fond du Lac villagers to recognize Mang'osid's American-sanctioned authority. He was deeply and genuinely perplexed when he came to realize that the other villagers, far from recognizing Mang'osid's authority, openly contested it. The issue of a land sale was at the heart of much of the villagers' unease with Mang'osid, who had spent a decade cultivating friendly relationships with a number of American officials, but many villagers were also troubled by a second compelling issue. These villagers believed Mang'osid had assumed power that was not rightfully his, relying on his connections with American officials, rather than the villagers themselves, to enforce his claim to political pre-eminence. Ely was stunned when he realized that the Fond du Lac community contended within itself over such serious political issues as the legitimate exercise of political power. His view of Native politics was predictably flat and generic, reflecting the Anglo-American construction of Native politics that saw little political authority and accordingly assumed that there was little political activity. After five contentious years, the Fond du Lac community succeeded in forcing the missionary to leave. Although he was a close observer of village life and Ojibwe culture during those years, Ely never grasped the Ojibwe political process, nor did he learn how to work within it.[11]

Ojibwe Counterpoint

In spite of Edmund Ely's failure at Fond du Lac, neither he nor any of his fellow missionaries ever abandoned the idea that conversion and civilization had to be accomplished inseparably from one another. Enmeshed as they were in their own culturally constructed reality, it did not occur to them that Native peoples might seek to appropriate some elements of the program they offered to put to their own uses. Among the Ojibwes, in whose villages the missionaries ultimately established a number of missions, there were several views regarding the missionaries' presence. Certain Ojibwe leaders sought political ties with the United States and hoped that, by inviting American missionaries into their communities, they could solidify an alliance with the new political power in the region. Other Ojibwes, well aware of the potentialities inherent in literacy, encouraged missionaries to establish schools in their communities.[12] This latter position was popular with much of the fur trade community as well. Head factors assisted missionaries in moving to and settling into Ojibwe villages. They transported their possessions, provided them with board and lodging in their houses, raised funds to pay teachers' salaries and, most importantly, enrolled their own children in the fledgling missions' schools.[13]

While the missionaries did not imagine that Native people would attempt to pick and chose among their offerings, at every village where missionaries settled, Ojibwes sought to make clear that this was exactly what they had in mind. At Leech Lake in Minnesota, an Ojibwe father named Butterfly was "very glad" when William T. Boutwell offered to teach his son to read and write over the winter of 1833-34. "'[C]ould my son be taught to read as the white people read,'" said Butterfly, "'. . . I don't know what I could do for you.'" Yet at the same time, Butterfly gave instructions to the fur trader with whom his son would board, that Boutwell was "not to learn him prayers, in either English, French or Indian" (Boutwell to Greene 18 Dec. 1883). Similarly, the Ojibwes at Yellow Lake in present-day Wisconsin tried to set the missionaries straight at the start, in the process revealing their prior familiarity with the outlines of the argument the missionaries advanced. "They would retain their customs & habits," they told Frederick Ayer in 1833 when he commenced a mission in their village, "If the Great Spirit had designed they should be instructed they would have had his word communicated to them before." Clearly, the Yellow Lake villagers had had enough conversations on religious subjects with Europeans to be familiar with the arguments about cultural change and civilization. That they had also glossed a term, Great Spirit, to describe an indigenous spiritual being in terms comprehensible to Europeans, further revealed that their prior discussions of Christianity had been of some depth and sophistication.[14]

Such blunt assertions disconcerted the ABCFM missionaries, for they had initially been "treated very kindly by the Indians" when they arrived at Ojibwe villages (Ayer to Green 4 Oct. 1833). In their search for explanations, they betrayed no awareness of indigenous wants and needs. In a striking demonstration of the replicative nature of the entire Christianization and civilization project, the missionaries proved incapable of imagining that human beings could have any wants or needs different from their own. The answer to Ojibwe resistance lay not in their commitment to their own culture, but instead in another universalizing construct, one embedded in the very process of conversion to Christianity and, in the missionary view, as old as humanity itself. Ojibwes rejected the message of the gospels, the missionaries realized, because "[a]ll mankind are corrupt by nature," preferring the easy life of sin and "wickedness" over "seek[ing] the Lord Christ & Salvation." To the original sin of pride, the missionaries soon added the baleful influence of the Catholic Church, for it took only a few months' residence in fur trade towns and Ojibwe villages for them to realize that there had been (and continued in their own times to be) a sporadic formal Catholic presence and a lively lay Catholic religiosity in the Great Lakes region. Though this recognition coexisted uneasily with their continued insistence that the region was a wilderness, the Protestant missionaries incorporated western Christianity's bitterest rivalry into their interpretation of Ojibwe reluctance to embrace New England Calvinism. "[I]gnorant, wicked Catholics" "put forth all their efforts" to impede Ojibwe progress toward the "light of pure Christianity."[15]

The Challenges of "Race"
If Native political realities were more complicated than the American Board missionaries anticipated, they were confronted with an equally complex and heterogeneous social reality in the western Great Lakes. They had expected their frontier to be populated by two distinct, exclusive, and easily identifiable racial groups—"Indians" and "whites." While they persistently collapsed Ojibwes, Odawas, Menominis, Ho-chunks and the region's other indigenous nations into the generic, replicable construct of "Indians," the missionaries remained deeply perplexed when they confronted people who could not be understood within their binary construct of "race." The Great Lakes region was home to a large number of such persons, ethnically and racially heterogeneous, the descendants of generations of Native women who had married the men of the fur trade, many though not all of whom were French. Present day scholars know them as the Métis, the French word meaning "mixed-race." But the Métis were not simply the descendants of the fur trade; they remained crucial to its continued operation. They were its self-perpetuating workforce, its multilingual interpreters and its cultural intermediaries.[16]

Métis self-conceptions were variable and contradictory and changed dramatically over time and space. In the early 19th century, individuals and families in the western Great Lakes understood ethnicity in multiple ways. Many considered themselves French; others, such as Elizabeth Thérése Fisher Baird, noted their descent from multiple tribal nations and prominent Native families. Still others, such as the Métis man who talked in 1850 to the visiting German botanist Johann Georg Kohl, proudly displayed their blended ethnicity. This unnamed man "had engraved both his French coat of arms and his Indian totem (an otter) on his seal-ring" (297). And, to the consternation of the missionaries, such identities seemed fluid and changeable. They were situational, dependent upon where people found themselves. Young William Johnston, descendant of a distinguished Anglo-Ojibwe family, described an instance of this situational ethnicity when he related his reception at the village of Leech Lake. Learning "from some remarks that I made" what Johnston's clan, or totem, affiliation was, village members of that same clan "claimed relationship with me." They further behaved as clan mates were supposed to, declaring that Johnston "should partake of what they had" and presenting him with food, "a bag of rice." Such a multiplicity of identities offered the missionaries a profound challenge.[17]

Missionary struggles to grasp the "race" of the Métis population, and their sense of its utter foreignness, are well demonstrated in the several names they used to try to create an identity for this population. Initially, they called them "Frenchmen" and "Canadians" interchangeably, sometimes creatively blending the two as "Canadian Frenchmen." They quickly added racial identifiers, though, referring to "French half-breeds," "mixed breed[s]," and "half-bloods" within a few months of their arrival. Whether racialized or not, the fact remained that Métis identity was fluid and shifting, and could not be easily defined using the missionaries' criteria of distinctly bounded races of "Indians" and "whites."[18]

The fact that the Métis were Catholic further complicated the missionaries' efforts to restructure the social reality of the Great Lakes. Through their religion and their French ancestors, the Métis possessed knowledge of—and laid a claim to—a European heritage. Both by words and cultural practice, they contested missionary interpretations of the "civil." They challenged the missionaries on broad theological points such as infant baptism and the mediatory role of saints. It was more respect-ful to address Jesus through his mother, they argued, a practice that accorded well with Native etiquette, too, incidentally. Especially when one made a request or asked a favor of a powerful spiritual being, polite indirection was far preferable to the missionaries' blunt demands for health, protection and food.[19]

On a second level, the Métis also countered the socioeconomic reorganization at the heart of the missionaries' construct of civilization by demonstrating that their reli-gious tradition was more suited to the harsh realities of Great Lakes life. True to their New England heritage, the missionaries sought to enforce sabbatarian practices of no work or travel on Sundays at the trading posts and indigenous villages where they resided. Such demands could only appear foolhardy, even life threatening, in an envi-ronment where the weather could be ferocious and could change suddenly. Métis Catholicism recognized that, when a blizzard lifted or Lake Superior calmed, travelers broke camp and marched, whether it was Sunday or not. It was no sin against God to seek safety from severe weather as quickly as possible. The missionaries soon learned through painful experience the truth of this, but it rankled that they had had to cede the point. They wrote angrily in their private diaries about the smirks and snide comments they were forced to endure when Métis voyageurs encountered missionaries who were traveling on Sundays. In such a circumstance, Sherman Hall gave vent to the exasperated quote in the title of this paper. "[T]o Labor in the midst of heathenism and where the errors of the Romish Church prevail," he fumed, ". . . is discouraging indeed." In both words and deeds the Métis presented powerful challenges to the missionaries' vision of "the civil" and they knew it. Although their religious ideology told them converting the heathen would be easy "once they could be made to feel the power of the gospel on their hearts," the reality proved different.[20]

Conclusion

In a new and confusing locality, the missionaries sought to contain mutability and replace it with sameness. Although no early 19th century missionary used or even conceptualized a word such as "cloning," their efforts to replicate in the Great Lakes country their idealized version of western culture and one of its religious traditions represented an effort at doing just that. Although the missionaries believed the salvation of human souls was their primary and most compelling objective, they believed with equal fervor that Native peoples must "change their present habits of life for those of civilization." They deeply and willingly implicated themselves in the larger Anglo-American colonization project. "Civilizing" and Christianizing Native peoples were never simply processes of religious and social change; however, they always entailed a drastic shift in power relations. Native peoples would be subordinated, not simply by "bringing them under the influence of the gospel," but also by subjugating them to the temporal power of the United States. While the missionaries never questioned the linkage between these two goals, they anguished over their inability to convert Ojibwes to a religion they fervently believed was universal in its appeal. What they never understood was that Ojibwes recognized early on the colonialist implications inherent in the missionary project.[21]

The ABCFM missionaries had arrived in the western Great Lakes with a well developed understanding of what constituted the "civil," and who the "Indians" were. They also brought with them a constructed history for the region that erased both its indigenous past and its European past, remaking it into that blank slate Americans called a frontier. The reality they encountered was nothing like what they expected and they spent two decades in the region attempting, with very limited success, to transform it and its peoples into that wilderness of their imagination. Their failure is a powerful reminder that the cloning of western religion and culture was always contested. It never proceeded with the smoothness of a surgical operation. Native peoples did not conform to the generic constructs, such as the "Indian" or the "heathen", that the missionaries created for them. Neither did they accept nor or reject each element the missionaries sought to introduce. Their actions were far more complicated, involving complex deflections and reconfigurations of the colonialist challenge to their cultures, religions and life ways. Perhaps this is nowhere better expressed than in two contemporary, contradictory facts: on one hand, the unreal, generic construct of the "Indian" has come to dominate 20th and 21st century Anglo-American discourse about Native peoples; on the other, the Great Lakes region remains home to multiple indigenous communities and a Native population numbering in the tens of thousands. Such a multi-layered reality serves as a caution that the process of replicating western culture is never a foregone conclusion.

Notes

1. For the likely derivation of the name "Ojibwe," see Warren 35–37, 39; see also Hickerson 44; and Schenck 17–28.

2. For towns of origin and education, see American Board 19 June 1832. For Yankee nationalism, see Boutwell, "Diary" 4 July 1834.

3. Ayer to Greene 1 Dec. 1833 ("ease of haymaking" and "perishing heathen"); Hall, "Journal" 5 Aug. 1831 (taverns); Boutwell, "Diary" 21 June 1832 (June weather). For expectations of social leadership, Boutwell to Greene 26 Jan. 1832; and Hall and Boutwell.

4. Greene to Hall and Boutwell 10 June 1831. See also Hall, "Journal" 4 Sept. 1831; Boutwell to Greene 25 June 1832 (first sermon preached); Ayer to Greene 4 Oct. 1833; Hall, "Journal" 13 May 1832 (first "white" women); Ayer to Greene 23 Mar. 1835 and 3 Apr. 1835 (first schoolhouse at given locale); and Hall, "Journal" 5 Aug. 1831 to 26 Sept. 1831 (travel with fur trade brigade).

5. Greene to Hall and Boutwell 10 June 1831 ("pioneers," "Indians who are remote" and "but little effected by intercourse with white men"); Hall and Boutwell ("unbroken wilderness"); Hall, "Journal" 11 Aug, 1831 ("beyond the limits of civilization").

6. Hall to Greene 17 Oct. 1834. For a detailed description of the voyage to LaPointe, including the number of people present, see Hall, "Journal" 5 Aug. 1831 to 26 Sept. 1831. For prior French colonization, see Tanner 36–47. For British colonization, see Tanner 48-67. For LaPointe, see Tanner 32–33. 40–41, and 57–58.

7. Hall, "Journal" 13 Aug. 1831 ("boundless wilderness"); Coe to Evans 23 Nov. 1828 ("Minister, Schoolmaster"); all remaining quotes from Hall, "Journal" 30 Aug. 1831. See also Hall to Greene 14 June 1832 (for cultivated fields and livestock).

8. Ely to Greene 4 Sept. 1839. For a discussion of the ABCFM in its historical and denominational context, see Berkhofer 1–15. For the New England Calvinist tradition in which the ABCFM missionaries were nurtured, see Stout.

9. For U.S. Federal Indian policy, see Prucha. Williams' most well-known ethnographic writings on the Native peoples of southern New England are in his volume *Key.*

10. Hall and Boutwell. For "sachem," see Salwen 160–176, esp. 166–168, 170, and 171; Conkey, Boissevain, and Goddard 177–193, esp. 177–178. For "sagamore," see Simmons 190–197, esp. 193–194; for "werowance," see Feest, "Nanticoke" 240–252, esp. 24–242, and Feest, "Virginia" 253–270, esp. 261–262.

11. Ely, "Diaries" 8 Mar. 1836. For a fuller discussion, see also Kugel, "Religion" 126–157.

12. For Ojibwe expectations regarding the missionaries, especially their efforts to solidify a political alliance with the United States, see Kugel, *Main Leaders.*

13. Hall to Greene 17 Sept. 1831 (traders transport possessions); Ely, "Diaries" 17 Aug. 1833 (traders provide board and lodging); Hall to Greene 14 June 1832 (traders' fundraising efforts); Evarts to Greene 27 July 1829 (traders' eagerness for schools).

14. Ayer to Greene 1 Dec. 1833. Whether the construct "Great Spirit" accurately represented an Ojibwe spiritual understanding is not as clear. See the views of Hultkrantz and Vecsey. For a new study that examines the interconnectedness of spirituality with political power, see Miller.

15. Ely, "Diaries" 15 May 1836 (mankind corrupt), 20 May 1836 ("wickedness"), 19 May 1836 ("seeking the Lord"), 14 Feb. 1834 ("ignorant Catholics"); Hall and Boutwell ("light pure of Christianity"). For the

missionaries' growing awareness of the strong Catholic presence, see Hall to Greene 14 June 1832; and Hall and Boutwell.

16. Jacqueline Peterson, one of the first American scholars to examine the Great Lakes Métis, notes that the term "Métis" and its variant spelling, Metif, were known and used by some Anglo-Americans resident in the Upper Great Lakes in the 1830s and 1840s; however, none of the ABCFM missionaries ever mentioned or used the term. See Peterson, "Many Roads" 35–71. Work on Métis communities in the United States has blossomed in the last 20 years. See Peterson, "Prelude"; Anderson; Thorne; Murphy; Sleeper-Smith; and Foster. Canadian studies date back to Giraud's masterwork Le Métis, and include Brown, Kirk; and Devine.

17. Kohl qtd. in Peterson, "Prelude" 54; Johnston 177. For Baird's discussion of her multi-tribal descent, see Baird. For theorizing the practice of "situational ethnicity," see Hart 88–113.

18. Hall to Greene 16 Aug. 1838 ("Frenchmen" and "Canadians" used interchangeably); Ayer to

Greene 1 Dec. 1833 ("Canadians"); Hall and Boutwell ("Canadian Frenchmen"); Boutwell to Greene 25 June 1832 ("French half breeds"); Hall to Greene 17 Oct. 1834 ("mixed breed[s]"); and Ayer to Greene 3 Apr. 1835 ("half blood[s]").

19. For infant baptism, see Ely, "Diaries" 19 Sept. 1833, 21 Feb. 1836, and 20 Mar. 1836. For the mediatory role of saints, see Ely, "Diaries" 20 Mar. 1836 and 20 May 1836. For addressing Jesus through his mother, see Ely, "Diaries" 20 May 1836. See also Ely, "Diaries" entries for 1836 for numerous theological, geographical and historical arguments between Ojibwe villagers, Métis fur trade workers and Edmund Ely.

20. Hall to Greene 2 June 1841; Hall to Greene 24 Oct. 1838. For sabbatarian efforts, see Ely, "Diaries" 22 Feb. 1836, and 22 May 1836; Greene to Hall and Boutwell 10 June 1831. For the dilemma posed by weather-related travel on Sundays, see Ely to Greene 25 Sept. 1833.

21. All quotes from Hall to Greene 17 Oct. 1834. For missionary attempts to understand why their religious message lacked appeal, see Hall to Greene 8 Feb. 1835.

Works Cited

American Board of Commissioners for Foreign Missions. "Complete List of Dakota and Ojibwa Missionaries," American Board of Commissioners for Foreign Missions Papers, Box 1, Minnesota Historical Society. Originals at the Houghton Library, Harvard University, Cambridge, MA.

Anderson, Gary Clayton. Kinsmen of Another Kind: Dakota-White Relations in the Upper Missouri Valley 1650–1862. Lincoln: U of Nebraska P, 1984.

Ayer, Frederick, to David Greene. American Board of Commissioners for Foreign Missions Papers, Box 1, Minnesota Historical Society. Originals at the Houghton Library, Harvard University, Cambridge, MA.

Baird, Elizabeth T. "O-De-Jit-Wa-Win-Wing: Comptes du Temps Passe." Henry S. Baird Collection, Box 4. State Historical Society of Wisconsin.

Berkhofer, Robert F., Jr. Salvation and the Savage: An Analysis of Protestant Missions and American Indian Response, 1787–1862. New York: Atheneum, 1976.

Boutwell, Williuam T. "Diary Kept by the Reverend Thurston Boutwell, Missionary to the Ojibwe Indians, 1832–1837." William T. Boutwell Papers, Box 1, Minnesota Historical Society. Originals at the Houghton Library, Harvard University, Cambridge, MA.

Boutwell, William T., to David Greene. American Board of Commissioners for Foreign Missions

Papers, Box 1, Minnesota Historical Society. Originals at the Houghton Library, Harvard University, Cambridge, MA.

Brown, Jennifer S.H. *Strangers in Blood: Fur Trade Company Families in Indian Country.* Vancouver: U of British Columbia P, 1980.

Coe, Alvan, to Jeremiah Evans. American Board of Commissioners for Foreign Missions Papers, Box 1, Minnesota Historical Society. Originals at the Houghton Library, Harvard University, Cambridge, MA.

Conkey, Laura E., Ethel Boissevain, and Ives Goddard. "Indians of Southern New England and Long Island: Late Period." *Handbook of North American Indians.* Ed. Bruce G. Trigger. Gen. ed. William C. Sturtevant. Vol. 15. (Washington, DC: Smithsonian Institution P, 1978. 177–193.

Devine, Heather. *The People Who Own Themselves: Aboriginal Ethnogenesis in a Canadian Family, 1660–1900.* Calgary: U of Calgary P, 2004.

Ely, Edmund F. "Edmund F. Ely Diaries." Edmund F. Ely and Family Papers, MHS. Originals in the St. Louis County Historical Society, Duluth, Minnesota

Ely, Edmund F., to David Greene. American Board of Commissioners for Foreign Missions Papers, Box 2, Minnesota Historical Society. Originals at the Houghton Library, Harvard University, Cambridge, MA.

Evarts, Jeremiah, to David Greene. American Board of Commissioners for Foreign Missions Papers, Box 1, Minnesota Historical Society. Originals at the Houghton Library, Harvard University, Cambridge, MA.

Feest, Christian F. "Nanticoke and Neighboring Tribes." *Handbook of North American Indians.* Ed. Bruce G. Trigger. Gen. ed. William C. Sturtevant. Vol. 15. Washington, DC: Smithsonian Institution P, 1978. 240–252.

———. "Virginia Algonquians." *Handbook of North American Indians.* Ed. Bruce G. Trigger. Gen. ed. William C. Sturtevant. Vol. 15.

Washington, DC: Smithsonian Institution P, 1978. 253–270.

Foster, Martha Harroun. *We Know Who We Are: Métis Identity in a Montana Community.* Norman: U of Oklahoma P, 2006.

Giraud, Marcel. *Le Métis Canadien: Son Rôle dans l'Histoire des Provinces de l'Ouest.* Paris: Institut d'Ethnologie, 1945.

Greene, David, to Sherman Hall and William T. Boutwell. American Board of Commissioners for Foreign Missions Papers, Box 1, Minnesota Historical Society. Originals at the Houghton Library, Harvard University, Cambridge, MA.

Hall, Sherman. "Journal of Rev. S. Hall." American Board of Commissioners for Foreign Missions Papers, Box 1, Minnesota Historical Society. Originals at the Houghton Library, Harvard University, Cambridge, MA.

Hall, Sherman, to David Greene. American Board of Commissioners for Foreign Missions Papers, Box 3, Minnesota Historical Society. Originals at the Houghton Library, Harvard University, Cambridge, MA.

Hall, Sherman, and William T. Boutwell, to the Prudential Committee (May 1833). American Board of Commissioners for Foreign Missions Papers Papers, Box 1, Minnesota Historical Society. Originals at the Houghton Library, Harvard University, Cambridge, MA.

Hart, William B. "Black 'Go-Betweens' and the Mutability of 'Race,' Status, and Idnetity on New York's Pre-Revolutionary Frontier." *Contact Points: American Frontiers from the Mohawk Valley to the Mississippi, 1750–1830.* Eds. Andrew R.L. Cayton and Fredrika J. Teute. Chapel Hill: U of North Carolina P, 1998. 88–113.

Hickerson, Harold. *The Chippewa and Their Neighbors: A Study in Ethnohistory.* New York: Holt, Rinehart and Winston, 1970.

Hultkrantz, Ake. *Belief and Worship in Native North America.* Syracuse: Syracuse UP, 1981.

Johnston, William. "Letters on the Fur Trade." Ed. J. Sharpless Fox. *Historical Collections of the Michigan Pioneer and Historical Society* 37 (1909–1910): 132–207.

Van Kirk, Sylvia Van. *Many Tender Ties: Women in Fur Trade Society, 1670–1870.* Winnipeg: Watson & Dwyer, 1980.

Kohl, Johann Georg. *Kitchi-Gami, or Wanderings Around Lake Superior.* London: Chapman and Hall, 1860.

Kugel, Rebecca. "Religion Mixed with Politics: The 1836 Conversion of Mang'osid of Fond du Lac." *Ethnohistory* 37 (Spring 1990): 126–157.

———. *To Be the Main Leaders of Our People: A History of Minnesota Ojibwe Politics, 1820–1898.* East Lansing: Michigan State UP, 1998.

Miller, Cary. *Ojibwe Leadership in the Early Nineteenth Century.* Diss. U of North Carolina. 2002.

Murphy, Lucy Eldersveld. *A Gathering of Rivers: Economy, Race and Gender Along the Fox-Wisconsin and Rock Waterways, 1737–1832.* Lincoln: U of Nebraska P, 2001.

Peterson, Jacqueline. "The Many Roads to Red River: Métis Genesis in the Great Lakes Region, 1680–1815." *The New Peoples: Being and Becoming Métis in North America: Manitoba Studies in Native History.* Eds. Jacqueline Peterson and Jennifer S.H. Brown. Winnipeg: U of Manitoba P, 1985. 35–71.

———. "Prelude to Red River: A Social Portrait of the Great Lakes Métis." *Ethnohistory* 25 (Winter 1978): 41–67.

Prucha, Francis Paul. *The Great Father: The United States Government and the American Indians.* Abridged ed. Lincoln: U of Nebraska P, 1984.

Salwen, Bert. "Indians of Southern New England and Long Island: Early Period." *Handbook of*

North American Indians. Ed. Bruce G. Trigger. Gen. ed. William C. Sturtevant. Vol. 15. Washington, DC: Smithsonian Institution P, 1978. 160–176.

Schenck, Theresa M. *"The Voice of the Crane Echoes Afar." The Sociopolitical Organization of the Lake Superior Ojibwa, 1640–1855.* New York: Garland, 1997. 17–28.

Simmons, William S. "Narragansett." *Handbook of North American Indians.* Ed. Bruce G. Trigger. Gen. ed. William C. Sturtevant. Vol. 15. Washington, DC: Smithsonian Institution P, 1978. 190–197.

Sleeper-Smith, Susan. *Indian Women and French Men: Rethinking Cultural Encounter in the Western Great Lakes.* Amherst: U of Massachusetts P, 2001.

Stout, Harry S. *The New England Soul: Preaching and Religious Culture in Colonial New England.* New York; Oxford UP, 1986.

Tanner, Helen Hornbeck, ed. *Atlas of Great Lakes Indian History.* Norman: U of Oklahoma P, 1987.

Thorne, Tanis Chapman. *The Many Hands of My Relations: French and Indians on the Lower Missouri.* Columbia: U of Missouri P, 1996.

Vecsey, Christopher. *Traditional Ojibwa Religion and Its Historical Changes.* Philadelphia: American Philosophical Society, 1983.

Warren, William Whipple. "History of the Ojibways, Based Upon Traditions and Oral Statements." *Minnesota Historical Society Collections* 5 (1885): 35–37, 39.

Williams, Roger. *A Key to the Language of America, or An Help to the Language of the Natives in that Part of America Called New England: Together with Briefe Observations of the Customs, Manner, and Worships, etc. of the Aforesaid Natives, in Peace and Warre, in Life and Death . . .* London: Gregory Dexter, 1643.

Thamyris/Intersecting No. 25 (2012) 187–204

The Yanqui Makeover

Toby Miller

[T]he human condition is now so thoroughly medicalized that few people can claim to be normal.[1]

If we are talking about assassinating world leaders, that is very close to the American mainstream. I bet if you took a poll right now of whether we should assassinate Kim Jong II, we could get 85 per cent of Americans to say we should. (Chuckles.) I think when Pat Roberston says things like that he is actually representing . . . about two-thirds of the country. (Laughter.)[2]

Ready for a free, fun, no-hassle virtual makeover? The Makeover-o-Matic virtual makeover game lets you try on virtual hairstyles, makeup and accessories with your own photo or a model photo. Find your best online virtual makeover look and style using the latest beauty products, without the risk! Select from hundreds of hairstyles, cosmetic colors and accessories in the privacy of your own home. Blend, highlight, mix and match to create your new online look. What are you waiting for? Go ahead and get beautiful![3]

The grand promise of the United States is that how its people were born need not define them forever. Instead, they can clone themselves from some more desirable model. The means to realize the ultimate Yanqui dream—self-invention through the commodity—is, at least paradoxically, about replication through appropriation. Some of this has to do with an old Hegelian longing for ethical substance. The ethical incompleteness inscribed in Yanquiness, courtesy of a people coming from the underclass of Europe and Asia, the enslaved of Africa, and the dispossessed of the Americas, encourages an all-powerful personal self-criticism. Such processes invite faith and consumerism as means of surviving and thriving. *One* alternately

Image Courtesy: www.adbusters.org

loving and severe world of superstition (AKA religion) is matched by a *second* alternately loving and severe world of superstition (AKA consumption).

In times of cultural and economic dynamism and uncertainty, these superstitions coalesce with old myths about meritocracy and religion as the heart of the nation. Yesterday's grand industrial-era projects of land reclamation and skyscraper construction have contemporary religious and nanotechnological equivalents in evangelism and biomedicine. Faith and pharmacology offer the prospect of absolute control/development of people through three techniques: beliefs that provide zero-signified interpretations and secure patriarchal dominance; industrial drugs that destroy or augment memory, block fertility, create hypermusculature, and defy resistance to bacteria; and micro-machines that give sight and hearing to the disabled—or take them away. The next phase, genetic engineering, promises to alter the who, what, when, where, and how of being human. These projects provide a convenient entry to the phenomenon of reinvention, of the makeover, in its contemporary dimensions—as mega-churches, pills, machines, and surgeries, they can easily be counted, so restless is the search for new selves forged from a *detritus* that can be blended with desired others. Using the formula for cultural-industry success—repetition and difference—the self can be made over.

In this chapter, I seek to demonstrate how demographic difference and economic change have helped to generate two powerful modes of cloning sameness with difference: faith and pharmaceuticals. Both faith cloning and pharmaceutical cloning invest in transformation, through the consumption of a repertoire of selves. The self-as-project, undertaken via commodities, dominates a formerly human and natural landscape. The corollary is the simultaneous triumph and emptiness of the sign as a source and measure of value. Quests for the self are undertaken as quests for objects, which are made to woo consumers, to glance at them sexually. Perfumed and beautiful in ways that borrow from the subjects of romantic love, they reverse that relationship: people learn to love from objects. Wolfgang Haug's term "commodity aesthetics" captures this division between what commodities *promise*, by way of seduction, and what they are *actually about*, as signs of production (17, 19, 35). For the public, this is "the *promesse du bonheur* that advanced capitalism always holds before them, but never quite delivers" (Benhabib 3). In tracing the semiotic history to this state of affairs, Jean Baudrillard discerns four phases. Beginning as a reflection of reality, the commodity sign is transformed into a perversion of reality. A representation of the truth is displaced by false information. Then these two delineable phases of truth and lies become indistinct. Underlying reality is lost as the sign refers to itself, with no residual need of correspondence to the real. It has adopted the form of its own simulation (10–11, 29, 170). Along the way, "human needs, relationships and fears, the deepest recesses of the human psyche, [have] become mere means for the expansion of the commodity universe" (McChesney and Foster). The apparently spiritual, collective world of faith, and the apparently commercial, individual world of pharmacology, meet in this makeover lane.

Self-Invention

Life is very much a project in the United States, where religious and medical commodities are both signs and means of change—but not straightforwardly individual ones. Hence, we see the aptness of the cloning metaphor as a simultaneously collective and individual, faith-based and science-based road to transcendence. This duality of disciplinary governance and free choice is the grand national paradox. Many of us arriving here from other sovereign states do so cognizant of the country's claim to being *laissez-faire*, and are perhaps attracted by it. We, in fact, encounter the most administered society we have ever experienced, albeit through civil society as much as the state (to the extent that the two can be disaggregated).

The great national makeover is not solely narcissistic, though that figures into the story. It is about an entire *ethos* of self-invention that replicates a narrow band of norms—hence, perhaps, the perverse U.S. fixation on "character," a seemingly magical component of masculinity that is referred to with inquisitorial reverence in election campaign after election campaign. Such rituals—when the leading man in the drama of U.S. politics is selected—offer a good example of self-invention through media candidacy. Distinctions are avidly drawn between "personality"—the psychological cards one is dealt—and "character"—how one plays them: nature versus management. Failings that derive from one's "personality" (which seems to be about fun and the id)

From dawn to dusk, life is laid out across a bewildering array of public and private institutions, with various forms of government present every day and in every way, along with politically unaccountable intrusions by god-bothering and business bureaucrats, not to mention the moralistic third sector of venture philanthropists, nosy foundations, and do-gooder associations. Even the summer break from school is orchestrated for young people via the bizarre ritual of camp, while those preparing for college entry must ritualistically embark on volunteerism to boost their application packets. Simply "being"—leading life without a bumper sticker avowing one's elective institutional affinities—seems implausible. Such is the administered society out of control—in the name of individualism. Wander through virtually any bookstore across the country and you will be swamped by the self-help section, edging its way closer and closer to the heart of the shop, as the ancestral roots of an unsure immigrant culture are stimulated by today's risky neoliberal society. The Hollywood promise of the makeover, of turning an off-screen farmgirl into a film star, or an on-screen librarian into a siren, is at the heart of such cloning enterprises. Fitting in means being individual, and expressing individuality means selecting from a menu.

can be overcome by strengths that can be developed through "character" (which seems to be about repression and the ego/superego). In the 2000 election, George Bush's character was routinely valorized by the *bourgeois* media as distinct from the Republican norm, because of his putative compassion and bipartisan tendencies. He was not evaluated on the measurable materiality of his public service—spectacular public-educational underachievement and record high rates of execution under his governorship of Texas—or his recreational drug record, nepotistic affirmative-action entry to the Ivy League, and sordid business history. It took years for *Newsweek's* alarming 2003 cover story "Bush and God" to highlight the policy implications of his alcohol-addiction and business-failure-fueled conversion to evangelical Protestantism, and its effective use as electoral appeal (Republicans were overwhelmingly supported across class lines by white Protestants during the 2003 Iraq crisis and the 2004 presidential election). Conversely, Al Gore's character was routinely problematized in 2000 because of his fund raising activities on behalf of the Democrats, and putative tall tales about inventing the freedom of the internet, inspiring the romance of *Love Story*, and uncovering the pollution of the Love Canal. He was not evaluated on the measurable materiality of his public service—spectacular economic growth and record high rates of educational attainment under his vice-presidency. Non-governmental organizations and state programs instantiate this obsession with character: the Character Counts! Coalition, the Aspen Declaration on Character

Education, the Character Education Partnership, the Character Education Network; and so it goes—civil society as behavioral governance (Newport and Carroll; Pew, *Religion*; Park).

All this palaver works as a grand metaphor for managing the differences and difficulties of language, history, race, gender, class, age, health, and faith that color the nation's history. The discourse on character references the risk and opportunity embodied in the longest-standing makeover aspect of U.S. society, immigration: the coterminous pleasure and pain of a "touch-and-go" existence, of a suddenly anonymous personal history, of "individual independence and differentiation"—of the "right to distrust" (Simmel)—alongside the need to clone new selves from available models. For immigration's interplay of repetition and difference is finally making the U.S. look truly American. The first great wave of immigrants at the turn of the 20th century left the country 87% white/Euro-American, a proportion that remained static through the 1950s. During the 20th century, the U.S. population increased by 250% (the equivalent figures are under 60% for both France and Britain). In the past decade, the country's Asian and Pacific Islander population increased by 43%, and its Latino population by 38.8%. Of the 100 million net additions to the population between 1967 and 2006, the plurality was Latino. Between those two groups, and African Americans and Native Americans, about 100 million U.S. residents can now define themselves as minorities ("Hispanic"; "Centrifugal"; Pew Hispanic). As diversity increases, whiteness becomes less normal and more conscious of its desire to replicate, with evangelicals sending spousal straights to the bedroom to have unprotected sex in the name of duty.

At the same time, successive population waves—no longer just white ones—have fled the inner city, and the nation has just become the first in the world with more than half its people living in suburbia (a quarter of whom are minorities). Seventy-five per cent of new office space is being constructed there. As this historic demographic shift continues, the trend from a rural to an urban to a suburban country, middle-class people are increasingly disarticulated from subsistence, from the state, and from the experience of rural and urban life. And economic life for many U.S. residents is becoming worse and worse. By contrast with European welfare systems, the capacity to escape poverty in the U.S. has diminished over the last three decades of neoliberalism and suburbanization, thanks to a gigantic clumping of wealth at the apex of the nation, atop a poor, unskilled, and unhealthy base. Forty-six million residents are indigent, the same number lack health insurance, and 52 million are functionally analphabetic. Access to money and net worth are massively stratified by race and gender. For instance, in 2003, black men earned 73% of the hourly wage rate for white people. And the gaps are widening. In the two decades following 1979, the highest-paid 1% of the population doubled its share of national pre-tax income to 18%. Incomes of the top 1% increased by 194%; the top 20% by 70%—and the bottom 20% by just 6.4%. In 1967, chief executive officers of corporations were paid 24 times the average wage of employees. Thirty years later, they received 300 times that amount. Over Bush's first term, profits rose by 60%, but wages by just 10%. In 2004, after-tax corporate profits grew to their highest proportion of Gross Domestic Product since the Depression. In the three years following 2003, hourly wages declined by 2%, adjusted for inflation, while productivity rose. In California, where I live, the local economy is larger than at least 180 sovereign states around the world, depending upon the measures used. But working-class family income has increased by 4% since 1969, while its ruling-class equivalent has grown by 41%. Nationally, corporate profits are at their highest level in five decades, and wages and salaries have the lowest share of the national pie on record. For the investment bank UBS, we inhabit a "golden era of profitability." But almost half the population does not see hard work as the means to a better life, and two-thirds say they have no savings (the national rate is the lowest since the Depression).[4] This bizarre re-concentration of wealth in the hands of the *bourgeoisie* is unprecedented in world history since the advent of working-class electoral franchises. No wonder *The Economist* captioned a photo of the Queen of England greeting George Bush and his "Desperate Housewife," Laura, as "Liz, meet the royals." No wonder Warren Buffet avowed in his 2003 letter to Berkshire investors that "If class warfare is being waged in America, my class is clearly winning" ("Ever Higher").

As immigration has become more diverse and complex, and wealth has been systematically redistributed upward, vast numbers of people have coped, I suspect, by re-pledging themselves to two key cloning technologies as means of transformation: mega-churches and Selective Serotonin Reuptake Inhibitors (SSRIs). These developments are reshaping a tendency toward reinvention through cloning that is central to the mythology and lived experience of the entire nation. Consider the bizarre makeover of evangelicals: an almost physical, trance-like transmogrification from a faith based in ideas to something that, ironically, resembles transubstantiation (Luhrmann). The outcome? Here is a recent demography of nativists:

> [H]airy-backed swamp developers and corporate shills, faith-based economists, fundamentalist bullies with Bibles, Christians of convenience, freelance racists, misanthropic frat boys, shrieking midgets of AM radio, tax cheats, nihilists in golf pants, brownshirts in pinstripes, sweatshop tycoons, hacks, fakirs, aggressive dorks, Lamborghini libertarians, people who believe Neil Armstrong's moonwalk was filmed in Roswell, New Mexico, little honkers out to diminish the rest of us.

Is this the irritated rant of an urban hipster, mercilessly mocking those beyond the world of downtown lofts and polymorphous pleasure? Did these words drop from a laptop as it hurtled across the fly-over states? No. The quotation comes from a true son of the mid-West. Garrison Keillor, host of the seemingly nativist but globally-syndicated radio program *A Prairie Home Companion*, was responding to the latest wave of right-wing reaction to the cultural difference and economic injustice that color U.S. life. With his concerns as a backdrop, I shall examine faith-based and pharma-based cloning in turn.

Faith

Religious rapture draws on a long history. For settlers and slaves alike, faith provided reasons to flee, forms of succor, and means of collective identification. Religion maintained ethnic solidarity in a new environment, leavened a lack of class bearings, gave solace through the horrors of slavery, and delivered social services away from the brutality of capital and the plutocracy of the state. Most recently, it has been stimulated by the economic riskiness of everyday life, which we might date rhetorically to a 1971 report for Presidential advisors that referred glowingly to "the development of flexible citizens . . . the kind of citizen the twenty-first century is going to need."[5] That neoliberal, anti-welfare flexibility has generated the economic disaster enumerated above.

So what has been the citizen response? Unlike any other First World country, most U.S. residents connect belief in God to morality and wealth. The vast majority of the population attests to the existence of a devil and individuated angels; 45% of people think aliens have visited Earth; three times more people think there are ghosts than was the case a quarter-century ago, and over a third think houses can be haunted; 84% say there is posthumous survival of the soul, up 24% since 1972; only 25% subscribe to evolution; 29% claim to have witnessed divine healing; 35% assert that the Bible is the literal word of "God"; almost two thirds anticipate millennial doom and rebirth; and, in the South, 44% believe that lightning is sent by God to punish wrongdoers (the same national proportion that has seen Mel Gibson's anti-Semitic, directing-under-the-influence paean to sado-masochism, known as *The Passion of the Christ*). Seventy-nine per cent of U.S. citizens identify as Christian, with 41% converts to fundamentalist evangelism across a bizarre array of groups, including 23% of the population that is subject to the peculiarities of charismatic possession, speaking in tongues and laying on of hands to heal disease. Eighteen per cent are aligned with the religious right. The latter are the most skeptical people in the Yanqui population about environmental protection. Apparently, there is no future for the planet. God's design is to destroy it, then deliver true believers to safety in a kinky theological draft of wind. The population's embrace of these superstitions places the United States alone among nations with advanced economies and educational systems. The 96% of people who believe in a higher power, and 59% who state that religion is crucial to their lives, represent more than twice the proportions for Japan, South Korea, Western Europe, and the former Soviet bloc.[6]

In the public sphere of politics, the "values" rhetoric of the right is both a diversion from class linkage and an index of cultural bigotry, achieved under the sign of sameness. Core ideas are cloned by over 300 right-wing "coin-operated" think tanks in Washington for use at specific sites of superstition. Funded by some of the wealthiest U.S. foundations and families, such as Olin, Scaife, Koch, Castle Rock, and Smith Richardson, these organizations extravagantly ideologize on everything from sexuality to foreign policy. Ghost writers make their resident intellectuals' prose attractive, as part of a project that is concerned more with marketing opinion than conducting research—for each "study" they fund is essentially the alibi for an op-ed piece. The corollary numbers for media coverage and, hence, access to everyday homes, are striking. Progressive think tanks had just a one-sixth share of media quotations compared to reactionary institutions during the 1990s. In the decade to 2005, the right averaged 51% of citations, progressives 14%. The people who appear on the three major television network newscasts as policy wonks are indices of this success: 92% of such mavens are white, 85% are male, and 75% are Republican. In all, 90% of news interviewees on the major networks are white men born between 1945 and 1960—a fine instance of cloning sameness for leadership. The audience for their grandstanding comprises a second-tier grassroots network stretching across the National Right to Life Committee, the American Family Association, the Liberty Alliance, the Eagle Forum, the Family Research Council, the Christian Action Network, and the Christian Coalition.[7]

The civil-society tactics of the right, from protests to op-ed pieces, come from somewhere uncomfortably close to the left: "they" cloned "our" methods. Having learned from progressive social movements that the personal and the cultural were political, the right declared itself the ideological foe, not only of subaltern groups seeking enfranchisement, but also of liberal, humanistic expressions of universality and the secular. Minorities and feminists had protested anti-defamation with great effect, so why shouldn't the right protest the defamation of its values—fundamentalism, homophobia, and nationalism? Such methods mimicked the rhetoric of civil rights and subject positions pioneered by progressive social movements. The umbrella term for these practices, "culture war," originated during Ronald Reagan's Presidency and became media orthodoxy when Republican Congressman Henry Hyde sought to condemn flag-burning as "one front in a larger culture war" in 1990.[8]

Consider these instances of the right cloning the left's use of cultural spectacle. For example, the National Rifle Association was for a long time a rather mild-mannered Clark-Kentish advocate for field sports. Following an internal *coup* in the mid-1970s, it left New York City for the wilds, campaigned for people owning guns as a Constitutional right/responsibility—and overtly copied tactics from the civil-rights movement. The same period marked the advent of the Moral Majority, again drawing on the rhetoric and methods of civil rights. Ten years later, this indebtedness to civil rights activism was carried forward by the United Shareholders Association, the consumerist politics of which disempowered workers and turned corporations into ventures of speculation rather than generators of infrastructure. Then evangelical Christians modeled their marriage movement on anti-tobacco activism. Today, both Stanford and UCLA feature organizations dedicated to undoing "institutional racism"—a concept long-derided by the white right that it now perversely embraces as a sign that groups such as the Movimiento Estudiantil Chicano de Aztlán, formed at the height of creative Chican@ cultural politics in the 1970s, has become so powerful on campus that it must be stopped for fear of its effect on whites. In 2004, the Sierra Club fended off a takeover by anti-Latin@s who positioned their nativist candidacy as environmental. All these groups were underwritten by far-right think tanks and foundations, artful practitioners of cultural politics they cloned from progressives and validated through the discourses of morality and religion. The mega-church is a fine instance of cloning, an amalgam of stadium rock and mall dross. By 2006, there were over a thousand such things, as defined by churches with weekly attendances in excess of two thousand people. That number had doubled since 2001, as had their average attendance. They were using satellites more and more, and four mega-church pastors were featured on the *New York Times*' bestseller list, with tens of millions in sales.[9]

Pharma

In addition to religiosity, a *superstitious* response to cultural difference and economic threat, there is a *rational* and equally far-reaching reaction to such changes: pharmacology, that strange meeting point of the external and the internal where commodities encounter emotions, mediated formally and informally through professional knowledge and intervention, and mass-produced in pill form. Pharmaceutical corporations promote fast and efficient solutions to life's problems—stop reading and start swallowing. Cosmetic pharmacology offers keys to contemporary U.S. personhood. Nowadays, '"big science" and "big technology" can sit on your desk, reside in a pillbox, or inside your body" (Clarke, et al.) alongside big faith. One models the brain; the other models what it believes.

If the self is "a cultural invention" (Kessen) and we are *en route* to what Erik Davis calls "the posthuman self," then the newest "darlings of Wall Street"—pharmacorps— are its manufacturers (Healy, *Creation* 2, 353). The drug makeover experience clearly appeals to upwardly mobile people who have decided to abandon former existences. They are living out the latest trend in a cloning nation: "SSRIs, hormones, brain boosters, neurotransmitters." Instead of old-style recreational objects that Yanquis liked to put in their mouths (alcohol, tobacco, coffee, and illegal substances), which promised instantaneous joy and release tied, in some cases, to death, disability, pain, contempt, or incarceration, the new substances, legal and controlled, offer a permanent overhaul (Davis; Elliott, "American Bioscience"). No huddling outside the office building, no stains on the paperwork or keyboard, no obvious need to be like others. No quick pleasure, no hangover, no nightly snoring or morning cough driving those around you to distraction, no staggering to the bathroom to be ill, no breath-lessness walking up two flights of stairs, no emanations from the mouth, hair, or clothes to mark one out. Instead, a discreet, discrete, daily dose backs up the gains made the day before within one's not-so-hard drive of a body. Once the decision has been made to take these reformatting technologies, they "melt invisibly into the texture of the everyday" (Davis). This is quiet cloning.

The psy-function (psychoanalysis, psychiatry, psychology, and psycho-pharmacology) is split between the discourses of swallowing and speaking, most ignobly illustrated by a 1971 debate between Heinz Lehmann (for pharmacology) and Herbert Marcuse (for psychoanalysis). While Lehmann was addressing the audience, Frederick Qunes, who had helped organize the event, threw a cream cake in his face. The incident is legendary in the psy-function. Just as symbolically, the renowned Chestnut Lodge psychodynamic center was sued in the 1980s for malpractice because it denied drugs to a patient. While the case did not set a legal precedent—terms were agreed—it furthered a developing discourse that juxtaposed clinically-trialed drugs against impressionistic speech. Since the cake fruitlessly flew and the chestnut privately settled, pharmaceutical corporations and their prescribing delegates have become hegemonic, utilizing the slogan "You can't talk to disease" to great effect (Healy, *Creation* 175; Rose; Breggin 11–13, 17, 23, 122). As they have found, you *can* vend invisible goods that will disarm it and clone normativity, then leave the content of speech up to god-botherers.

The first major psychoactive drug was Chlorpromazine (sold as Thorazine). It came onto the market in 1954, featured immediately in numerous print advertisements. Combined with increased governmental employment of therapists, the new arrival reversed the institutional removal of the mentally ill from public life. Two years later, the number of mental hospital patients declined for the first time since the previous century. Patients were not the only ones to come out. Whereas almost all U.S. psychiatrists were hospital-based in 1940, by 1957 over 80% were not. The key corporations manufacturing these exit passes from asyla—Sandoz, Rhône-Poulenc, Geigy, Ciba, and Roche—convened many collusive meetings between 1953 and 1958. They set up a network of psycho-pharmacology, paid clinical researchers to exchange information, and founded the anachronistically-named Collegium Internationale Neuropsychopharmacologium to invent a classical heritage. Merck also played a part, distributing 50,000 copies of Frank Ayd's 1961 book *Recognizing the Depressed Patient* to doctors around the world. This product placement success-fully promoted depression as something ordinary and diagnosable in general prac-tice. Advertisements in medical journals trumpeted families reuniting, men returning to work, and women embracing the home—a cultural cloning that could be chemically produced. One famous promotion for Thorzine depicted the pill on a leather couch: it had displaced the patient, not just the therapist! With the advent of Medicare and

Medicaid as part of the "Great Society" reforms of the 1960s, public hospitals lost even more inmates. State governments utilized new forms of funding to shift them into non-traditional institutions, such as private nursing homes, halfway houses, and outpatient services, which were simultaneously ideologized as democratic by the emergent community care movement. This policy disaster was enshrined by the Supreme Court in *Olmstead v. L.C.* in 1999 (Herman 257–259; Rubin; Healy, *Antidepressant* 47, 75–76).

Antidepressants offered highly specific interventions, albeit with systemic effects. Although called "magic bullets," implying precise targeting, their effect was much wider: they shifted "health to the center of Western politics and culture" (Healy, *Antidepressant* 1). By the turn of the 21st century, 38 million people in the U.S. had tried Prozac. Over 10 million new prescriptions were written for it in 1999 alone. In 2004, 91 million people took prescription drugs regularly, and only a quarter of the population had never done so. Sixty-four per cent of households filled three billion prescriptions a year. In a period of minimal inflation, U.S. expenditure on pharmaceuticals doubled in the ten years to 2000, to U.S. $100 billion. A decade ago, U.S. residents averaged seven prescriptions per year; now it is twelve (Goode; Fox; Rowe).

Drugs are planned for the "sleep market" (Marsa) and to enhance memory—matters of far greater interest to pharmacorps than the treatment of illness (Breithaupt and Weigmann), since their military and educational market potential outstrips the temporal and spatial limitations of disease. Companies are forever developing new products to deal with newly defined maladies, such as baldness, obesity, and impotence. TV commercials promote pills to counter hair loss, weight loss, and erection loss. In fact, everything barring Lacanian loss.

What used to be part of drug subculture—a pill that transforms the self—is now central to corporate capital. To quote the *New York Times*, "Big Pharma Ogles Yasgur's Farm." So we find Viagra sponsoring a tour by Earth, Wind & Fire, the '70s rhythm and blues/soul/funk group, because its manufacturer, Pfizer, wants to attract consumers who once associated popular music with illegal recreational drug use, but might now be open to a legal, lifestyle equivalent (Leland). For its part, commercial television offers politician Bob Dole, baseball player Rafael Palmeiro, race car driver Jeff Fuller, and football coach Mike Ditka needing help with erections, and a car race named after a cigarette company includes Viagra as its secondary sponsor, while football player Ricky Williams was found seeking alleviation from anxiety. More money is spent promoting psychiatric "wonder drugs" in the U.S. than on medical school and residency training—in 1998, Eli Lilly spent U.S.$95 million just to market Prozac (Jaramillo, Scherer; Moynihan; Bloom).

Rather than forming illicit informal relationships with others through the shared experience of ingestion, the new drugs forge a new relationship with the self that becomes nearly invisible—a pre-party preparation, the perfect makeover. Or they can become public badges of membership through water cooler discussions about whether last week's Prozac has taken hold yet, almost like evangelicals' seemingly insatiable need for recognition of their status as "born again" (a charming critique of their mothers). These drugs fulfill the meritocrat's dream—to learn the code, to crack the means of making oneself anew, to leave as something more than one arrived as—and to do so in a seamless way that does not draw attention to itself unless desired. What may have begun, through confession and therapy, as a search for authentic feelings—the real me revealed—turns commodified cloning into authenticity (Elliott, *Better* 22, 29–30), just like the search for meaning that characterizes the culture of faith.

For Prozac guru Peter D. Kramer, psy-pharmacology may be "the American ideal" (Elliott, *Better* xi). Instead of illness cured, one type of wellness substitutes for another (Elliott, *Better* 50–51). Some say "the scientific management of *production*, so prevalent in the early days of the twentieth century, has been displaced by a new scientific management of *consumption*" (Hansen, et al. 1). The *British Medical Journal* derides these commercial projects as "disease mongering" for profit[10] and the *Los Angeles Times* wonders about the will "to treat . . . benign personality traits" (Gottlieb).

These changes are not only about individual choice. For instance, corporate intranets provide employee assistance programs for easy access to therapy around the clock. Cost pressures militate against individual and even group psychotherapy, encouraging both self-help software and company-sponsored electronic listeners. The American Psychological Association offers "Questions to Ask Your Employer's Benefits Manager" on its web site as part of a "Consumer Help Center" (Hansen, et al. 56, 106, 123), and the HSM Group's "Productivity Impact Model" estimates the cost of employee depression to company revenues. It operates on the assumption that 50% of depressed workers are "untreated" and miss between 30 and 50 days of work per year as a consequence. To start the process, simply log on to <depressioncalculator.com>; the neoliberal employer's perfect wake-up page, no doubt. And in order to ensure a neat articulation among the politics, economics, and culture of drugs, and despite criticism from the Association of American Physicians and Surgeons, George Bush's administration introduced a New Freedom Commission on Mental Health, comprised of former drug company mavens, to screen every person for mental illness. Children were the first targets for mandatory evaluation, because the Commission's pharmacorps members regarded schools as ideal testing venues for identifying 50 million potential customers. This was happening even as the International Committee of Medical Journal Editors and the New York Attorney General were criticizing the pharmaceutical sector for hiding negative clinical trials from professional and public evaluation (Graham, "Bush"; Graham, "Big Brother"; Executive Summary; "Trials").

Conclusion

The cosmic ambivalence about the self that comes with being an immigrant under-class culture is also an animator of capitalist innovation and retardation, and social chaos and cohesion. The outcome is contradictory, because superstition often con-jures up terror in the face of science. Superstition and innovation do not always play well together.

But while that struggle may be grimly fascinating, progressives must pose harsh questions as we await the crescendo when creepy Christianity and psy-function phar-macology clash, as they inevitably will, given the problems faith has with science and pleasure. We must ask what it would mean to seek salvation in the secular world, the here and now, and to do so without divine intervention, the psy-function, or corporate commodities. Could we enjoy the notion of the self as a piece of art, to be enjoyed through unpaid labor, in a way that did not postpone pleasure, defer income, or embroil us in commodity relations disguised as medicine? That would direct us to Kant's call for self-knowledge as an autotelic drive rather than an instrument, as an end in itself rather than a means toward some endlessly deferred or recurring achievement (Manninen). Such self-knowledge could produce a wisdom that tran-scended cultural politics through religiosity, and self-control through pharmacology—what Kant envisaged as *"man's emergence from his self-incurred immaturity,"* independent of religious, governmental, or commercial direction (54).

Is such an alternative viable, a world where a person can "hunt in the morning, fish in the afternoon, rear cattle in the evening, criticize after dinner . . . without ever becoming hunter, fisherman, shepherd or critic" (Marx and Engels 53)? A world that rebuts dehumanizing commodity fetishism, turning instead toward the Xhosa saying that "a person is a person through other persons?" A world where we live between the promise of cosmopolitanism and the loss of national identity (Canclini 50) rather than as "desiccated calculators . . . rational-choice rodents moved exclusively by the short range and the quantifiable" (Nairn), with "freedom to choose" only once "the major political, economic, and social decisions have already been made?" (Mosco 60).

Notes

1. New Scientist qtd. in Hansen, et al. 12.

2. Ross Douhtat, assoc. ed., *Atlantic Monthly*, at a public forum qtd. in Pew Research Center, *In Pursuit.*

3. http://beauty.ivillage.com/0,,9jlxfdd5,00. html.

4. Higher"; "Breaking Records"; Yates; Hutton, *Declaration* 133, 148; Taibo 24; UBS qtd. in Greenhouse and Leonhardt; Wallechinsky.

5. Qtd. in Mattelart.

6. Hutton, "Crunch"; Mann 103; Pew Internet; Gallup; Grossberg 140–141; Pew, *Spirit*; Newport and Carroll; Pew, *Religion*; Pew, *Trends*; Baylor.

7. Alterman 85; Dolny; Claussen 56; Love; Rendall and Broughel.

8. Qtd. in DiMaggio.

9. Hutton, *Declaration* 85, 104; Coltrane; Lovato; Thuma, Travis, and Bird.

10. Qtd. in Ahmed.

Works Cited

Ahmed, Kamal. "Britons Swallow Cure-All Drugs." *The Observer* 26 Jan. 2003.

Alterman, Eric. *What Liberal Media? The Truth about Bias and the News.* New York: Basic, 2003.

Baudrillard, Jean. *Selected Writings.* Ed. Mark Poster. Stanford: Stanford UP, 1988.

Baylor Institute for Studies of Religion and Department of Sociology, Baylor University. *American Piety in the 21st Century: New Insights to the Depth and Complexity of Religion in the US* (2006).

Benhabib, Seyla. *The Claims of Culture: Equality and Diversity in the Global Era.* Princeton: Princeton UP, 2002.

Bloom, S. G. "Sex-Free Bliss?" *Salon.com* 23 May 2000.

"Breaking Records." *The Economist* 12 Feb. 2005: 12–13.

Breggin, P. R. *Toxic Psychiatry: Why Therapy, Empathy, and Love Must Replace the Drugs, Electroshock, and Biochemical Theories of the "New Psychiatry."* New York: St. Martin's, 1994.

Breithaupt, Holger, and Katrin Weigmann. "Manipulating Your Mind." *European Molecular Biology Organization* 5 (2004): 230–232.

Canclini, Néstor Garcia. *Latinoamericanos Buscando Lugar en este Siglo.* Buenos Aires: Paidós, 2002.

"Centrifugal Forces." *The Economist* 16 July 2005: 4–7

Clarke, Adele E., Laura Mamo, Jennifer R. Fishman, Janet K. Shim, and Jennifer Ruth Fosket. "Biomedicalization: Technoscientific Transformations of Health, Illness, and U.S. Biomedicine." *American Sociological Review* 68 (2003): 167, 164.

Claussen, Dane S. *Anti-Intellectualism in American Media: Magazines & Higher Education.* New York: Peter Lang, 2004.

Coltrane, Scott. "Marketing the Marriage 'Solution': Misplaced Simplicity in the Politics of Fatherhood: 2001 Presidential Address to the Pacific Sociological Association." *Sociological Perspectives* 44 (2001): 395.

Davis, Erik. "Take the Red Pill." *AlterNet.org* 1 Sept. 2000.

DiMaggio, Paul. "The Myth of Culture War: The Disparity between Private Opinion and Public Politics." *The Fractious Nation? Unity and Division in American Life.* Ed. Jonathan Rieder. Assoc. ed. Stephen Steinlight. Berkeley: U of California P, 2003. 79–97.

Dolny, Michael. "Spectrum Narrows Further in 2002: Progressive, Domestic Think Tanks See Drop." *EXTRA!Update* July–Aug. 2003.

Elliott, Carl. "American Bioscience Meets the American Dream." *American Prospect* 39 (June 2003).

———. *Better than Well: American Medicine Meets the American Dream.* New York: Norton, 2003.

"Ever Higher Society, Ever Harder to Ascend." *The Economist* 1 Jan. 2005: 22–24.

Executive Summary: "The President's New Freedom Initiative for People with Disabilities: The 2004 Progress Report" (2005).

Fox, Susannah. *Prescription Drugs Online.* Washington: Pew Internet & American Life Project, 2004.

Gallup Polls 2002–2003. <gallup.com>.

"The God Slot." *The Economist* 16 Sept. 2006: 38.

Goode, Erica. "Once Again, Prozac Takes Center Stage, in Furor." *New York Times* 18 July 2000.

Gottlieb, Scott. "Cashing in on the Real and Imaginary Health Anxieties of Americans is a Lucrative Business." *Los Angeles Times* 23 July 2000.

Graham, Jordanne. "Big Brother in Your Medicine Cabinet." *Intervention Magazine* 28 Nov. 2004.

———. "Bush Wants to be Your Shrink." *Intervention Magazine* Aug. 2004.

Greenhouse, Lawrence and David Leonhardt. "Real Wages Fail to Match a Rise in Productivity." *New York Times* 28 Aug. 2006.

Grossberg, Lawrence. *Caught in the Crossfire: Kids, Politics, and America's Future.* Boulder: Paradigm, 2005.

Hansen, Susan, Alec McHoul, and Mark Rapley, with Hayley Miller, and Toby Miller. *Beyond*

Help: A Consumer's Guide to Psychology. Ross-on-Wye: PCCS, 2003.

Harris, Patrick. "Wake Up: The American Dream is Over." *The Observer* 8 June 2006.

Haug, W. F. *Critique of Commodity Aesthetics: Appearance, Sexuality and Advertising in Capitalist Society.* Trans. Robert Bock. Cambridge, MA: Polity, 1986.

Healy, David. *The Antidepressant Era.* Cambridge, MA: Harvard UP, 1997.

———. *The Creation of Psychopharmacology.* Cambridge, MA: Harvard UP, 2002.

Herman, E. *The Romance of American Psychology: Political Culture in the Age of Experts.* Berkeley: U of California P, 1996.

"Hispanic and Asian Populations Expand." *New York Times* 30 Aug. 2006.

Hutton, Will. "Crunch Time for Uncle Sam." *The Observer* 5 Jan. 2003.

———. *A Declaration of Interdependence: Why America Should Join the World.* New York: Norton, 2003.

Jaramillo, Deborah L. "Pills Gone Wild: Medium Specificity and the Regulation of Prescription Drug Advertising on Television." *Television & New Media* 7 (2006): 272.

Kant, Immanuel. "*Political Writings.* Trans. H. B. Nisbet. Ed. Hans Reiss. 2nd ed. Cambridge: Cambridge UP, 1991.

Keillor, Garrison. "We're Not in Lake Wobegon Anymore." *In These Times* 26 Aug. 2004.

Kessen, William. "The American Child and Other Cultural Inventions." *American Psychologist* 34 (1979): 815.

Leland, John. "Big Pharma Ogles Yasgur's Farm." *New York Times* 29 July 2001.

Lexington. "It's a Man's World." *The Economist* 7 Aug. 2004: 28.

Lovato, Roberto. "Fear of a Brown Planet." *The Nation* 28 June 2004.

Love, Maryann Cusimano. "Global Media and Foreign Policy." *Media Power, Media Politics.* Ed. Mark J. Rozell. Lanham: Rowman & Littlefield, 2003. 246.

Luhrmann, Tanya M. "Metakinesis: How God Becomes Intimate in Contemporary U. S. Christianity." *American Anthropologist* 106 (2004): 518–528.

Mann, Michael. *Incoherent Empire.* London: Verso, 2003.

Manninen, B. A. "Medicating the Mind: A Kantian Analysis of Overprescribing Psychoactive Drugs." *Journal of Medical Ethics* 32 (2006): 100–105.

Marsa, Linda. "Sleep for Sale." *Mother Jones* Jan.–Feb. 2005: 20.

Marx, Karl, and Frederick Engels. *The German Ideology: Part One.* Ed. C. J. Arthur. New York: International, 1995.

Mattelart, Armand. *The Information Society.* Trans. Susan G. Taponier, and James A. Cohen. London: Sage, 2003.

McChesney, Robert W., and John Bellamy Foster. "The Commercial Tidal Wave." *Monthly Review* 54 (2003): 1.

Mosco, Vincent. *The Digital Sublime: Myth, Power, and Cyberspace.* Cambridge, MA: MIT P, 2004.

Moynihan, Ray. "The Intangible Magic of Celebrity Marketing." *PLoS Medicine* 1 (2004): 102–104.

Nairn, Tom. "Democracy & Power: American Power & the World." *openDemocracy.net* 19 Jan. 2003, 16 Jan. 2003, 23 Jan. 2003, 4 Feb. 2003, 20 Feb. 2003.

Newport, Frank, and Joseph Carroll. "Support for Bush Significantly Higher Among More Religious Americans." *Gallup Poll Analyses* 6 March 2003.

Park, Nansook. "The Role of Subjective Well-Being in Positive Youth Development." *Annals of the American Academy of Political and Social Science* 591 (2004): 41.

Pew Forum on Religion & Public Life. *Religion and the Environment: Polls Show Strong Backing for Environmental Protection Across Religious Groups* (2004).

———. *Spirit and Power: A 10-Country Survey of Pentecostals* (2006).

Pew Hispanic Center. *From 200 Million to 300 Million: The Numbers Behind Population Growth.* (2006).

Pew Internet & American Life Project. *Faith Online* (2004).

Pew Research Center. *In Pursuit of Values Voters.* (2006).

———. *Trends 2005* (2005): 17.

Pew Research Center for the People & the Press. *Religion and the Presidential Vote.* (2004).

"Productivity Impact Model: Calculating the Impact of Depression in the Workplace and the Benefits of Treatment." *H. S. M. Group,* 2004. <depressioncalculator.com>.

Rendall, Steve, and Tara Broughel. "Amplifying Officials, Squelching Dissent." *EXTRA!Update* May–June 2003.

Rose, Nikolas. "Neurochemical Selves." *Society* 41 (2003): 51.

Rowe, Jonathan. "Drug Ads Sell a Problem, Not a Solution." *Christian Science Monitor* 21 Aug. 2006.

Rubin, Lawrence C. "Merchandising Madness: Pills, Promises, and Better Living Through Chemistry." *Journal of Popular Culture* 38 (2004): 370–372.

Scherer, Michael. "The Side Effects of Truth." *Mother Jones* May–June 2005.

Simmel, Georg. "The Metropolis and Mental Life." Trans. Kurt H. Wolff. *Sociological Perspectives: Selected Readings.* Eds. Kenneth Thompson and Jeremy Tunstall. Harmondsworth: Penguin, 1976. 88–89.

Skocpol, Theda. "The Narrowing of Civic Life." *American Prospect* June 2004: A5–A7.

Taibo, Carlos. "Hegemonía con Quiebras." *Washington Contra el Mundo: Una Recopilación de Rebelión.org,* Ed. Pascual Serrano. Madrid: Foca, 2003.

Thelen, David. "How Natural are National and Transnational Citizenship? A Historical Perspective." *Indiana Journal of Global Legal Studies* 7 (2000): 552.

Thumma, Scott, Dave Travis, and Warren Bird. *Megachurches Today 2005: Summary of*

Research Findings. Hartford: Hartford Institute for Religion Research and Leadership Network, 2006.

"Trials and Tribulations." *The Economist* 19 June 2004: 62–63.

Wallechinsky, David. "Is the American Dream Still Possible?" *Parade* 23 April 2006.

Webster, Bruce H., Jr., and Alemayehu Bishaw. *Income, Earnings, and Poverty Data from the 2005 American Community Survey.* U.S. Census Bureau, American Community Survey Reports (2006): ACS-02.

Yates, Michael D. "A Statistical Portrait of the U. S. Working Class." *Monthly Review* 56 (2005): 12–31.

Part Four: The Cloning Imaginary: Proliferations of a Fantasy

Thamyris/Intersecting No. 25 (2012) 207–218

Twin Enemies

Gabriele Schwab

Like so many other Southern California kids, Sandra grew up in a pink tract house in the Los Angeles suburban sprawl. Her city was called Irvine, and she had overheard her dad saying that the Irvine Company advertised the city as "the best planned community in the world." She had puzzled over this, especially because the "Irvine Company" seemed to be some almighty organization that owned everything, including the public parks and the shopping center where she went with her parents and friends. The Irvine Company, Dad said, controlled every inch of public space and life, and had to approve everything from the color of houses to what you could and could not plant in your garden. This included not being allowed to dry your laundry in your own back yard or being required to have a two-car garage, even if you were a single person living in a small house! Sandra remembered her father's anger when he had to take out a eucalyptus tree because it grew higher than the other trees in the neighborhood. "The Irvine Company has bought the City Council," he had shouted in a rage that day. Her mom's sarcastic response was, "What else is new? It has been like this for the last hundred years." "No, it's getting worse," he had snapped back at her. "At the beginning of the century, you could at least paint your houses in shades of brown and beige and ochre. Now it's pink and pink and pink like every little girl's room in the compound!"

One of her dad's colleagues called Irvine an "edge city," a term invented by a former University of California-Irvine history professor, now famous for having long ago predicted all the eco-disasters that had come to haunt California during the past decades. Sandra liked the word. It reminded her not only of living on the edge of the real thing, L.A., but also of being on the edge, her most familiar mode of being. Perhaps it was because she always felt watched by her mother. Sometimes Sandra had the impression that her mother observed and studied her as though she were conducting an educational experiment of sorts. It made her feel so uncomfortable that she used to squirm out from under her mother's coldly scrutinizing eyes. It had become even worse since Mom started to wear the fashionable algae gloss contacts that gave her eyes an almost surreal green sheen. There was something distant about her mother, too, as though she were distracted from herself, always here and yet not quite here. Those new eyes made it worse. You couldn't even see yourself in her pupils anymore. Sandra often felt intruded upon, judged by invisible eyes and beholden to an unknown ideal.

At least her mother had insisted that they moved to a neighborhood that was child-proof, Sandra thought. Her mom was big on childproof. She had taken Sandra to the new Ikea store in Fashion Island that distinguished itself from the other four Ikeas in the area with the label *Ikea Plus*. Sandra liked the huge neon sign that was visible at night from the freeway with a different color for each letter. Her favorite was the huge magenta "P" at the beginning of "Plus". At *Ikea Plus,* her mother had selected a child-proof kid's room, including a bunk bed with a safety net to prevent the child sleeping on top from falling out of her dreams. Sandra was a single child, but they had bought the bunk bed for sleepovers, because all of her friends had bunk beds and the ones with the safety nets were all the rage. They also had bought a childproof kitchen at the time. It came with a miniature copy, a "kitchen within a kitchen" so to speak, for little girls to learn how to cook right next to their mothers. Sandra's mother had even given her a small cupboard with mini-containers for spices, sugar and salt. After school, Sandra liked to run around with friends or go to the pool with her Chicana nanny. Sandra remembered that, when she was little, she would get lost because all the streets looked the same. One day, many years ago, she had run home and, when she burst through the front door, everything had changed—the furniture, the pictures, the curtains and all. She really freaked out and screamed for her mom. Then this neighbor lady whom she didn't even know appeared and told her she was in the wrong house. Luckily, that day she had worn the bracelet with her phone number and street address, which the city council had introduced as mandatory for children under reading age. But that incident seemed to have happened such a long time ago! On Saturdays, her dad used to take her to one of her team's soccer games and, after-ward, they stopped at McDonald's. This was a little secret they shared, because Mom hated McDonalds. She claimed the hamburgers were made from the meat of mass produced lab rats discarded by UCI's Center for Reproductive Assistance after com-pleting its experiments on stem cells and reproductive rodent cloning. Dad told her not to listen to Mom's apocalyptic fantasies. But despite her mom's strange ways, Sandra loved her, and all the more because Mom always told her she was really, really special. "There is no other kid like you here," she said. "You are completely unique." And when her mom heard her speaking Spanish with her nanny, she would get dreamy and say, "At your age, I had only one language. You are so lucky. I wonder how it will change your brain." That always freaked Sandra out a little. Changing the brain felt scary.

Sandra also had a little secret with Mom. She used to take her to Starbucks and allowed her to have a double decaf iced mocha, even though she was only eight years old. She liked pretending that she was high on real caffeine. Mom said that, with her, one couldn't tell the difference anyway. Mom was a rather well known, if somewhat controversial local artist with her studio in the remodeled garage of their house. The studio was off limits, almost like a sacred space. When Mom worked there, nobody was allowed to disturb her. Sandra had adapted reluctantly to this rule, but found a way to climb a tree outside that allowed her to see the studio from above, almost like a bird. She liked to sit there peaking through the huge skylight her father had built into the garage roof. From this lofty hiding place, she watched her mom working with paper and brushes, pots and tubes of color and fine pencils, scissors and glues. Her mom was obsessed with green acrylics and used the color so abundantly that it gave her studio the feel of a greenhouse with artificial plant life. That was one of the things that made her art so controversial. Her critics said that she celebrated the increasing replacement of natural life with artificial simulacra. Sometimes Sandra stayed on the roof for a long, long time, oblivious of the world around her. It made her feel safe and gave her space for daydreaming. It also was a secret she had all to herself. She loved secrets, and the best were those not shared by anyone in the whole world, not even Mom or Dad. At the same time, she wished she had somebody to share her secrets with and dreamt of having a little puppy to whom she could tell everything she knew and saw and felt, and who wouldn't be able to tell on her or betray her like the friend at school who had told the teacher about the secret hiding place adjacent to the school yard where Sandra changed the clothes her mother made her wear because she hated them. Better to have an imaginary friend like Carla whom Sandra could call upon whenever she felt lonely and who followed her everywhere. Most importantly, Carla could make herself invisible and did so whenever Sandra's mom was around.

It was on one of those days when she sat in the tree that Sandra discovered a whole series of blown-up photos newly pinned to the studio wall. Since Sandra couldn't see them too well, she got her dad's binoculars and was surprised to find photo after photo of herself from all the way back when she was a little baby to the last photo Mom had shot of her just a few weeks ago. That was another story. When her mom took photos of her, she always went through these elaborate rituals of dressing Sandra in particular ways. There were even a few occasions when Mom had the nanny sew dresses that she described in minute detail. After making her wear one of these new dresses, Mom also made her hair up in old-fashioned ponytails or braids, all specially for the photos. For Sandra, this was an ordeal rather than a pleasure, even though she liked how the photos turned out. She liked them despite the fact that she often felt the photos looked as though they were of an actress playing her role rather than of her as she saw herself. It was when Sandra saw one of those photos on the studio wall that her curiosity got the better of her. She could barely wait until her mom went on errands that day. Then, for the first time in her life, she did what she had always dreamt of doing—she took the key to her mom's studio out of the hiding place she had spied long ago and sneaked into the studio. Her heart beating—she called it a Starbuck's high—she stood there mesmerized, gazing at the wall. Something was weird, something felt wrong but she couldn't quite figure out what. All the photos of her came in pairs—almost as though she had a twin sister— except one showed her in her familiar surroundings and the other right next to it in a house or a garden she had never seen. She felt a sudden pang of fear, but didn't understand what she was afraid of. It was almost like being in a dream where everything is strange and alien, but uncannily familiar at the same time. When had her mom taken these photos and why couldn't she remember the house so different from the one in which they now lived? Sandra also felt that she looked slightly different in the photos her mom had placed on the left side. Perhaps it was the paper with its slightly fading colors and a strange touch of yellow. Everything seemed somehow weird when she came to think of it. And what was her mom doing with those photos anyway? Wasn't she a painter? Sandra stood transfixed while, in her mind, she wanted to run away, close her eyes, and forget about the pictures. Wishing she had never come to her mom's studio, she finally fled, running back into the house, all stirred up and confused. As she tried to think of something else—play a video game, read a book, call a friend on her new solar-powered cell phone or simply anything— the photos kept intruding like an obnoxious ad on her favorite TV show.

After her mom came back, loaded with shopping bags, groceries and a bunch of yellow and purple orchids, Sandra kept stealing secret glances at her, almost as though she could figure everything out just by looking. "Mom, did we ever live in a different house?" she tried. "Of course not, honey, you know that! Why on earth did you ask, silly?" "Never mind," Sandra almost yelled back at her mom, already on the way outside. She ran up to what little remained of the hills behind their housing complex and sat down near a dry cactus field, looking over the city, the skyscrapers near the ocean and the airport in the distance. Then she started crying silently, not knowing why. She stayed until dark and, at the dinner table she had to listen to her mother's probing questions about what was wrong with her. Sandra brushed her off, lips and heart sealed. It was that night when she had the first of a long series of nightmares about being lost in a place she had never seen, a scenario that would stay with her as a recurring dream in ever-new variations. After hours of tossing and turning, she finally took her blanket and crawled into her parents' bed, curling up with her mom who didn't even wake up.

"What are you painting these days, Mom?" Sandra asked a few days later. "I'm not painting actually; I'm doing a collage," her mom replied. "What kind? Can I see?" Sandra begged. "No, you are still too young. One day when you're ready, I'll show you." Her mom stayed firm, regardless how often Sandra tried to make her give in and share her work on the collage. Things became tense in the house and the distance between Sandra and her mother grew so wide that she yearned for the days before her confusing discovery. Something had definitely and irrevocably changed, she felt, but was unable to understand what. Her father seemed oblivious to everything and went about his routine but, to Sandra, even the outings with him didn't feel the same anymore. This is why she was half relieved when her mom announced that she was to go to her grandmother's on her first vacation ever without her parents. Grandma lived out in the desert and insisted on staying there, even though the increasingly frequent sandstorms, deadly heat waves and torrential floods had turned the towns in the Southwestern deserts almost into ghost towns. The overdone and almost frantic preparations for this trip gave Sandra a welcome distraction from her troubles at home. Her mother prepared her suitcases and loaded the car as though she were moving to the moon. Since Grandma's divorce, she had lived all by herself in Joshua Tree in her stunningly beautiful house high up on a hill, overlooking mountain ranges with huge boulders on one side and badlands on the other. She had been able to afford it, she said, because people were fleeing the storms and the heat. Sandra was excited because she loved her grandmother. On the occasions she had visited Grandma with her parents before, she had seen neither storms nor floods and thoroughly enjoyed the desert hikes, feeling the sun wrap her skin in a hot blanket and taking in the noise of small rodents amid the empty desert quiet. The day they arrived at Grandma's house after what seemed a way too long and tedious car ride, Sandra was so impatient she almost wished her mom would leave right away. But Grandma had prepared dinner for everybody and then they had to go and see the sunset before her parents finally drove home.

Sandra spent a whole month with Grandma, during which they went on daily hikes to different parts of the desert. Sandra's favorite was Barker's Dam, a small trail that took them to a dry riverbed where they sometimes saw mountain goats. The trail then took them back in a large loop to a set of huge boulders with ancient rock paintings. Sandra always climbed up to her most cherished spot with a small turtle hidden under the largest rock's roundly carved roof. They usually set out for their hikes early in the morning before it got too hot. In the evenings, Grandma took her up to the mountains at Key's View to see the sunset. "Look, all the way back there behind the Salton Sea," Grandma said. "That's Mexico!" The very idea that you could sit on a hill and look from one country to another country excited Sandra. They would sit there for a long time, wrapped in their coats to protect them from the sudden drop in temperature. Sandra became all still inside, looking over the badlands and losing herself in her own dreams, quietly, just thinking.

During their daily hikes, Sandra was thrilled to see mountain sheep, coyotes, snakes and different types of small ground animals and bugs. Most of all, she loved the bats at night because her grandmother told her they were spiritual guides. Before going to bed, Grandma read her stories on the porch from the many books that filled the shelves along the walls all over the house. When Grandma was busy in the house, Sandra loved to browse through these books on her own. This is how, one day, she came across an old album of photos. Excited, she opened it, yet froze instantly when her eyes fell upon some familiar looking pictures. There they were, picture after picture of the house she had seen in her mom's photos! And there she was herself in that house! But no, she was with Granny who looked so much younger. Suddenly it dawned on her. This was not her but her mother, looking like her identical twin. In panic, she ran to Grandma, crying almost, "My mom, is this my mom? She looks like me!" Her grandmother turned all pale and silent. Then she took a deep breath and sat Sandra down. "We need to talk," she said quietly, but Sandra could feel her hidden agitation. "You were not supposed to see these pictures yet, my little one," Grandma explained almost soothingly. "Why do you think your mom never had any childhood photos around? She thought it was too early for you to know." "Know what?" Sandra cried in a flurry of panic.

They talked through half the night until, overcome by sheer exhaustion, Sandra finally fell asleep in Grandma's arms. She was her mother's clone! Sandra still couldn't quite grasp the magnitude of this revelation. She wanted to understand, but didn't want to understand. She didn't want to know and wanted to make her whole world go away. Like all the kids, she had, of course, heard the story of Dolly, the sheep they had cloned in the last century. It was part of the biology lessons at school and the teachers always made a point of telling how shocking the story of Dolly was when it first hit the news. Also, as Sandra remembered from school, Dolly had been a feeble copy of the original sheep and had had trouble carrying her own weight and keeping herself on her feet. Cloning techniques were perfected during the last century, her teacher had said, but Sandra didn't even know they could clone humans! "And why would her mother want a cloned child?" Sandra asked in utter despair. Because of a genetic problem that ran in her father's family, her parents couldn't have children, her grandmother explained. Rather than taking the risk of adoption or *in vitro* fertilization, her mother had suggested they volunteer for the first national human cloning program launched at UCI's Center for Reproductive Health. Slowly, her grandmother revealed to Sandra the whole story behind this devastating family secret. She talked and talked. Sometimes Sandra found her lost in thoughts or absentminded, almost as though she was really telling the story to herself as much as to Sandra. Some of the things she explained, Sandra didn't understand, or they seemed outlandish to her. At the time, there had been a big, though somewhat secretive, almost conspiratorial, advertising campaign in medical journals that Sandra's mother had found in her gynecologist's office. They selected only 20 mothers from all over the country who volunteered to have cloned children who would be monitored throughout their lives. The secrecy surrounding the project was partly an attempt not to revive the huge scandal that had erupted at UCI's Fertility Center a half-century earlier when assisted reproduction was still in its early years. "Imagine," Grandma said, "they swapped eggs and embryos among unknowing couples and failed to cover up their tracks! Those children must have grown up all confused over who their parents were! I still remember the lawsuit when a Christian couple sued a Jewish couple that had received their biological child. They claimed visitation rights so that they could teach their child 'the right religion!' Crazy days those were! Reproductive wars and religious wars all in one! We've never quite grown out of this mess. But look how different your mother was! Despite the fact that I was firmly opposed to her idea, I understood even at the time that it was your mother's dream to have a child unmistakably hers and hers alone. She wanted you to be something very special, different from other children. She thought you would be exactly like her and imagined you would become closer to her than children who come with genetic differences. She was also excited because she felt she could see herself grow up in a different life." "But I'm not her. I've never been like her. I'm different and I hate her!" Sandra screamed in a rage so huge it threatened to swallow her up. It took weeks before it began to settle in a dark hidden space inside her while, on the outside, she became taciturn and meek. Even being with Grandma didn't feel right anymore.

At the end of her vacation, Sandra knew she didn't want to return home. She never wanted to go back and never wanted to see her mother ever again. But her mother insisted and came to fetch her. Grandma had pleaded to give Sandra more time to adjust, but her mother was adamant. She had to drag a screaming child into the car. On the way home, Sandra didn't say a word while her mother tried to smooth-talk her into understanding what was, to Sandra, horrible beyond belief. Once they had returned home, Sandra settled into a mode of mute defiance and withdrawal. She became hostile and, from then on, refused to let her mother touch or cuddle her. One day, she broke into her mother's garage and destroyed the collage with the twin clones. Her father walked through the house, hissing to his increasingly distressed wife, "I told you so!" That's what Grandma had said on the phone the night she told Mom that Sandra had found out—"I told you so!" Sandra had silently listened in on the conversation because she hated secrets now. She also hated remembering all those remarks about being her mother's spitting image that used to make her feel so good when she was a little kid.

When, after months and months, Sandra's mom was at the end of her rope, she made an appointment for Sandra with a psychotherapist specializing in identity disturbances resulting from assisted reproduction fantasies. After all, they were not alone in struggling with psychological problems emerging from the new technologies of genetic screening, engineering and enhancement. After spending 50 minutes alone with Sandra, the therapist emerged from his office and pronounced almost laconically, "I guess there is some boundary work in order here!" Sandra thought she had detected a sneer in his voice when she told her story and an almost disgusted look at her mother when he saw her in the waiting room. But perhaps it was just her imagination. These days, she didn't quite trust her feelings anymore, and she hated being dragged to a therapist as though it was she who had a problem. Yet, she also felt helpless enough to give in to her mother's decision, especially because her father, passive as ever, was no help in the first place. After Sandra had returned from the desert and all the tensions and outbursts with her mother started, her father became involved in what Sandra secretly termed his vanishing act. He returned later and later from work, often after Sandra had gone to bed. Sometimes she didn't see him for days. And, instead of taking her to the beach, to soccer or on their secret MacDonald's outings on weekends, he now claimed he had brought work home from the office and needed to withdraw for a while. Sandra had never felt so lonely and, often, she wished she could simply disappear and hide somewhere where nobody knew her and especially where nobody knew her mom. The worst was that, soon after the family secret was revealed, her mother and grandmother had a falling out of sorts over differences concerning how to handle "the incident" as they now called it. They left Sandra out of the loop concerning the details of their disagreement, but she became the victim of its effects. She saw her grandma less and less, and her mother refused to let her visit with Grandma without her being present.

As the years passed, things began to settle. At least, this is what it looked like on the surface. Sandra stayed in therapy with various therapists for nearly seven years. Sometimes she went to family therapy with her mom, sometimes with both parents. She never forgave her mom. She never got over hating her. When her mom pleaded with her, telling her she just wanted them to have the perfect mother-daughter love, Sandra screamed, "You never loved me. You only loved yourself. You never even wanted me to have a life of my own!" A few years down the road, her parents divorced and Sandra moved with her father to another city two hours up the coast. There she developed an obsession with trying to find out whether any of the girls she saw in the street with their mothers could possibly be her mother's clone. "There must be others like me," she thought, even though she had no idea what it would have meant and what difference it would have made if her idea were confirmed. Her obsession with resemblances became so bad that she completely lost trust in her own judgment. Did this girl really look like the spitting image of her mother or did she just imagine it? This was also the time when she began fantasizing about a twin sister she called Carla. Soon Sandra spent hours daydreaming about her life with Carla. In the intricate interior dialogues Sandra composed, they shared the most illicit thoughts and secret wishes. It deeply satisfied Sandra to know that it was the very intimacy her mother craved so much that she freely gave to Carla instead. Imagining they were both born as mother's clones, Sandra's greatest delight consisted in spinning tales of truculent revenge with Carla. "Shared revenge is double revenge," she would exclaim in a gleeful bond with her imaginary twin. It was in those idle hours of fantasizing about Carla that she could escape the immure abode of her loneliness, at least temporarily. But while she shifted more of her energies to the lofty world of daydreams, she increasingly retreated into a defiant and hostile withdrawal from the world around her. She became obsessed with making herself look different from her mother and developed a darker and darker Gothic style, mainly because it was what her mom had always hated most. Her make-up looked almost white under her black hair and eyebrows, and her black lipstick and nail polish enhanced the haggard look she had acquired after she took pleasure in starving herself. She had bought the blackest color contacts she could find, which made her eyes look huge and almost unearthly. Her father followed his own gospel of tolerance and was determined to give his daughter space. He missed no occasion to hint at the fact that he now was on her side rather than her mother's. But even though Sandra now hated her mother, it bugged her that her father kept trashing Mom, as though he had never been part of the deal in the first place. He ranted against "all those 21st century pseudo-feminists who boasted about their freedom from sperm and sex! SS-feminism," he sneered full of venom and contempt. Yet, Sandra didn't forgive her father either for allowing her mom to act on her dream. To be sure, he tried his best to be a good father again after the divorce. He came home after work to spend time with her and help her with her homework. She had gotten worse and worse at school, mainly because she couldn't muster any interest in whatever subjects she had to study. She had even lost her childhood interest in books, painting and music. Her mind always seemed to wander elsewhere, and she didn't care a bit whether she flunked school, went to college or was bent on a career of selling hotdogs as her father jokingly said. "They wouldn't let a Goth behind a hot dog stand," Sandra retorted. "Perhaps I'll become a mortician!" But Sandra's father kept engaging her and defended her when she got into trouble at school. He convinced her teachers to cut her some slack. After all, she was diagnosed with PTSD. So he patiently sat down with her during long evening hours to study math or history and, in their free time, he thought of activities or even trips they could take together. Yet, somehow Sandra knew there was no real connection between them. Perhaps there never had been but, at least, they used to have fun together. Now it rather felt as though they strained to fulfill a role. Sandra didn't even know who her father really was. A stranger. She no longer knew what she felt for him—nothing really, except some lingering resentment. She felt lonelier than ever. Sometimes she was tempted to convince her father to let her stay with her grandmother. But then again, she never acted on the impulse. Wasn't that where everything had started?

One day, however, when Sandra was about to go out with her father for dinner, she caught him looking at her in a particular way. She didn't even quite know how she figured out and suddenly understood what was happening. In a state of shock, it dawned on her that, since a few months ago, her own father had begun courting her—yes, that's what it really felt like—courting. It must have begun right after she had made inroads in her therapy in the treatment of her anorexia and had almost achieved a legitimate weight again. She just hadn't seen what she didn't want to see, but now the insight had come to her in the glimpse of an eye, so to speak. She completely freaked out. All she heard was a shrill scream as though it came from elsewhere. Then Sandra heard herself shouting at her father, telling him he was a creep, a pervert, worse than scum, worse even than her sick and perverted mother! He just stood there, sheepishly confessing that Sandra reminded him so much of her mother when she was young that he couldn't help it. He would, of course, never think of acting on it, he tried reassuringly. Sandra stared at him, turned on her heel, packed up her things and left. She moved to an undisclosed address. After that, she saw her mom a few more times in joint therapy sessions. She never mentioned the incident with her father and never revealed her new address to her mother either. That she needed privacy was all she said and that was it. Uncannily, however, her mother and she had become more intimate than they had ever been. They knew each other inside out. They had, in fact, become intimate enemies for life. Yet, in total denial and with a stubborn tenacity that made Sandra cringe each time, her mom kept talking about healing things between them. Sandra retaliated with sheer hostility.

One day, in a confused bout of self-pity, despair and false hope, her mom fulfilled Sandra's old childhood wish and surprised her with a puppy. It was a week after Sandra had revealed in therapy that she had always felt alone. Other kids had siblings or at least a puppy, but all she had had was parents who never seemed to understand her. They had met at the therapist's office and her mother asked her afterward to accompany her to her car. There she handed her a little basket with a puppy, a golden retriever. Sandra was speechless. She took the basket, turned on her heel and left without so much as a distant but polite thank you. She drove home in such inner turmoil that she could barely stay on her side of the road. What she hated most was the feeling that her mother had given her what she would have loved most. If only it hadn't come from her mother. She simply couldn't take it anymore. In a wild fit of deadly rage, Sandra threw the puppy against the wall and then buried it under a jasmine tree, crying her eyes out. That's when Sandra became afraid of herself. She had a feeling that her rage was bottomless and out of control. She began hating herself almost as much as she hated her mother. Another flash of insight told her what she had to do. In the middle of the night, she drove all the way back to her mother's house, took the key out from under the decoy stone and silently entered through the back door. She took off her shoes, carefully walked in her socks to the kitchen and placed a note, beautifully calligraphed in acrylic green letters, next to her mother's new automatic Starbucks coffee maker. The note said: "Claiming the life you never gave me, I kill your fake immortality. Listen to what I won't tell you. Sandra."

Sandra vanished into the night, humming an old tune. She smiled to herself as she heard Carla's footsteps following her at a distance. For the first time, she felt free as a bird. Nobody ever saw her again.

Dead Ringer – Knock Off

Carole-Anne Tyler

I. Dead Ringer

[The story is the same through until the psychotherapist episode; the following is appended to that by way of continuing and completing it differently.]

"When, after months and months, Sandra's mom was at the end of her rope, she made an appointment for Sandra with a psychotherapist specializing in identity disturbances resulting from assisted reproduction fantasies. After all, they were not alone in struggling with psychological problems emerging from the new technologies of genetic screening, engineering and enhancement. After spending 50 minutes alone with Sandra, the therapist emerged from his office and pronounced almost laconically, "I guess there is some boundary work in order here!" Sandra thought she had detected a sneer in his voice when she told her story and an almost disgusted look at her mother when he saw her in the waiting room." (Gabriel Schwab)

"Well, Alexandra," her mother said, looking up from the magazine she was holding, "it's rather like children's therapy, isn't it, to start with a story—and one with a lot of drawings in it at that. You are not a clone. All children feel they are trapped by what they make of their parents' hopes for them. This is classic Oedipus. And the business about refusing the longed-for gift from the mother or being the mother's puppy," she said, rolling and unrolling the magazine as she spoke quietly, but firmly, "that's a bit obvious, isn't it? The whole scene is rather jarring. We both know Alexandra could never be so violent. Nothing has prepared us for that."

"Mom, stop treating me like I'm one of your head cases; I'm your daughter," Sandra wailed, her voice taking on the hysterical tones she had vowed to avoid, because she was not going to let her mother get to her again, as she always did.

Biting her lip until she drew blood, she continued in more even tones, "And stop calling me Alexandra. I told you Dad and I legally changed my name. Why don't you get it? I'm only 13, but I got this story published in a real magazine. Doesn't that mean anything to you?" She heard with consternation the whine that always came into her voice when she asked that question, as she had on countless other occasions for different, yet similar reasons. Once again, she was conscious of how she always became a parody of herself. She flattened her dramatically outstretched arms to her sides, shifting her feet to bring her knees and ankles together in a posture of closed-off primness that, like the open arm-waving, was the other gesture with which she punctuated conversations with her mother. For a minute, the two mirrored each other in silence, for Sandra's demure pose was characteristic of her mother too.

"All right, *Sandra*," her mother said, with just a trace of a sigh in the emphasis she gave the name. "Suppose you tell me what you think the story means. Suppose you tell me why you wanted to have me read it in a publication, and why I had to read it here, in my office."

Sandra stared stonily at her mother. Her throat tightened—the only sign of the wave of outrage she was struggling to repress. Why did her mother always have to ask such questions so patiently, so disinterestedly, as though nothing could quicken her to the emotional outbursts Sandra could barely contain? What was the use when her mother asked them like that, like a needle stuck in the groove of one of the old record albums she loved, unaware of how she pierced Sandra's all too tender feelings as she played them? Sandra reached into the Coach bag she had bought with her Bat Mitzvah money, which was just a bit nicer than the one her mother owned, and pulled out the bottle of anti-depressants. Slowly, with great deliberation, she twisted off the childproof cap and turned the bottle upside down, releasing the capsules in a hail of green and white that hardly marred the pastel perfection of the Oriental rug on which they rained down. She got up from the couch on which she had been sitting, the couch which complemented the carpet, the wall coverings, and even the folk collectibles her mother had chosen for this space in partial emulation of Freud, though their hushed tones made them disappear a little too conspicuously into the silence the room spoke, the whole of it too pearly pretty, a conch horn muted into a pink and peach ear. "You know, Mother, I'm surprised you aren't concerned that I was prescribed Prozac when there is such a high suicide rate among teens who use it," she said. And she ground the drug into the wool pile as best she could on her way out the door. She knew now what she had to do.

Late that night, Sandra made her way silently into her mother's bedroom, clutching an African fertility statue she had pilfered from her office. Raising it high above her head, Sandra brought it down as hard as she could on her mother's face, which crumpled into a bloody flower on the pillow, like some more lurid version of the office carpet's roses. Again and again, Sandra beat her, raising and lowering the stone figure just as her mother would the stylus when she was trying to catch the right groove in a record. But all Sandra heard was the sound of her own voice as she sang out, "I take the life you never gave me. Why can't you listen to what I can't tell you? Why can't you listen to what I can't tell you?"

[or how about this ending?]

II. "Knock Off"

Sandra reached into the Coach bag she had bought with her Bat Mitzvah money, which was just a bit nicer than the one her mother owned, and pulled out the bottle of anti-depressants. She knew what she had to do. That night, she took all her anti-depressants . . . and flushed them away in the guest-room toilet. "Bitch," she muttered, watching them swirl in the water cyclone like snowflakes in the paperweight Citizen Kane let fall at the start of her mother's favorite film. Then she opened her suitcase and pulled out the other outfit she had packed for this visit, the secret one she had bought at the mall with the Christmas money her parents had given her to spend on school clothes. "Bitch," she said again as she struggled into the leopard skin halter top and equally tight black leather mini and matching thigh-high boots. "How do you like that, bitch," she half snarled to the mirror as she curled her lips into a bitter line and painted them scarlet. She straightened and smiled at what she saw framed in the glass, the very picture of one of the cheap little tarts in a teen runaway movie-of-the-week. "You wanted to see yourself grow up in a different life, Mom. All right, Sandra's really going to do Alexandra now." She ripped a sheet from the little rosebud dotted notepad her mother, the thoughtful hostess, had left by the guestroom phone on the nightstand next to the bed. "I take the life you never gave me," she wrote, the pen carving deep into the page. "Fuck you!" she added. She paused and tapped the pen against her teeth, eyes narrowed. Then sneering at the cliche, she asked herself, "Shall I sign it 'Randy Sandy?'" Shaking her head, she folded it in half with a violent gesture and sealed it with a bloody kiss that blotted her lipstick before dropping it on the bed and climbing out the window just above it, suitcase in hand, to head to the bus stop. Beside the note was its signature, the only other mark of Sandra's presence in her mother's home that night: a tiny, high-heel hole that pierced the heart of one of the pink and cream cabbage roses on the bed quilt.

Destiny – Eternity

Nancy Postero

I. Destiny

Because this was California, Sandra began seeing a therapist shortly after the terrible revelation. Sometimes she went with her mother and father, but mostly she went alone, trying to make sense of the unimaginable story of her own beginning. Who was she, she pondered, who or what? At first, she was just mad at her mother for being selfish, for failing to think about the effect her decision would have on Sandra. What kind of mother love was that? She moved out as soon as she could, when she was seventeen, and went to live with her grandmother in the desert. She found the desert peaceful, and her grandmother was a helpful sounding board for her anguished teenage ruminations. Why did the world play this nasty trick on her? How could she figure out who or what to be if she was merely a copy of someone else? Did this mean she was doomed to repeat her mother's life? Her mistakes? Was she a prisoner of her own genes?

She couldn't help herself; she began to look obsessively at her grandmother's photo albums, containing pictures of her mother at Sandra's age. Looking from different angles to find differences, she was horrified at the similarities. She began to tape them up in her bedroom, around her mirror, on the walls, then on the bed frame next to her so that she saw them first thing when she woke up. Soon, she found herself taking photos of herself, Polaroids, digital photos, blowing them up and making collages on the walls. Her grandmother finally pushed her and this increasingly bizarre work out into the garage. "She'll get through this phase," she thought. "It's probably just her way of working it all out." Late nights would find Sandra drinking espresso and assembling her works, looking at herself in mirrors, at her face, her body. "Am I just a collection of genes, and molecules? Where is the "me" in this body, in this duplicated, copied body?"

The works became bigger, more jagged, and now began to include bits of text, phrases that Sandra excavated from her therapy journals: "self, selves, selfish . . .," "other, another, mother . . .," "clone, lone, alone. . .," along with images and headlines from press accounts of animal cloning experiments. Soon, she took her work outside, to big canvases she built in the desert. When her high school art teacher saw them, things heated up and, before she knew it, an L.A. art dealer was at her door, asking her to do a show. Sandra couldn't believe it—here it was again, the eerie repetition she was scared would be her destiny. Wasn't she doing just exactly what her artist mother had done? Could she not be free, even while expressing her own fury? "But hell," she thought, "I'll show my mother who is the real artist!"

The show was a sellout, and she did not hesitate to relate to critics and buyers the original story that had inspired her work. The press hounded her, harassed her parents, and made her a star. "The technology generation's Frida," they said, "whose very life and work point out the fractured constructed nature of the self." The next few years were a blur of creating art, going to galleries and parties, and displaying her "anguished clone" persona. One highlight was a show called Copies, a joint installation in a London gallery with the Singh twins, Sikh artists from Liverpool who paint together and present themselves as one artist. At the accompanying conference entitled "Cloning Cultures," academics considered the difficult issues presented by the work, the blurry boundaries between difference and sameness, and between the simulacrum and the authentic.

For Sandra, the attention and the money were nice, but they did not erase the doubts that continued to eat at her insides, keeping her up at night. On the show's opening night, all she could hear was the voice inside her, saying, "Impostor, this is your mother's talent, not yours." She envied the Singh twins their apparent peace, not to mention their companionship. With all the ghosts in her head, Sandra still felt alone. Stalking moodily through the gallery with her third glass of champagne gripped tightly in her paint-stained hands, she came to a sudden stop. Was that really Richard Gere in front of one of her pieces? Was he buying it? When the gallery owner introduced them, Gere told her he loved the work, a big piece with refracted images of Sandra and her mother layered over and over on top of one another. For a Buddhist like him, it was a beautiful reminder of the many incarnations through which all beings must go. "We are all recombinations of past life forms, forced to live in bodies not of our choosing. Your work reminds me that the body is a dangerous illusion. It is the soul that we must remember," he said.

You can guess the rest. Inspired by this new perspective, Sandra decided to investigate Buddhism, spent several months on a meditation retreat in Northern California where she did not speak or look into mirrors, and eventually decided to embrace her karmic position. She became all compassionate, forgave her mother, and they now run an exclusive art studio and yoga spa center in Big Sur. Twins get a two-for-one discount.

II. Eternity

Sandra and her parents managed to work through the painful emotions resulting from the revelation of her birth, thanks to a lot of counseling and the intervention of Sandra's grandmother, who provided a safe haven for her when she just couldn't cope with the home environment. While Sandra never felt very close to her parents after that, she finally accepted the belief that their motives had been, well, if not good, then at least not terrible. At least she was wanted, which was much more than many of her unhappy school friends could say. She promised her parents that she would keep their family secret, although it made her feel uncomfortable, almost dirty. So the years passed and Sandra grew up, never revealing her unusual pedigree, even when people commented on how much she took after her mom. Even when she dyed her hair jet black and bought funky thrift store clothes to make herself look as different as possible, she still felt her secret was obvious. She became withdrawn and quiet.

In college, she was drawn to gender studies—she wasn't sure why. Perhaps it was a life of silences and erasures? Through her classes and the meetings at the women's center on campus that her counselor suggested she attend, Sandra began to acquire a circle of friends whom she felt might understand her. She became more outgoing, and gradually came to think that maybe graduate school might work for her. For her senior thesis, she decided to study a new women's group she had heard of— feminists Wiccans, who combined goddess worship with a radical separatism. "It's a bit extreme," she thought, "but that makes a good case study, right?" Over the months of participant observation, Sandra was drawn into the group, and found the rituals much more meaningful than she could have imagined. She began to dream about the goddess, and found herself humming their lovely chants as she wrote up her field notes. One night, the group did a trance-induced shamanic voyage. Sandra had not intended to go this far, but she went along with it to see what it was all about. In the middle of her trance, as the drums pounded rhythmically, she found herself face to face with herself—or was it her mother?—naked, covered with garlands of flowers, surrounded by adoring women who were touching her, addressing her as Mother. When she came out of the trance, sobbing, she told the group her long-held secret, that she was her mother's clone. She was astonished by their response. Instead of the horror she expected to feel from her witchy friends, their faces lit up. "You were born just from a woman? This was a man-less reproduction?" "Yes," she admitted. She'd never thought of it that way. The women were jubilant; here was a way to increase their family without men, a way to erase all traces of men, and to glory only in the woman as giver of birth. "Your mother is like a new Virgin Mary to us, and you are the Christ womanchild!" In their celebration, they lifted her up, tucked flowers in her hair, and chanted their ancient songs to the Mother goddess.

All of Sandra's shame lifted and, although she was unsure what it would mean, she assented to the role the women offered. She became a member of the group, learned their religion, and presided over their rituals. Their numbers grew as word got out that the goddess had taken corporeal form. New songs were written, new rituals imagined and enacted. Then came the hard consensus work of group process. Over the following months, the group decided that this was an opportunity not to be passed up. If Sandra was a man-less woman child, then what could happen if she, too, were cloned? Wouldn't each step be purer, less tainted? Much to her surprise, Sandra's disgrace became the hope of this new family, and she agreed. A year later, a new baby goddess was born. A year later, another one arrived. And a year later . . .

The Contributors

Ackbar Abbas is professor of comparative literature at UC Irvine. He has written on fascination and fakes. He is currently working on Chinese cities and cinemas, and 'Poor Theory'.

Rosi Braidotti (B.A. Hons. Australian National University, 1978; PhD Cum Laude, Université de Paris, Panthéon-Sorbonne, 1981; Senior Fulbright Scholar, 1994; Honorary Degree 'Philosophiae Doctrix Honoris Causa', University of Helsinki, 2007; Knight in the Order of the Netherlands Lion, 2005; Honorary Fellow of the Australian Academy of the Humanities, 2009) is Distinguished University Professor and founding Director of the Centre for the Humanities at Utrecht University. She was the founding professor of Gender Studies in the Humanities at Utrecht (1988–2005) and the first scientific director of the Netherlands Research School of Women's Studies. In 2005–2006, she was the Leverhulme Trust, Visiting Professorship in the Law School of Birckbeck College, University of London. In 2001–2003, she held the Jean Monnet Visiting Chair at the Robert Schuman Centre for Advanced Studies of the European Institute in Florence. In 1994–1995 she was a fellow in the School of Social Science at the Institute for Advanced Study at Princeton. Her books include *Patterns of Dissonance*. Cambridge, Polity Press, 1991; *Nomadic Subjects: Embodiment and Sexual Difference in Contemporary Feminist Theory*. New York: Columbia Univ. Press, 1994; *Metamorphoses: Towards a Materialist Theory of Becoming* Polity Press, 2002; *Transpositions. On Nomadic Ethics*, Polity Press, 2006 and *La philosophie, lá où on ne l'attend pas*, Larousse, 2009. In 2011 a thoroughly revised second edition of *Nomadic Subjects* was published by Columbia University Press in New York.

Scott Coltrane is Dean of the College of Arts and Sciences at the University of Oregon and a sociologist whose research focuses on fathers and families. He is the author of several books, including Family Man, Gender and Families, Families and Society, and Sociology of Marriage and the Family, and over 75 scholarly journal articles or chapters in edited collections. His most recent research projects investigate the impact of economic stress on Mexican American and European American fathers and stepfathers and the influence of public policies on father involvement.

M. Robin DiMatteo received her Ph.D. (1976) in Psychology and Social Relations from Harvard University. Her research focuses on health care delivery – specifically on communication in the medical interaction. Using complex methods of interpersonal interaction analysis, she and her graduate students examine verbal and nonverbal communication in the "micro-social environment" of the medical visit. They examine how information is gathered and conveyed between physician and patient, and how trust and commitment to adherence develop. Professor DiMatteo has published numerous meta-analytic studies on the prediction and management of patient adherence to preventive and treatment recommendations, focusing on patients' beliefs, behavioral constraints, depression, social support, illness severity, and provider-patient communication. She is currently examining the role of patients' socio-economic vulnerabilities and health literacy in their adherence, and has developed and validated training programs for providers and patients to reduce communication gaps and improve adherence. With colleagues Leslie R. Martin, Ph.D. and Kelly Haskard-Zolnierek, Ph.D., Dr. DiMatteo is author of "Health Behavior Change and Treatment

Adherence: Evidence-Based Guidelines for Improving Healthcare" published in 2010 by Oxford University Press.

Philomena Essed (Ph.D., Cum Laude, University of Amsterdam; Honorary Doctorate, University of Pretoria) is professor of Critical Race, Gender and Leadership studies, Antioch University, *PhD in Leadership and Change Program* and affiliated researcher at Utrecht University, *Graduate Gender Program*. Before joining the Antioch faculty she worked as a transnational scholar at the University of Amsterdam (1993–2005) and the University of California, Irvine (2001–2005). Best known for introducing the concepts of *everyday racism* and *gendered racism,* her work has been adopted and applied in a range of countries, including the US, Canada, South Africa, Sweden, Finland, Russia, the UK, Switzerland, Australia and translated into German, French, Italian, Portuguese and Swedish. Books and co-edited volumes include *Everyday Racism; Understanding Everyday Racism*; *Diversity: Gender, Color and Culture*; *Race Critical Theories; Refugees and the Transformation of Societies;* and *A Companion to Gender Studies* (selected 'outstanding' 2005 academic reference, American Librarian Association). Her current work is on *human dignity*. In progress is a volume on *Dutch Racism.*

A life-long commitment to social justice, theory and practice are mutually constitutive of Essed's career. Among others, she has been Member of the Dutch *Selection Commission of Members of the Judiciary* (SRM, 2003–2010) and, since 2004, Deputy Member of the Dutch *Equal Treatment Commission.*

In April 2011 she was honored with a Knighthood from *Queen Beatrix* of the Netherlands.

Christine Ward Gailey is Professor of Women's Studies and Anthropology at the University of California, Riverside. She has published extensively on gender and kinship, state formation, and feminist epistemologies. Her most recent book is *Blue Ribbon Babies and Labors of Love: Race, Class, and Gender in U.S. Adoption Practice* (University of Texas Press, 2010).

David Theo Goldberg is Director of the system wide University of California Humanities Research Institute and Executive Director of the MacArthur-UCI Research Hub in Digital Media and Learning. The latter is the international center coordinating all research for the MacArthur Foundation initiative in connected learning. He is a Professor in Comparative Literature and Criminology, Law and Society and an Affiliate Professor of Anthropology at UC Irvine. He has written extensively on digital media's impact on higher education, on race and racism, law and society, and on critical theory. He has raised more than $30m for the University of California in research funds and endowment.

Rebecca Kugel teaches Native American History at the University of California, Riverside. Her research focuses on the history of the Ojibwes and other Native peoples of the Great Lakes region, emphasizing the operation of the historic political system in the eighteenth and nineteenth centuries. Her current research examines the construction of Great Lakes indigenous political speech and its use of distinctive metaphors. She has additional research interests in the cultural constructions of race among Great Lakes Native peoples and in Native women's history. She is the author of *To Be The Main Leaders of Our People; A History of Minnesota Ojibwe Politics, 1825–1898* (1998), and co-editor, with Lucy Eldersveld Murphy of *Native Women's History in Eastern North America before 1900; A Guide to Research and Writing* (2007).

Eileen Luhr is assistant professor of history at California State University, Long Beach, where she teaches courses in United States history, religious history, history and theory, and history pedagogy. Her first monograph, *Witnessing Suburbia: Conservatives and Christian Youth Culture* (University of California Press, 2009), examines the connection between conservatism, religion, youth culture, and suburbanization during the late twentieth century. Her current project, *Pilgrims' Progress*, explores religious journeys and American power in a global context.

Toby Miller (August 9, 1958) is a British-Australian-US interdisciplinary social scientist. He is the author and editor of over 30 books, has published essays in more than 100 journals and edited collections, and is a frequent guest commentator on television and radio programs. His teaching and research cover the media, sports, labor, gender, race, citizenship, politics, and cultural policy, as well as the success of Hollywood overseas and the adverse effects of electronic waste. Miller's work has been translated into Chinese, Japanese, Swedish, German, Spanish and Portuguese. He has been Media Scholar in Residence at Sarai, the Centre for the Study of Developing Societies in India, Becker Lecturer at the University of Iowa, a Queensland Smart Returns Fellow in Australia, Honorary Professor at the Center for Critical and Cultural Studies, University of Queensland, CanWest Visiting Fellow at the Alberta Global Forum in Canada, and an International Research collaborator at the Centre for Cultural Research in Australia. Among his books, *SportSex* was a *Choice* Outstanding Title for 2002 and *A Companion to Film Theory* a *Choice* Outstanding Title for 2004. Born in the United Kingdom and brought up in England, India, and Australia, Miller earned a B.A. in history and political science at the Australian National University in 1980 and a Ph.D. in philosophy and communication studies at Murdoch University in 1991. He taught at Murdoch, Griffith University, and the University of New South Wales and was a professor at New York University from 1993 to 2004, when he joined the University of California, Riverside. Miller is now chair of a new Department of Media & Cultural Studies and lives near the ocean in Los Angeles.

Ross D. Parke, Ph.D., is a Distinguished Professor of Psychology, Emeritus and past Director of the Center for Family Studies at the University of California, Riverside. His interests include fatherhood, the relation between families and peers, ethnic variation in families, and the impact of the new reproductive technologies on families. He has served as Editor of *Developmental Psychology* and the *Journal of Family Psychology,* and as Associate Editor of *Child Development.* He was president of the Division of Developmental Psychology of the American Psychological Association and of the Society for Research in Child Development. He received The G. Stanley Hall award from the Division of Developmental Psychology of APA, the Distinguished Scientific Contribution award from SRCD and the Graduate Student Mentoring Award from the graduate division of UC Riverside. He is author of several books including *Fathers* and *Fatherhood* and coauthor of *Throwaway Dads* (with Armin Brott) and *Child Psychology: A contemporary perspective* (with E. Mavis Hetherington and Mary Gauvain) which appeared in its 7th edition in 2008. With Alison Clarke-Stewart, he recently published *Social Development.* He has co-edited several books on families, history and child development including *Children in Time and Place, A Century of Developmental Psychology* and most recently *Strengthening Couple Relationships for Optimal Child Development.* He is currently working on a new book *Future Families: Diverse forms, Rich Possibilities.*

Nancy Postero is an Associate Professor in the Anthropology department at UC San Diego. Formerly a human rights lawyer and a radio journalist, she received her PhD from UC Berkeley in 2001. Her work focuses on the intersection of neoliberalism and multicultural citizenship. She has carried out fieldwork with the Guaraní people of lowland Bolivia since 1994. Along with numerous articles on indigenous politics in Bolivia, she is the author of *Now We Are Citizens, Indigenous Politics in Post-multicultural Bolivia* (Stanford University Press 2007) and the co-editor with Leon Zamosc of *The Struggle for Indigenous Rights in Latin America* (Sussex Press 2003). Her new work examines the "post-neoliberal" moment in Latin America and the agenda of decolonization in contemporary Bolivia.

Carole-Anne Tyler is Associate Professor of English at the University of California at Riverside. Her publications and teaching focus on gender and sexuality, literary and media theory, film and television, and modern and contemporary fiction, the interests central to her first book, *Female Impersonation* (Routledge 2003). Her current project, *Reading "as a Woman,"* explores the gaze, the voice, and "feminine desire" in feminist and queer theory beginning with the 1980s debates the title recalls and closing with current claims for new queer forms of sociality or the "anti-social." Her awards include an American Council of Learned Societies Fellowship, a U.C. President's Research Fellowship in the Humanities, and fellowships at the U.C. Humanities Research Institute and U.C. Riverside's Center for Ideas and Society.

Verena Stolcke is Professor Emeritus of social anthropology at the Departamento de Antropologia Social y Cultural, Universitat Autónoma de Barcelona. Born in Germany in 1938, she was educated at Oxford University [D.Phil., 1970]. She conducted field and archival research in Cuba in 1967–68 and in Sao Paulo, Brazil, between 1973 and 1979. She is the author of *Marriage, Class, and Colour in Nineteenth Century Cuba* (Cambridge: Cambridge University Press, 1974, reprinted by the University of Michigan Press in 1989 and 2003; published in Spanish under the title *Racismo y Sexualidad en la Cuba Colonial.* Alianza Editorial, Madrid, 1992); *Coffee Planters, Workers, and Wives: Class Conflict and Gender Relations on Sao Paulo Plantations, 1850–1980* (Oxford: St. Antony's/Macmillan 1988); "Women's Labours: The Naturalisation of Social Inequality and Women's Subordination," in *Of Marriage and the Market*, edited by K. Young, C. Wolkowitz, and R. McCullagh (London: Routledge and Kegan Paul 1981), "New Reproductive Technologies, Old Fatherhood," *Reproductive and Genetic Engineering* I (I); "Is Sex to Gender as Race Is to Ethnicity?" in *Gendered Anthropology*, edited by Teresa del Valle (London: Routledge, I993). Recent articles are "Talking Culture. New boundaries, new rhetorics of exclusion in Europe", *Current Anthropology* 36 (1) February 1995; "The 'Nature' of Nationality" in *Citizenship and Exclusion* edited by Veit Bader (London: Macmillan Press Ltd., 1997) and "El sexo de la biotecnología" in *Genes en el laboratorio y en la fábrica* edited by Alicia Durán & Jorge Riechmann (Madrid: Editorial Trotta, 1998). She has also published on feminist theory, more recently, "La mujer es puro cuento: la cultura del género", *Quaderns de l'Institut Càtala d'Antropología*, serie monográfica: A propósito de cultura, 19, 2003; "La influencia de la esclavitud en la estructura doméstica y la familia en Jamaica, Cuba y Brasil", *Desacatos. Revista de Antropología Social*, CIESAS México, no. 13, invierno 2003; and "A New World Engendered. The Making of the Iberian Transatlantic Empire", edited by Teresa A. Meade & Merry E. Wiesner-Hanks (eds.), *A Companion to Gender History, Serie: Blackwell Companions to History* (Oxford: Blackwell Publishing 2004). A new line of research is published in "Los mestizos no nacen sino que se hacen" in *Identidades Ambivalentes en América Latina (Siglos XVI–XXI)* edited by Verena Stolcke & Alexandre Coello. And recent articles are "A propósito del sexo", *Política y Sociedad*, vol. 46, nos. 1 y 2, 2009, and "Qué tiene que ver el género con el parentesco? in V. Fons, A. Piella y M. Valdés (coords), *Procreación, crianza y género. Aproximaciones antropológicas a la parentalidad* (Barcelona: PPU. Promociones y Publicaciones Universitarias, S.A. 2010).

Gabriele Schwab received her Ph.D. in English, American and Romance Literatures at the University of Konstanz, Germany, in 1976 and her Ph.D. in Psychoanalysis from the New Center for Psychoanalysis, Los Angeles in 2009. She is Chancellor's Professor of English and Comparative Literature and Faculty Associate in the Department of Anthropology as well as a member and former Director of the Critical Theory Institute at the University of California at Irvine. She is the recipient of a Guggenheim Fellowship and a Heisenberg Fellowship. Her books include *Subjects without Selves* (Harvard UP, 1994), *The Mirror-and the Killer-Queen* (Indiana UP, 1997) *Haunting Legacies: Violent Histories and Transgenerational Trauma*, (Columbia UP, 2010), *Imaginary Ethnographies* (Columbia UP, 2012, in press). *Samuel Beckett's Endspiel mit der Subjektivität* and *Entgrenzungen und Entgrenzungsmythen* appeared in German. *Literature, Power and Subjectivity*, translated by Tao Jiajun with a preface by Sola Liu, appeared in Chinese in 2011. Edited volumes include *Accelerating Possessions: Global Futures of Property and Personhood*, co-edited with William Maurer, (Columbia UP, 2006), *The Cultural Unconscious and the Postcolonizing Process*, co-ed. with John Cash, Special Issue of *Postcolonial Studies; Derrida, Deleuze,*

Psychoanalysis (Columbia UP, 2008). Her work has been translated into Bulgarian, Chinese, French, German, Japanese, Korean, Portuguese and Spanish. Works in progress include *Children of Fire, Children of Water* with Native American writer Simon J. Ortiz.

Heleen van den Hombergh has a background in tropical forestry and rural development (Wageningen University and Research Centre). She did her PhD, University of Amsterdam, on socio-environmental coalition building and campaigning in Costa Rica. For several years van den Hombergh was in charge of supporting international networks at Oxfam Netherlands (Novib) where she got introduced to global concerns associated with gentech agriculture. Currently she is senior advisor at the International Union for the Conservation of Nature (National Committe of the Netherlands) and works as a freelance advisor and coach.

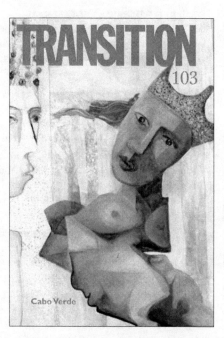

Tulsa Studies in Women's Literature

Publishing scholarship on women's writing for 30 years

SUBMIT

Guidelines at
www.utulsa.edu/tswl

rodopi

Orders@rodopi.nl—www.rodopi.nl

Destruction in the Performative

Edited and with an introduction by
Alice Lagaay and Michael Lorber

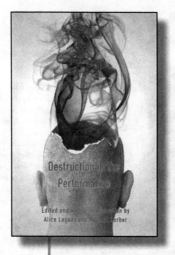

Cultural transformation tends to be described in one of two ways: either with reference to what comes about, is created or emerges in the process of change or with reference to what is destroyed or obscured in that process. Within a performative paradigm, that is, from a perspective which focuses on the manner in which social and cultural reality is constituted or brought about by human activity, theorists have, in recent years, tended to underline the productive aspects of transformation by emphasising the creative thrust of performative processes and events. In so doing, this perspective has tended to overlook the extent to which a certain destructive element may in fact be inherent to such performative processes. Drawing upon a range of historical and contemporary constellations of socio-cultural change and a variety of different types of events and activities, the articles in this volume describe different forms of destruction and their respective role in processes of transformation.

Their shared aim is to explore the manner in which destructivity, such as the destabilisation and destruction of orders, subjects and bodies, can be grasped by concepts of performativity. In other words, to what extent may a certain destructive dynamic be inscribed within this very notion?

Amsterdam/New York, NY
2012. 212 pp.
(Critical Studies 36)
Paper €42,-/US$57,-
E-Book €42,-/US$57,-
ISBN: 978-90-420-3457-0
ISBN: 978-94-012-0741-6

USA/Canada:
248 East 44th Street, 2nd floor,
New York, NY 10017, USA.
Call Toll-free (US only): T: 1-800-225-3998
                          F: 1-800-853-3881

All other countries:
Tijnmuiden 7, 1046 AK Amsterdam, The Netherlands
Tel. +31-20-611 48 21 Fax +31-20-447 29 79
Please note that the exchange rate is subject to fluctuations

CPSIA information can be obtained at www.ICGtesting.com
Printed in the USA
LVOW042055210912

299723LV00002B/163/P